STARK MAD
ABOLITIONISTS

STARK MAD ABOLITIONISTS

LAWRENCE, KANSAS, AND
THE BATTLE OVER SLAVERY
IN THE CIVIL WAR ERA

ROBERT K. SUTTON
Foreword by Bob Dole

Skyhorse Publishing

Skyhorse Publishing books may be purchased in bulk at special discounts for
sales promotion, corporate gifts, fund-raising, or educational purposes. Special
editions can also be created to specifications. For details, contact the Special
Sales Department, Skyhorse Publishing, 307 West 36th Street, 11th Floor,
New York, NY 10018 or info@skyhorsepublishing.com.

Skyhorse® and Skyhorse Publishing® are registered trademarks of Skyhorse
Publishing, Inc.®, a Delaware corporation.

Visit our website at www.skyhorsepublishing.com.

10 9 8 7 6 5 4 3 2

Library of Congress Cataloging-in-Publication Data is available on file.

Cover design by Rain Saukas
Cover photo credit: Sarin Images / Granger, NYC

Print ISBN: 978-1-5107-1649-0
Ebook ISBN: 978-1-5107-1651-3

Printed in the United States of America

Dedicated to the memory of my mother and father
Robert H. Sutton and Evelyn W. Sutton
and to my mother-in-law
Florence R. Davidson

Contents

Foreword

Growing up and attending school in Russell, Kansas, we were steeped in the early history of our state and its founders. We learned that the earliest settlers were given the choice of whether they wanted slavery or not under the concept of popular sovereignty in the Kansas-Nebraska Act that created the territory.

Pro-slavery advocates from Missouri were willing to go all out to bring Kansas into the slave-state fold. Meanwhile, antislavery proponents were just as determined that Kansas would be free. The first salvo in the first battle came with the election for a territorial legislature in 1855. Today, we hear accusations of voter fraud or voter suppression, but in Kansas's first territorial election, there was no question of voter fraud. Thousands of Missourians, having no intention of living in Kansas, crossed the border and voted to elect members of the territorial legislature who would do their bidding. This was the first step in their efforts toward making Kansas a slave state. The pro-slavery legislature went on to pass legislation protecting the institution of slavery, submitting the Lecompton Constitution to Congress in an effort to protect the institution of slavery when Kansas was admitted to the Union.

On the other end of the spectrum, antislavery proponents did everything they could to make Kansas a free state. Bob Sutton tells the story of Amos Adams Lawrence, an extraordinary man from Boston who "waked up" one morning as a "stark mad abolitionist" and devoted a substantial portion of his energy and fortune to ensure that Kansas would become a free state. Lawrence became the treasurer and benefactor of the New England Emigrant Aid Company, an organization that encouraged antislavery activists from the Northeast to leave everything behind and emigrate to Kansas, with the primary purpose of making the territory a free state. Many settled in the community—Lawrence, Kansas—that they named for their benefactor. They battled the pro-slavery legislature by establishing their own, albeit illegal, government. They created and elected members to their own legislature, and drafted and submitted their constitution to Congress, seeking admission for Kansas as a free state.

The battle that started as a war of words eventually became a war of violence called "Bleeding Kansas." In time, the antislavery side prevailed and Kansas was admitted to the Union as a free state on the eve of the Civil War. Kansans wholeheartedly supported the war, sending nearly all eligible men, or almost 20 percent of the entire state's population, to fight for the Union. Thirty-eight percent of Kansas's soldiers were casualties of the war, among the nation's highest per capita.

But the wounds opened in the territorial period did not heal with statehood. In 1863, the Confederate guerrilla chieftain William Clarke Quantrill led a force of four hundred ruthless killers into Lawrence, Kansas, killing some two hundred men and boys and burning most of the buildings in town to the ground.

Balanced with the savagery of Quantrill's attack, money and food poured into Lawrence from all over the country. Amos Adams Lawrence donated thousands of dollars in relief money after the raid and at the same time underwrote the initial funding to establish my alma mater in Lawrence—the University of Kansas. The residents of Lawrence were resilient and quickly rebuilt their town. Amos Lawrence and other benefactors set aside substantial portions of their relief money to aid the hundreds of children whose fathers were killed in Quantrill's raid or in other battles of the Civil

War. One key benefit: these children could attend the University of Kansas free of charge—quite a progressive program for the 1860s.

Bob Sutton does a wonderful job of capturing our state's early history. His Kansas roots run deep. Sutton's ancestors were among the earliest pioneers in Kansas, arriving and settling in Sutton Valley in Anderson County in early 1855. Sutton's great-grandfather, Isco "Pony" (shortened from Napoleon) Sutton, served in the 16th Kansas Cavalry during the Civil War. In this carefully researched book, Sutton reminds us that 150 years ago our country underwent its most challenging transition period to date. The nation was fundamentally torn over the institution of slavery, and Kansas was at the center of that debate. In this scholarly but readable book, Sutton explains why the stakes were so high during this most momentous time in our history.

—Bob Dole
Former US Senator from Kansas

Preface

IN 1831, ALEXIS DE TOCQUEVILLE left his native France and traveled to the United States, ostensibly to visit American prisons. But his journey carried him well beyond the penal system. He immersed himself in American culture, economics, politics, and society and recorded his observations in his *Democracy in America* (1835). Even today, most scholars recognize Tocqueville's work as the most perceptive study of early nineteenth-century America. His purpose was to explain the United States to his fellow French people, but over time, we have come to recognize that he also described America to Americans. Among his many findings, Tocqueville noted that "western migration is an extraordinary phenomenon, in which [Americans] band together in search of fortune. The restless spirit which drives people to move west is very good for the country, because it prevents the population from being concentrated in only a few places."

The phenomenon of westward expansion, fascinating to Tocqueville, also captured my imagination at a very early age. As a young child, my grandparents regaled me with the stories of their parents emigrating to Oregon. My great-grandfather traveled to Oregon by himself at age seventeen—with only the shirt on his back—and my great-grandmother was three weeks old when her family left Missouri on the Oregon Trail. My father also shared the accounts of his family's frequent moves, ending with their settlement in

Kansas. My great-great-grandfather, James Sutton, settled in Kansas in 1855. He brought his family from Osage County, Missouri, and settled in a region that would become part of Anderson County. James's parents were from New Jersey. They moved to Pennsylvania, then to Hamilton County, Ohio, where James was born in 1809. He moved to Indiana, to Illinois, to Osage County, Missouri, then on to Kansas.

James's son—my great-grandfather, Isco Napoleon "Pony" Sutton—fascinated me as well. Pony Sutton joined Company L, of the 16th Kansas Cavalry, late in the Civil War. The story that was passed down through the generations was that he was wounded four times and, as a result, died at an early age. From the depositions in his pension record, however, we learned that he contracted dysentery while in service and died from complications of the disease at age forty. Before he died, he was twice elected sheriff of Anderson County, and, in 1882, he was elected to the Kansas State House of Representatives as a member of the Greenback Party

Clearly, my ancestors on both sides of the family moved west to better themselves and the lives of their families. But the preparations required for each move must have been staggering. They needed to dispose of their property, purchase enough supplies and equipment for their journeys, and bid farewell to friends and family. Then, when they arrived at their destinations, they had to start from scratch. Whether they acquired land, started businesses, or went in search of jobs, most were confident, but unsure, of future success.

As Tocqueville observed, my ancestors and most pioneers moved to the West seeking their fortunes. Some were successful; others were not. There were exceptions, such as the Mormons who moved to Utah, hoping to free themselves from religious persecution. Others, such as the American fur trappers, combined adventure with their search for wealth. And still others headed west—not for financial gain, but to weaken the institution of slavery and bring about its ultimate destruction. They acted when Congress passed the Kansas-Nebraska Act of 1854, opening up settlement in these two territories. Embedded in this law was the principle of popular sovereignty that allowed the citizens to decide whether or not they wanted slavery in their future states. Knowing little about the land and even less about their chances for economic success, abolitionists willingly left their lives behind to settle in Kansas, with the primary purpose of doing everything in their power to keep slavery out of their new home.

Their task was daunting. But to ease the prospect of traveling to and settling in this alien land, businessmen in the East were willing to risk vast sums of money to facilitate the migration. One such northeastern businessman, Amos Adams Lawrence, in his own words, went to bed one night a conservative businessman, and "waked up a stark mad abolitionist." As quickly as he awakened, he combined his fortune and his energy with others in the New England Emigrant Aid Company to encourage abolitionists to emigrate to Kansas by making the trip as painless as possible. This financial support was crucial, but in addition to the challenges of building new lives in Kansas, immigrants quickly discovered that the pro-slavery residents of neighboring Missouri were just as passionate that Kansas should become a slave state. These Missourians were willing to stop at nothing to achieve their goal.

The epicenter of the antislavery movement, which also became the prime target for the pro-slavery side, was the community of Lawrence, Kansas. When Lawrence was more a dream than a reality, the first pioneers voted to name the community after Amos Adams Lawrence, recognizing his generous financial support. Whenever needed, Amos Lawrence opened his pocketbook to ensure that Kansas would become a free state, and that the town that bore his name would thrive. Amos Lawrence and many of the major players in the story have recorded their experiences. Whenever possible, as we whisk you back 150 years, we will share the challenges, the struggles, the tragedies, and the triumphs of Lawrence—the town and the person—through the eyes of the participants.

Acknowledgments

TWENTY-FIVE YEARS AGO, WHEN I published my first book, my mother-in-law extracted a promise from me. She made me promise that I would write another book. Well, Mom, it took some time, but I kept my promise. I just wish you and my mom and dad were still here to see this new volume.

Writing a book now is very different from the experience twenty-five years ago. Word processors were readily available, but the development of the Internet, with its amazing resources we now take for granted, was only in its infancy. Now, with the push of a computer button, researchers can access materials that for generations were only available in physical repositories. The Kansas State Historical Society and the University of Kansas, in partnership and with a major grant from the federally funded Institute for Museum and Library Services, has created a website that has proven to be an absolute gold mine of resources. Territorial Kansas Online has assembled government documents, diaries, letters, photographs, maps, newspapers, rare secondary sources, and historical artifacts from the collections of these two institutions. Researchers such as I can access scanned handwritten documents to capture the feelings experienced by the original writers, but as an added benefit, most letters are transcribed for easier reading. Photographs and scanned images of museum artifacts are constantly added to the site. I wish I could individually thank each person involved in developing this website. I cannot begin to tell you how valuable your work has been to writing this book.

A number of individuals have been important to bring this project to fruition as well. First, my agent, Greg Aunapu, saw the potential of this book and connected me with Joseph Craig at Skyhorse Publishing. Denise Roeper and Katherine Kiger provided excellent copyediting and proofreading. I am grateful to you all for producing this volume. I owe a huge debt of gratitude to Robert Shimp, a former National Park Service colleague, who, on his own time, spent hours combing through the Amos Adams Lawrence Papers at the Massachusetts Historical Society. Robert: I cannot thank you enough. Also former colleagues, Jeff Patrick, the librarian/historian and Ted Hilmer, the superintendent at Wilson's Creek National Battlefield provided a treasure trove of materials related to the participation of Kansas soldiers in the Battle at Wilson's Creek. Thanks to Rick Hatcher, also of the National Park Service, for compiling the information on the battle. Katie Armitage, a Lawrence historian, directed me to a number of important sources and brought me up to date on how Lawrence currently commemorates the anniversary date of Quantrill's Raid. Julie McPike with the Freedom's Frontier National Heritage Area guided me to valuable resources and provided encouragement as I worked on this book. Sara Keckeisen and Lisa Keys at the Kansas State Historical Society, Kathy Lafferty at the University of Kansas, Anne E. Cox at the State Historical Society of Missouri, Anne E. Cox at the State Historical Society of Missouri, and Isabella Donadio at Harvard University Portrait Collection, were enormously helpful in obtaining images from their collections.

When I completed the first draft, Nicole Etcheson, whom I consider the leading historian on the "Bleeding Kansas" period, graciously agreed to read the draft and offered enormously valuable insights, suggestions, and corrections to the document. David Martin and Glenn Willoughby also read and offered valuable critiques on the draft manuscript. My son, Lee David, offered helpful suggestions and edits as well. Thanks to your careful readings, the final product is much improved.

Finally, to quote the famous baseball player Lou Gehrig, I feel like the luckiest man on the face of this earth to be married to my wonderful wife, Harriet Davidson. We have a strong and enduring partnership in nearly every way imaginable. So, when I asked her to take the time from her busy schedule to read my manuscript, she took it along on trips, got up early, and stayed up late to read the entire document. Her insights, her corrections, her critiques, and her suggestions have immeasurably improved the final product. More than this, from start to finish, Harriet has been a wonderful sounding board. She would enthusiastically support many ideas, tell me others needed more work, and for still others, she would help me relegate them to the trash heap. Through the whole process, her love, support, and thoughtfulness kept me going. I appreciate you more than you will ever know.

Introduction

IN THE SUMMER OF 1787, Congress was, for all intents and purposes, dysfunctional. Many members of the United States in Congress Assembled—the official title of the body under the Articles of Confederation—were in Philadelphia as delegates to the Federal Convention, deliberating over a new constitution. On most days, the remaining members of Congress could barely pull together a quorum to do business; on other days, not enough were present to even make a quorum. In the middle of the summer, however, Congress was back in business. The Reverend Manasseh Cutler, a lobbyist from Massachusetts, came to the seat of government in New York City on behalf of the Ohio Company of Associates. His clients were Revolutionary War veterans and land speculators from New England. His job was to convince Congress to sell a large tract of land in Ohio to his company at a bargain price. The government was strapped for money, and Rev. Cutler made the convincing argument that his clients would put money in the government coffers, and, by advertising the availability of land far and wide, they would stimulate settlement in Ohio. To move the deal along, Cutler offered stakes in the land company to recalcitrant Congressmen in exchange for their votes.

Rev. Cutler was an outstanding salesman. As he was closing the deal to buy one and a half million acres, he made the case that potential settlers in Ohio or in other western lands needed assurances that stable governments, with orderly processes in place for admission to the union on equal footing with the original thirteen states, were necessary to encourage emigration. To that end, Rev. Cutler helped craft the Northwest Ordinance, which became one of the most important pieces of legislation in our nation's history.[1] The ordinance stated that at least three and no more than five new states would eventually be created in the area north and west of the Ohio River, up to the Mississippi River. Each would have been initially established as a territory. As it reached certain milestones, it would achieve more and more autonomy until each new territory could apply for statehood. When admitted as states, each would be equal in every way with the original thirteen. The ordinance stipulated that "religion, morality, and knowledge being necessary to good government," schools of all levels were important to ensure "the happiness of mankind" in each territory. Slavery was specifically prohibited in the allowed three-to-five new territories created by this ordinance. As with the land purchase, Rev. Cutler had to sweeten the pot to ensure that the president of Congress, Arthur St. Clair, would support the ordinance. Governors would be appointed, rather than elected, to make way for St. Clair to fill that position in Ohio.[2]

Rev. Cutler then traveled to Philadelphia to apprise the delegates of the Federal Convention what their colleagues were doing in New York. He wanted to ensure that his agreement, agreed upon with Congress in New York, would not be undermined in the new constitution. His mission was successful; with very little debate, Article IV, Section 3 of the new Constitution stated that "new states may be admitted by the Congress into this union. . . ." Further, under the same section, the delegates adopted the language that "Congress shall have power to dispose of and make all needful rules and regulations respecting the territory or other property belonging to the United States."

While the future admission of new states was straightforward, other issues before the convention were far more complicated, such as how to deal with the institution of slavery. Delegates debated at length as to whether slavery should even be allowed under the new government. After North Carolina, South Carolina, and Georgia threatened to walk if slavery was not protected, the delegates addressed slavery in three parts of the new Constitution. Slaves could be imported from outside the United States until 1808, individual slaves would be counted as three-fifths of a person in the census to bolster the power slave states held in the House of Representatives, and the fugitive slave clause provided for the return of escaped slaves to their masters. Many northern delegates believed slavery was on the road to extinction, making it easier to support the compromise.

For the first thirty years under the constitution, new states were admitted in an orderly fashion, under the basic framework established under the constitution and the Northwest Ordinance. The prohibition of slavery in the Northwest Ordinance only applied to that region. Under the new Constitution, Congress had the flexibility to balance equality in the admission of free and slave states. Everything seemed to be working well; that is, until Missouri sought admission as a slave state in 1819—at the time, there was not an obvious free territory ready for admission to maintain the balance between free and slave states. Senator Rufus King of New York led the northern, antislavery faction, when he argued that Congress had the power to prohibit slavery in any new state. Senator William Pinkney of Maryland advocated for the Southerners, arguing that states had a perfect right to choose slavery if they wished. Congress was deadlocked, until Senator Henry Clay from Kentucky proposed a compromise, in which Missouri would be admitted as a slave state, and to balance free and slave states, Maine, then part of Massachusetts, would be admitted as a free state. In addition, a line would be drawn at latitude 36°30′ (the southern boundary of Missouri); slavery would be illegal north of that line within the Louisiana Purchase.

As with most compromises, there was grumbling on both sides over the issue of slavery, but, in the end, most were willing to accept the agreement. One elder statesman who was deeply troubled by the compromise, however, was Thomas Jefferson. He confided to his friend John Holmes that "like a fire bell in the night, [news of the Missouri Compromise] awakened and filled me with terror. I considered it at once as the knell of the Union." He went on to say that "we have the wolf [the institution of slavery] by the ear, and we can neither hold him, nor safely let him go. Justice is in one scale, and self-preservation in the other." He was fearful that the nation he and other patriots had created might collapse over the institution of slavery.[3]

Over the next thirty years, Jefferson's concerns about the future of his country seemed unfounded. Numerous issues regarding slavery came before Congress, but the admission of free and slave states continued, and the balance remained equal. In 1850, however, another crisis emerged. California had exploded in population with the gold rush. It had not been organized as a territory, but it still desired admission to the Union as a free state. As Jefferson had prophesied, the issue was like "a fire bell in the night." There seemed to be no reasonable solution to the problem. Henry Clay, who orchestrated the Missouri Compromise, was not well, but he introduced a package of five bills that he hoped would work magic. In September 1850, and with the shepherding of Senator Stephen A. Douglas from Illinois, Congress reached a compromise by passing all five bills introduced by Clay. Texas would surrender its claim to what would become New Mexico, as well as its land north of the Missouri Compromise line. In return, the federal government would assume Texas's public debt. California would be admitted as a free state. The Utah and New Mexico Territories could choose if they wanted slavery or not under the concept of popular sovereignty. The slave trade, but not the institution of slavery, was banned in the District of Columbia. Finally, Congress enacted a stringent fugitive slave law, making it much easier for slave owners to reclaim their slave property.

The North was pleased to have another free state, and many could see the potential for other new free states created from the territory surrendered from Texas. Some, especially antislavery members of Congress, were happy to see the slave markets in the District of Columbia closed. But the new Fugitive Slave Act was a hard pill to swallow. The South was not pleased with most of the compromise, but many believed they had achieved a small victory with the Fugitive Slave Act. Under this law, special federal commissioners were appointed to handle fugitive cases. If they found for the slave owner, and returned the fugitive to servitude, they received $10. The hearing was not a jury trial and the fugitive could not provide a defense. The claimant only had to provide an affidavit or sworn testimony that he or she had a legal claim to the fugitive. If commissioners found against the claimant, they received $5. In other words, their financial incentive was to find in favor of the slave owner. US Marshals were required to aid in the capture of fugitives, and they could force bystanders to aid in apprehending a fugitive slave. Anyone who aided or provided food or shelter to a fugitive was subject to a $1,000 fine and six months in jail. Without normal legal protections, free blacks were vulnerable to capture and being sent south as slaves.

As the Fugitive Slave Act was in force, fugitive slaves—and even some free African Americans—fled to Canada—some three thousand in the three months after passage of the law. Many abolitionists, or fugitives such as Harriet Tubman, who assisted or guided slaves in their journeys on the Underground Railroad, simply saw the new law as an additional bother. They subscribed to a "higher law" that they considered above any earthly law. Other antislavery advocates, normally law-abiding citizens, were deeply conflicted with knowingly breaking a federal law but felt so strongly about the injustice of the law that they swallowed their apprehensions and aided fugitives. On the other side, Southerners, who had reluctantly agreed to the entire compromise, thinking the Fugitive Slave Act would protect their interests, were outraged that the federal government wasn't doing a better job of returning slaves to captivity and punishing those who helped slaves escape.

Clearly, the Compromise of 1850 was not functioning as well as its sponsors had hoped. Senator Douglas, who had successfully pushed through the earlier compromise, came up with a new plan that he hoped would calm the troubled political waters. He had introduced the concept of popular sovereignty with the establishment of the New Mexico and Utah territories, and now he proposed the same concept in the bill he introduced in 1854 to create the Kansas and Nebraska territories. He hoped that the concept of popular sovereignty would "triumph and impart peace to the country and stability to the Union."[4] He thought his idea made perfect sense. The US Constitution started with "We the People of the United States, . . ." which to Douglas meant that the people were the power behind the government to which none other was equal. So, the people should be the ultimate source to make decisions such as whether or not they wanted slavery where they lived. Douglas had another motive as well: he hoped the transcontinental railroad would be built in one of these territories, which would financially benefit him and his constituents.

Not everyone agreed with Douglas. Abraham Lincoln, who would run against Douglas for his Senate seat several years later, strongly disagreed. Lincoln argued that the decision as to whether or not slavery should be allowed in the territories had successfully rested with Congress, dating back to the Northwest Ordinance of 1787. In his Peoria Speech in 1854, Lincoln said that Congress was abdicating the responsibility it had held "through sixty-odd of the best years of the republic." Since Congress had successfully managed territorial issues since the creation of the republic, he saw no reason to change that now. Lincoln also made it very clear that he was emphatically against slavery, adding that "if the negro is a man, why then my ancient faith teaches me that 'all men are created equal;' and that there can be no moral right in connection with one man's making a slave of another."[5] So, to Lincoln, decisions concerning slavery in the territories should remain in the hands of Congress, and, if he had his way, slavery would be abolished in all territories as well.

Douglas and Lincoln disagreed on how Congress should legislate regarding slavery in the territories, but at least they both recognized that Congress had the authority to make laws for the territories. There was, however, another faction that did not agree with Douglas or Lincoln—the slaveholding South. While a number of senators from the South were begrudgingly willing to support the Kansas-Nebraska Act, most believed that neither Congress nor the people should be able to ban slavery in the territories. They based their argument on the Constitution as well, but rather than focusing on Article IV, they argued that the Fifth Amendment provided that no one could "be deprived of life, liberty, or *property* [emphasis added], without due process of law; nor shall private property be taken for public use, without just compensation." Slaves were property, and there should be no restrictions on people taking their slaves into territories on a temporary or permanent basis.

While the nation's leaders were debating the creation of new territories in Kansas and Nebraska under the principle of popular sovereignty, the Fugitive Slave Act created a spectacle in northern cities that was turning more and more people against slavery. Many northern conservative businessmen had, for the most part, stood on the sidelines and not taken much interest in the issues surrounding slavery. But as they witnessed the capture of escaped slaves who were brought before kangaroo courts without any chance to plead their cases, and then these slaves being returned in shackles to bondage, the businessmen could no longer ignore what was happening around them. One such businessman, George S. Hilliard, after he witnessed a fugitive being shipped off to bondage from Boston, was so deeply troubled by what he saw, he wrote to a friend that "when it was all over [the slave was led away in chains] and I was left alone in my office, I put my face in my hands and wept. I could do nothing less."[6] Amos Adams Lawrence, another wealthy conservative Bostonian, had the same reaction to the same incident, but instead of hanging his head in shame, he decided to take action, to do what he could to end the institution of slavery. He saw his opportunity, for at the same time the slave was returned to bondage, Congress moved from debating to passing the Kansas-Nebraska Act. Since Congress made the decision to allow these new territories to choose whether they wanted slavery or not, in an instant, he committed to investing a great deal of money and energy to make Kansas a free state.

PART I

THE AWAKENING

1 We Waked Up Stark Mad Abolitionists

FROM MAY 24 THROUGH JUNE 2, 1854, Boston was in an uproar. On May 24, Anthony Burns, a young African American enslaved man, who had escaped from his bondage in Virginia and settled in Boston where he worked at a men's clothing store, was captured by his owner on his way home from work. Burns's owner, Charles Suttle, tracked his whereabouts from a letter he had intercepted from Burns to his brother. There was no question that Burns was an enslaved man and was Suttle's property. Under the United States Constitution and the Fugitive Slave Act of 1850, there also was no question that Burns had no rights whatsoever.[7]

Although Burns had no legal claim to his freedom, to the citizens of Boston, his capture was an outrage. Antislavery lawyers representing Burns used several legal maneuvers to delay the hearing to send their client back to slavery. On May 26, a mob of some seven thousand black and white abolitionists, led by a Unitarian minister, the Reverend Thomas Wentworth Higginson, stormed the courthouse attempting to free Burns. When order was restored, one US Marshal was dead, and a dozen more individuals were injured. Abolitionists and federal troops faced off again the following day when the hearing began under heavy guard. Burns was represented by Richard Henry Dana and Charles M. Ellis, two of Boston's finest abolitionist attorneys. Unfortunately for Anthony Burns, the Fugitive Slave Act did not allow for legal representation,

Anthony Burns engraving by John Andrews. Surrounding Burns are scenes from his life. Lower left, sold at auction, next a whipping post, then his arrest in Boston. The next scene depicts his escape on ship from Richmond, then Burns escorted to Boston dock by federal marshals. Burns is possibly addressing the court, and finally Burns in slave prison in Richmond. Library of Congress.

so there was very little Dana or Ellis could offer as a defense. US Commissioner Edward G. Loring found for Suttle and ordered Burns returned to servitude.

President Franklin Pierce, although a Northerner, was committed to upholding the Fugitive Slave Act and was determined that Anthony Burns would be returned to servitude no matter the cost in dollars and manpower. So, on June 2, more than two thousand federal soldiers and marines cordoned off the streets of Boston. An estimated fifty thousand people watched as Anthony Burns was escorted in chains to an awaiting ship in Boston harbor. He was returned to Virginia and bondage. The government expense for the whole affair was $40,000.[8]

The story did not end on June 2, 1854. True, no more enslaved people were returned to bondage from Boston, so that part of the

Amos Adams Lawrence. Frontispiece in William Lawrence, ed, *Life of Amos A. Lawrence: With Extracts from His Diary and Correspondence* (1888).

story was over. The Burns affair had a profound impact on Amos Adams Lawrence, who was a patriarch of one of Boston's wealthiest and most powerful families. On June 1, the day before Burns was returned to slavery, Lawrence wrote to his uncle that "we went to bed one night old-fashioned, conservative, Compromise Union Whigs and waked up stark mad Abolitionists."[9]

We know very little of Amos Adams Lawrence's physical attributes. From the best image we have, he appears to be diminutive in stature, but that is based on conjecture, since no description of him survives. We know more about his persona. He was a deeply religious man, who was also absolutely devoted to his family. He was a very private man. He kept his innermost thoughts to himself, but fortunately for us, he shared his personal musings with his diary, which has survived. He shunned public attention whenever possible; he preferred communicating in writing rather than by the spoken word.

Lawrence fulfilled the adage of being born with a silver spoon in his mouth, with all of the benefits his noble birth implied. He was sent to a boarding school, Franklin Academy in Andover, Massachusetts, but was so unhappy there, he ran away for several days. He entered Harvard at age seventeen, but he left a year later when the college president suggested to his father that he needed private tutoring before he continued with his studies. Lawrence was sent to Bedford, Massachusetts, where he received private tutoring from J. Stearns; he then returned to Harvard, from which he graduated in 1835.

Amos Adams Lawrence was able to enjoy all of these advantages because his father, also Amos Lawrence, along with his uncle, Abbott Lawrence, built one of the largest and most successful wholesale mercantile businesses in the country. They also developed cotton and woolen milling enterprises in Massachusetts. When Amos senior retired from his business interests in 1831 at age forty-five, he devoted the remainder of his life to philanthropy, reportedly giving over $1 million to charitable causes, organizations, and projects.

So the younger Amos Lawrence grew up in a wealthy but generous household. He acquired both his father's business skills and passion for philanthropy. Shortly after he graduated from Harvard, Lawrence created a business niche as a commission merchant selling manufactured textiles produced in New England mills. Then in 1843, when he and his partner, Robert Mason, consolidated their interests into Mason and Lawrence, Lawrence was a successful textile merchant.[10] From the very beginning of his business successes, the younger Lawrence was generous with his money; so much so, in his personal diary entry from earlier in 1854, he wrote that he needed to continue with his business enterprises so he would be able to meet the demands of the charities he supported.[11]

It didn't take long for Amos A. Lawrence to connect his money with his "stark mad" abolitionism. On May 30, during the nine days of turmoil in Boston over Anthony Burns, President Pierce signed the Kansas-Nebraska Act into law. For Lawrence and other New England abolitionists, the Burns episode and the Kansas-Nebraska Act must have seemed like a perfect storm.

After extensive debate, divided along sectional lines, and with shepherding from Senator Stephen A. Douglas of Illinois, Congress adopted the Kansas-Nebraska Act. The law changed the paradigm in place since the Missouri Compromise of 1820, in which new territories above the 36°30' parallel would be free, and those below would be slave. Citizens in both territories could decide whether they wanted slavery or not under the concept of popular sovereignty.[12]

Amos Lawrence had followed the progression of the Kansas-Nebraska legislation for several months. He visited Washington, DC, to dine with his half-cousin, President Franklin Pierce, and his wife. While there, on April 13, 1854, he met Senator Stephen A. Douglas for the first time.[13] In his diary, he wrote that Douglas was "apparently desirous to make me his friend." The feeling was not mutual, however, for Lawrence went on to say that the senator from Illinois was "a very bright man and an ambitious and unscrupulous one," and noted that Douglas likely would have had a good shot at being elected president, except that his sponsorship of the Kansas-Nebraska bill likely killed those chances. When the law passed in May, Lawrence observed that while President Pierce believed that the new law would "forever allay agitation about slavery," he and many others saw the Kansas-Nebraska Act as "a fool-hardy scheme."

Lawrence was unhappy with the passage of the Kansas-Nebraska Act, but with this new law and the capture and return of Anthony Burns, he moved from the sidelines of the slavery issue to firmly within the antislavery camp. He wrote that the Burns incident "made one resolve in his mind the value of our union when such a scene [Burns's return to servitude] must be enacted here in order to support slavery and the laws." From that moment on, Lawrence put his efforts and his considerable fortune toward keeping slavery out of the new territories.[14]

Since Missouri, a slave state, was adjacent to Kansas, the conventional wisdom in the spring of 1854 was that Missourians would flood the new territory with settlers and slaves and make Kansas a slave state. For that reason, many antislavery advocates wrung their hands in despair. Some, like Lawrence, on the other hand, saw an opportunity to match wits and strength with the pro-slavery forces by beating them at their own game—to encourage such a high number of antislavery people to settle in Kansas, that when it came for citizens to decide whether Kansas would be slave or free, the antislavery side would win.

Shortly after Anthony Burns was returned to slavery, Lawrence wrote that he had "been made a trustee . . . [in an organization] to settle Kansas [with free residents] in advance of the introduction of slavery there."[15] The organization was the Massachusetts Emigrant

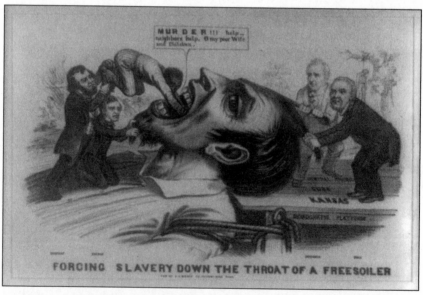

Cartoon, *Forcing Slavery Down the Throat of a Freesoiler*, by John L. Magee, 1856. The freesoiler's head rests on a platform marked "Kansas," "Cuba," and "Central America." Pro-slavery Democrats of that time wanted to extend slavery to these places. In the background, destruction and a man hanging from a tree. Library of Congress.

Aid Company, established by Eli Thayer, who was a member of the Massachusetts Legislature. Thayer had pushed through the incorporation of this company a month before the passage of the Kansas-Nebraska Act for the primary purpose of encouraging the settlement of Kansas by New England antislavery advocates. The company charter established a ceiling of up to $5 million in capital, which was used to make the journey from New England to Kansas as painless as possible. Company agents would find the easiest transportation routes and negotiate the lowest fares. Company scouts would find and survey the most desirable land and provide temporary housing until settlers could build permanent dwellings. The company also would invest in schools, mills, and other economic infrastructure, such that the community would be self-sufficient as quickly as possible. Thayer envisioned that investors would invest in the company and reap profits from their investments.

Just when enthusiasm for Thayer's plan was building, however, it looked as if the company might fold for lack of capital. Under the Massachusetts charter, board members were required to personally assume financial liabilities if the company failed. At this point, Amos Lawrence came to the rescue. Lawrence's friend and fellow Boston merchant, Patrick T. Jackson, recognized that Thayer had a great idea but not a good sense of business, so Jackson cajoled Lawrence into bringing his considerable business skills as well as his deep pockets to the company. Lawrence was delighted to join forces with Thayer and put his "stark mad" abolitionism to work, yet he had no idea how much hard work the project would entail or how much money he would contribute. Lawrence's son would later say that his father "had undertaken a piece of work which was as arduous as it was expensive."[16]

Thayer and Lawrence would work together for the next several years to make Kansas a free state. Thayer came from a prominent but not prosperous New England family. He worked his way through Worchester County Manual Labor High School and Brown University, became a teacher in Worcester, and founded the Oread

Eli Thayer, Library of Congress.

Institute—a school for young women. Regarding his passion to end slavery, Thayer later wrote that "during the winter of 1854, I began to have the conviction . . . that something had to be done to end the domination of slavery."[17]

With Lawrence on board, the organization was reorganized into a private company, which did not have the onerous requirements of liability for the board members. The new entity, the New England Emigrant Aid Company, was managed with three board members, with a new target capitalization of $200,000, which would be raised by selling $20 shares. The charter stated that the organization would "promote the emigration to Kansas Territory of persons opposed to slavery there, and to prevent, by all legal and constitutional means, its establishment there as well as in the Territory of Nebraska."

Thayer continued to hold to the notion that investors could expect returns on their investments. Lawrence did not share his optimism and privately cautioned his friends that they should only contribute funds if they could spare them, rather than invest with the expectation of a return. "I am willing to contribute to the cause," he wrote to a clergyman seeking his advice, "and I have already given a part of this away, and I intend to do the same with the balance," without expecting anything in return. Writing to another friend, he said that he believed his financial backing would contribute to the "impulse to emigration into Kansas which cannot easily be stopped."[18]

Before long, Lawrence grew increasingly worried that the demands for funds were becoming more than even his deep pockets could tolerate. In his diary, he wrote that the Emigrant Aid Company appeared as "a vigorous and rich company in the public prints, when in fact it is only an embodiment of the *feeling* of the people without *material* [*or financial*] strength." And a few weeks later, he wrote that "all expenditures thus far have been by myself, but I cannot go further without funds in hand."[19]

From his diary entries, it was clear that Amos Lawrence was committed financially and economically to the cause of keeping slavery out of Kansas Territory, even though that effort put a tremendous strain on his personal and business finances. Yet in none of his diary entries of other correspondence did Lawrence ever suggest that the source of his wealth was in any way incompatible with his antislavery passion. He, his father, and his uncle made their fortunes from buying, selling, and producing textiles—mostly made of cotton. Where did they get the raw cotton? Or, more to the point, who planted, picked, ginned, baled, and transported this cotton? The answer, of course, was the enslaved population in the American South—the same population for whom he was seeking freedom. Whether he had difficulty juxtaposing his antislavery views with his business dealings or not was and is a mystery. But if there was a conflict of conscience, it certainly did not dampen his commitment to the cause, nor did it stop him from recruiting other wealthy, likeminded friends to join the company.

One of Lawrence's first recruits was a friend, John Carter Brown, whom he tapped as the president of the company. The title of president was, by design, mostly honorary. But Lawrence was strategic in drafting Brown as president. First, he was from a prominent New England family, and second, he was a moderate Whig, with no radical political baggage. Brown attended most board meetings and allowed his name to appear on many of the company's circulars. Like Lawrence, much of the money Brown donated to the Emigrant Aid Company came from the backs of slaves and the institution of slavery he was trying to eradicate. His father and uncles made their fortunes from the "triangle trade." Slaves were shipped to the Americas from Africa in exchange for sugar, which was transported from the Caribbean to New England, where it was distilled into rum. Rum and other goods were then shipped to Africa, where the process started all over again. The Browns donated a large portion of their profits to the College of Rhode Island, and for their generosity, they were honored when the school changed its name to Brown University.

John Carter Brown, however, followed in the footsteps of one of his uncles, Moses Brown, who made an about-face from his brothers, separated himself from their slave-trading business, and became an early leader in the antislavery movement in Rhode Island. In addition to his antislavery passions, John Carter Brown amassed one of the largest collections of rare books at the time. His son donated the collection to Brown University, creating the John Carter Brown Library, one of the finest research libraries in the country today.[20]

Joining Brown, Thayer, and Lawrence on the board was Dr. Thomas H. Webb as the secretary. Like many who would join the cause, Dr. Webb was well educated, having attended Brown University and graduated from Harvard Medical School. Whether he was an unsuccessful businessman or lost interest—or both—his medical practice failed. His interest shifted to history and science, and he was one of the founding members and the first librarian of the Providence Athenaeum. Webb signed on early with Thayer and served as secretary until his death in 1866.

Webb was concerned that the wonderful idea of the Emigrant Aid Company would be stillborn. On May 24, 1854, he wrote to

Thayer that the whole scheme would be "perfectly Quixotic" since at that point the company was "endorsed by nobody" and that "not one of the [in]corporators has subscribed for a shilling's worth of Stock." But Webb also showed his determination to do his part to achieve success, writing: "I am ready and willing to put on the harness and work to the best of my ability and power." He did just that.[21]

Several months later, when the emigration to Kansas began, Webb negotiated reduced fares on the conveyances and assisted prospective travelers in their plans to relocate. Perhaps his greatest contribution, however, was to write, revise, and publish a circular each year, beginning in 1855, to "answer the numerous inquiries respecting Kanzas [sic; sometimes it was spelled with a z], daily addressed to the Secretary both by letter and in person."[22] Amos Lawrence recognized how hard Webb worked for the success of the company, and later wrote that he was "the truest man of all."[23]

In addition to Thayer, Lawrence, Brown, and Webb, many others contributed to the success of the venture. Few were as important as the Reverend Edward Everett Hale, a Unitarian minister from Worchester. Hale entered Harvard as a prodigy at age thirteen and graduated second in his class. His passion for liberating slaves was much like the passion for liberty of his great-uncle, Nathan Hale, who, when faced with his execution by the British in the Revolutionary War, regretted that he "only had one life to give for his country." Hale signed on as the company's chief publicist. Nine years earlier, Edward Hale had written a pamphlet—*How to Conquer Texas Before Texas Conquers Us*—advocating for abolitionists to settle in Texas to check the advancement of slavery there, which may or may not have planted the seed for the Emigrant Aid Company with Thayer. Hale threw his considerable energy into promoting the Emigrant Aid Company by making numerous speeches, writing articles, enlisting the help of clergymen around New England, and by publishing the book, *Kanzas and Nebraska* in September 1854, in which he described the territory, although he had never been there.[24]

The Reverend Thomas Wentworth Higginson—the same Higginson who led the mob trying to free Anthony Burns—passionately supported the Emigrant Aid Company, corresponded with the company's settlers in Kansas, and later led a group of antislavery emigrants to Kansas. As the Kansas antislavery movement became more militant, Higginson worked behind the scenes to provide guns to the settlers. He came from one of the bluest of blue-blooded Boston families. His ancestor, Francis Higginson, was a member of the first Puritan settlement to New England and the first minister of the Salem, Massachusetts, church. Thomas graduated from Harvard and entered Harvard Divinity School but left after a year, drawn to Transcendentalist Unitarian minister Theodore Parker. He returned to Harvard, finished his theology studies, and, in 1847, accepted a call as minister of the First Religious Society of Newburyport, Massachusetts, a Unitarian church known for its liberal religious views. He invited speakers such as Theodore Parker and Ralph Waldo Emerson to address his congregation. He railed against the poor treatment of white workers in northern mills and condemned the institution of slavery. But when he implied that his own congregation was not doing enough to end the institution, he was asked and agreed to resign.

In 1852, Higginson accepted the appointment as minister of the Free Church in Worchester, Massachusetts, a nondenominational congregation, which was more in tune with his radical social views. After the failed attempt to free Anthony Burns, and after the passage of the Kansas-Nebraska Act, he joined Eli Thayer and the others as a key member of the Emigrant Aid Company.

Religious leaders in New England often held a great deal of influence over their congregations. Some were held in such high esteem that their names and stature were universally recognized and revered. Such was the case with the Reverend Dr. Lyman Beecher. If his name was associated with any program or cause, other clergymen paid attention. So to take advantage of his prestige, and to hopefully bring some money into the company's coffers, Amos Lawrence drafted two circulars and obtained Lyman Beecher's permission to attach his name at the top of the list to "the Clergymen of New England," urging them and their parishioners to buy shares of $20 in the New England Emigrant Aid Company.[25]

Lyman Beecher was nearing eighty when he agreed to attach his name to the Emigrant Aid Company appeal. He was a patriarch among clergy, but he was also the head of one of the most famous families in America. His daughter Harriet married a professor of biblical literature named Calvin E. Stowe. The couple lived in Brunswick, Maine, where Calvin was a professor at Bowdoin College. There, in 1852, Harriet wrote one of the most influential books in American history, and one of the best selling books in the United States next to the Bible in the nineteenth century—*Uncle Tom's Cabin*. Uncle Tom and the other characters in the story drew sympathy to the plight of enslaved African Americans more than any other book in the 1850s.

Harriet's younger brother, Henry Ward Beecher, followed his father's footsteps into the ministry, and became one of the most dynamic and influential ministers in the 1800s. Following his graduation from Lane Theological Seminary in 1837, the younger Beecher ministered in two churches in Indiana, and then in 1847 he was called to establish a new church in Brooklyn, New York. Beecher achieved success overnight. His Plymouth Church grew in membership to over two thousand members—an early mega-church—in a building that seated three thousand and was frequently full. His style was the opposite of his father and nearly all other clergymen of the day. He was informal, often telling funny stories from the pulpit. He encouraged congregational singing, which is taken for granted today, but was nearly unheard of then.[26]

Following the Compromise of 1850 and the passage of the Fugitive Slave Act, Henry Ward Beecher began to preach against the evils of slavery from his pulpit, and allowed his church to become a station on the Underground Railroad for escaped slaves. He even brought attractive young slave girls into church and conducted a mock auction, working the congregation into a frenzy to donate enough money to buy their freedom. His church in Brooklyn became one of the bastions of the American antislavery movement. Henry Ward Beecher would play an interesting role in the Kansas struggle that would involve his name and an important symbol of his profession. But before he could take the stage, the antislavery pioneers for which his father's circular was trying to raise money had to settle in Kansas.

2 Nothing but a Beautiful Green Carpet

ADVOCATES FOR A FREE OR a slave territory would fight it out until Kansas was admitted as a free state on the eve of the Civil War. The pro- and antislavery slugfest that was about to begin, however, was not over virgin land. The land was already inhabited. Some people had lived there for generations; others were recent arrivals. Kansas was part of the Indian Territory, which in 1854 included what would later become nearly all of Oklahoma, about two-thirds of Kansas, and roughly half of present-day Nebraska. The Kansas-Nebraska Act that would set this conflict in motion did not ignore these indigenous peoples; in fact, it seemed to take their needs into consideration. But Sam Houston, a senator from Texas, understood that implied protection was very different from real protection. Houston noted that it was "not novel for [him] to seek to advocate the rights of the Indians upon [the floor of Congress] and elsewhere." He believed it was his duty "to protect the Indian against wrong and oppression, and to vindicate [Indians] in the enjoyment of rights which have been solemnly guaranteed to [Indians] by this Government."[27] Sam Houston was the only member of Congress to oppose the Kansas-Nebraska Act over the issue of American Indian rights there.

Sam Houston knew of whence he spoke. Six weeks after the passage of the Kansas-Nebraska Act, the Senate ratified a new treaty with the Delaware Indians, which required them to cede large portions of their reservation lands in northeastern Kansas and agree to provide rights-of-way through their remaining land for roads and access. The government was reneging on the 1829 treaty in which it promised that "the United States hereby pledges the faith of the government to guarantee to the said Delaware Nation *forever* [emphasis added], the peaceable possession and undisturbed enjoyment of [their permanent home], against the claims and assaults of all and every other people whatever."[28]

The Delaware Indians, as their name implied, had inhabited a wide area in the mid-Atlantic region, centered between the Hudson and Delaware Rivers. From the late 1700s on, they were forced to move further and further west, until the majority of the tribal members settled in Kansas. Their land in Kansas was substantial—nearly two million acres—and fertile. Further, the Delaware people proved to be successful farmers and ranchers, attracting many Delaware people who had scattered from earlier forced moves to congregate in Kansas to share in the bounty. Now, their livelihoods were threatened. To abrogate its 1829 treaty, the government agents cleverly negotiated with Delaware leaders who were amenable to the new treaty. Or, more likely, the leaders were not even sure what the treaty said—as evidenced by the signing of the new treaty with numerous "Xs." The lands ceded by the Delaware Indians became some of the most desirable lands for white settlement in Kansas. Eventually Kansas's other nations—the Shawnee, Ponca, Kansa, Kiowa, Osage, Otoe, and others—would be squeezed onto smaller reservations or removed from Kansas altogether.

Eli Thayer, Amos Lawrence, and other leaders of the Emigrant Aid Company were aware of the treaties, and instructed their agents to make sure that the land they selected for settlement did not have any encumbrances associated with former Indian lands. But before anyone worried about land in Kansas, they had to make the prospect of migrating more than one thousand miles to an entirely new and very different territory attractive. The goal, of course, was to lure strong antislavery advocates, but the promoters were cognizant that the passion to end slavery likely would not be enough to tip the balance in favor of emigration. They needed to provide incentives to potential emigrants.

An undated document in the Kansas State Historical Society Collection provides some insight into their thought processes to entice emigration. The Emigrant Aid Company would "organize emigration to the West." In doing so, there would be three benefits—one to the emigrants, another to the nation, and a third to the company itself. For the emigrants, the company would provide transportation, food, and shelter at the lowest possible cost while they were settling into their new homes, as well as assistance in helping them locate and secure home sites. The company would immediately assist in establishing newspapers, schools, and churches, "so that the morals and intelligence of their children shall not be forfeited by a life of semibarbarianism [sic] as often happens to settlers in the West."

The company would benefit the country because it would create new, free states. Further, western settlement would provide a safety valve, relieving the pressures of poverty and overpopulation in the East. The assistance provided by the company would provide a means for the urban poor to move west. In other words, what was "vicious here [in the East] will be virtuous there [in the West]."

Finally, the Emigration Aid Company itself would benefit, because new settlement would increase the value of the land. Investments in new mills and other machinery would further benefit the investors. And, if nothing else, "the pleasure of founding new and free states which bless everybody and injure nobody and of binding them forever to Massachusetts by the strongest ties of gratitude and filial love" would have benefits at least equal to, if not superior to, any monetary benefits.[29]

Of course, the efforts to organize, raise money, and facilitate the emigration to Kansas and fulfill these lofty ideals would have been to no avail if the Emigrant Aid Company could not recruit settlers and get them to Kansas. Eli Thayer, Amos Lawrence, and the other officers in the company understood that they needed to move quickly, so in June 1854, they hired Dr. Charles Robinson and Charles H. Branscomb to go to Kansas and conduct a reconnaissance to identify the best locations for settlement.

Dr. Robinson almost immediately became a key figure in the Emigrant Aid Company and in the settlement and politics of Kansas. Robinson was born in Massachusetts in 1818. He attended but did not graduate from Amherst, studied medicine, established a practice in Belchertown, Massachusetts, and married Sarah Adams in 1843. His wife died in 1846, throwing him into a deep depression, which forced him to leave his medical practice. In 1849, he joined the Congress and California Mutual Protective Association as the group's physician and headed to California to hopefully snap out of his depression and find his fortune. On the way to the goldfields, he traveled through Kansas and was immediately drawn to the land. In his diary entry for May 11, 1849, he wrote that "as far as the eye can reach, he sees nothing but a beautiful green carpet; . . . he hears nothing but the feathered songsters of the air, and he feels nothing but a solemn awe in view of this infinite display of creative power."[30]

Robinson, like many other prospectors, recognized quickly that the diggings meant hard work with little reward, so he settled in Sacramento, opened a restaurant, and became involved in land issues in California. Robinson led an effort to secure the rights of squatters to their land claims. He was elected to the California House of Representatives when it became a state and appeared destined to be a major figure. But in 1851, he left California and returned to Massachusetts. Romance beckoned.

While in California, he corresponded with Sara Tappan Doolittle Lawrence, a distant relative of Amos Lawrence. They had met in Massachusetts just before he headed west. It appears that Sara's charms held sway over the warm weather, business, and political prospects of California. A little more than a month after he arrived back in Massachusetts, the couple married. Charles and Sara settled in Fitchburg, Massachusetts, where he edited the local newspaper

Dr. Charles Robinson. Kansas State Historical Society.

Sara Robinson. Kansas State Historical Society.

and practiced medicine part time. Sara Robinson was an amazing woman, and her marriage to Charles was a true partnership. Charles would jokingly remark that she became so well known in the East, he was known as "the husband of Mrs. Robinson."[31]

In 1854, Robinson attended an antislavery meeting conducted by Eli Thayer and was immediately drawn to Thayer's plan to flood Kansas with antislavery settlers. Shortly after the meeting, he offered his services to the Emigrant Aid Company. With Robinson's journey through and affinity for Kansas on his way to California, he became the ideal candidate to scout settlement locations there. So, in June, Thayer and Lawrence hired Robinson along with Charles H. Branscomb to do just that.[32]

Charles H. Branscomb, Robinson's reconnaissance partner, was a young lawyer in Holyoke, Massachusetts. A native of New Hampshire, Branscomb attended Phillips Exeter Academy, graduated from Dartmouth College, and studied law in Cambridge Law School. He practiced law for about six years. Clearly he was drawn to the Emigrant Aid Company, and just as clearly, Thayer and Lawrence were drawn to him as well, offering him the opportunity to accompany Robinson to find the best location to start a settlement in Kansas. Lawrence agreed to finance the reconnaissance with up-front money and a note to draw on credit if necessary.

Robinson and Branscomb arrived in Kansas in early July. On the steamer trip up the Missouri River, they experienced what they would be up against in settling Kansas. Members of the Missouri Legislature boarded the riverboat in Jefferson City, boasting that they planned to do whatever it took to keep abolitionists out of Kansas. Robinson noted that during the conversation he "was a listener rather than a talker."[33] But when they arrived in Kansas Village (the future site of Kansas City), they found some of its businessmen more amenable. They arranged for the purchase of the Gillis House, a substantial brick hotel that would serve as temporary housing, and they further arranged to use Mr. Riddlesbarger's "commodious warehouse" as a temporary storage facility. From Kansas City, they agreed that Robinson would head up the Missouri River to Fort Leavenworth and that Branscomb would head up the Kansas River to Fort Riley, searching for the best land for settlement.

They knew that Delaware Indian lands under the new treaty would be sold to the highest bidder. The same would likely be the case with the Shawnee lands. So, to assist Robinson and Branscomb with land issues, Amos Lawrence hired James Blood, who was an expert in preemption and other land laws.[34] Blood scouted the land as well, and preferred a site near where the Wakarusa River entered the Kansas River, about forty miles west of the Missouri line. The site appeared to be unencumbered by any potential title issues.

When Robinson arrived back in Kansas City, a message was waiting that the first wave of emigrants was ready to leave Boston for Kansas. Robinson was directed to meet the party in St. Louis, then return to Boston. He sent a note to Branscomb to wait for the emigrants in Kansas City and guide them to the new settlement.[35] When the first group arrived, Blood and Branscomb guided them to the settlement, at first called Wakarusa.[36]

One of the earliest recruits to head west under the auspices of the Emigrant Aid Company was Dr. John Doy, a resident of Rochester, New York. He later described how he was attracted to the company. In June 1854, "in consequence of what was published in the news-papers . . . to settle Kansas with intelligent and industrious citizens from the Northern States, a public meeting was held at the Court House in Rochester, New York, to consider the propriety of sending a delegate to Massachusetts, where the movement originated."[37] He was selected as the delegate and was sent to meet with Thayer and officers of the Emigrant Aid Company in Boston.

Dr. Doy, a homeopathic doctor, originally from Hull, in Yorkshire, England, met with Thayer and several "leading citizens" of Boston, and was so impressed with the enterprise that he returned to Rochester and prepared for the journey to Kansas. He recruited Daniel R. Anthony, Susan B. Anthony's brother, to join the first party. From Thayer and others, Doy understood that he and the other members of the "first pioneer party" were "to ascertain if the soil was . . . fertile, well wooded and well watered," and thus "good agricultural and manufacturing country. If they found this to be the case," they were to inform the main party, which would follow soon after, that everything looked favorable.[38]

John Doy was one of twenty-nine who made up the first party. He and B. R. Knapp, a mechanic from Massachusetts, recalled the journey and early settlement. The party was made up of eleven mechanics, five farmers, two physicians, two speculators, a reporter, a clerk, a lawyer, a banker, a laborer, a merchant, a builder, an architect, and one who gave his occupation as a "sportsman." They left Boston on July 17, 1854, and arrived in St. Louis on July 20. The route took the party from Boston, through Rochester, Buffalo, and eventually to St. Louis.

Years after the city of Lawrence and the state of Kansas were well established, Ferdinand Fuller, George W. Goss, Dr. S. C. Harrington, and J. F. Morgan posed for this photograph. All four men were members of the first party to leave Boston for Kansas with the New England Emigrant Aid Company on July 17, 1854. Kenneth Spenser Research Library, University of Kansas.

According to Dr. Doy, when the party arrived in St. Louis, "we made a bargain with the captain of a steamboat the *Polar Star* to take us to Kansas City, Missouri, for twelve dollars a head. Everything went on well." He continued, writing that at "Lexington, Missouri, some of us strolled about on shore while the boat wooded, and certain persons, having learned who we were . . . informed us that a large party was waiting for us at Kansas City, and would give us a warm reception . . . as might induce us to go back." Doy and his companions were prepared, however, and "on nearing Kansas City, our little army of twenty-nine was drawn up in a line on deck, with rifles and revolvers all ready to give a fitting response to the promised warm reception." Nothing came of the incident, and the party "quietly went on shore in a body, and attended to our own business.[39]

In Kansas City, the party bought two yoke of oxen and a wagon and hired a four-horse team, wagon, and driver to carry their trunks, provisions, tents, and other baggage the rest of the way. Doy reported that "as soon as we crossed the line of Kansas, our driver said he had come as far as he had agreed, and must have more money, or he would go back. We reasoned with him, however, and he finally consented to go with us as far as the backbone hills," their final destination. They arrived at Wakarusa on August 1, 1854.

B. R. Knapp wrote that they established their camp and pitched their twenty-five tents, "which made a fine appearance, although a little soiled." The next day, Knapp and the others went to work setting up their claims to the land, "preparing for a permanent settlement." They paced off half-mile squares, marked the corners with stakes, and wrote on each stake that the owner claimed "160 acres of the lands within the bounds, from the date of the claim." Each owner registered and recorded his claim. Knapp also claimed eighty acres of timberland at Mount Hope, several miles from the "new city." Several members of the party made their claims and returned east, intending to come back with their families in the spring.[40]

Dr. Doy wrote that as the group were setting up their tents and staking out their claims, a squatter "stood by and watched our proceedings." Since with preemption laws, a squatter had first claim to the land, the group offered to buy him out. "He was sure, if [we] wanted it, his claim was worth at least five hundred dollars, and he wouldn't take a red cent less." Doy continued: "we made a bargain with him, and took possession on the first day August, AD 1854."[41]

Another member of the pioneer party, who staked a claim next to Dr. Doy, was twenty-three-year-old Samuel F. Tappan. Tappan was a member of one of the most prominent abolitionist families in New England. His cousins, Arthur and Lewis Tappan, were successful silk merchants in the Northeast who donated much of their fortunes to support antislavery programs and causes. Samuel could have stayed in Massachusetts and earned a comfortable living in his father's cabinet-making shop or in his extended family's profitable businesses; instead he joined the first party going to Kansas to do his part to ensure that the territory would be free. He frequently sent reports to eastern newspapers reporting on the free-state activities in Kansas, and later became an active "conductor" on the Underground Railroad.

Charles Robinson arrived back in Boston and prepared to lead the second party to Kansas. His partner on this trip was Samuel C. Pomeroy. Pomeroy was from an old New England family, graduated from Amherst College, and demonstrated clear antislavery credentials, having organized the Liberty Party in Massachusetts and serving in the Massachusetts Legislature as a member of the Free Soil Party.

This second party was much larger than the first, consisting of seventy-eight members, including women and children and four musicians from Hartford, Connecticut, who brought along their instruments. They left from the Boston and Worcester train station on August 29, 1854, with an impressive send-off, singing a hymn written for the occasion by noted poet John Greenleaf Whittier. They made it to Kansas City on September 6, and nearly everyone arrived in Wakarusa by September 11.[42]

Euphoria reigned among the New England abolitionists with the tremendous response to the summons to Kansas. But behind the scenes, Amos Lawrence worried that the Emigrant Aid Company was teetering on insolvency. He did not personally go to Kansas at this time. He believed that he could best serve the cause working from Boston. In his August 27, 1854 diary entry, he wrote that "the subscription goes slowly and hard: people have no confidence in land stock. . . . This is, and it has turned out as I supposed. Still it must not fail: Kansas must be a free state, if possible." On September 3, he reported that the first large party left for Kansas, and he lamented that "all the expenditures thus far [have] been met by myself, but I cannot go further without funds in hand: these must be raised soon." Then, at the end of September, he recorded that he had devoted a great deal of time to "the Kansas business," and if Kansas "and Nebraska do not become free states, it will not be for want of hard work to settle them."[43]

After the community organized, selected its officials, and began to settle into more permanency, the inhabitants debated whether their community should be called Wakarusa, Yankee Town, New Boston, or Plymouth. Instead, on October 6, they settled on Lawrence City in honor of Amos A. Lawrence, who everyone knew had contributed substantial money to the Emigrant Aid Company and the settlement of Kansas. One settler jokingly observed that "the name sounded well and had no bad odor attached to it in any part of the Union."[44] The residents of the new town probably were unaware that Lawrence would have preferred not to have his name attached to the town. His own choice would have been Wakarusa. To his diary, he wrote "1. That being a trustee . . . will cause my motives of action to be doubted and thus will lessen my influence. 2. It will create dissatisfaction among the other trustees. 3. The Indian name Wakarusa is excellent."[45]

The New England Emigrant Aid Company was remarkably efficient at populating Kansas with antislavery settlers, but it was not the only such organization, and Lawrence was not the only destination. Isaac Goodnow, a teacher in Providence, Rhode Island, heard a lecture from Eli Thayer and caught the bug to go to Kansas to join the antislavery cause, but he wanted to start a new community. Goodnow led another advance party in March 1855. He carried a letter of introduction from Thomas Webb to Samuel Pomeroy, which showed that even serious abolitionists had senses of humor. "This will introduce to you I. T. Goodnow Esq.," he wrote, "who not only is good now, but I trust will remain good thro' all time for freedom & justice."[46]

When Goodnow arrived in Kansas and conferred with Pomeroy, he decided to travel up the Kansas River to where it was joined by the Big Blue River, about 120 miles west of Kansas City. Two tiny settlements were already nearby that joined forces to create the community of Boston. In June 1855, not long after Goodnow arrived, a steamboat, carrying seventy-six members of the Cincinnati and Kansas Land Company, chugged up the Kansas River and landed at the settlement. Goodnow and the citizens of Boston agreed to join forces with the Cincinnati group, which instantly doubled the population. The Cincinnati group was committed to calling the community Manhattan—no one knows exactly why—but Goodnow and the others agreed to the name change, and it stuck.

The Cincinnati group also brought a printing press, parts to build a small gristmill, a steam engine, cooking stoves, seeds and agricultural implements, the components to build prefabricated buildings, and 153 barrels of whiskey. Manhattan would not have the violent future of Lawrence, but it remained a solid antislavery settlement. Goodnow also was instrumental in receiving a charter from the territorial legislature in 1858 to establish Blue Mount Central College just outside Manhattan. In 1863, after Kansas achieved statehood, and with the federal Morrill Land Grant College Act of 1862, the legislature transformed this private college that was teetering on the brink of insolvency into Kansas State Agricultural College, which later became Kansas State University.[47]

Other organizations, such as the New York State Kansas Committee, raised funds and sent antislavery emigrants to Kansas as well. Dozens of organizations were formed to encourage emigration to

Kansas. Most were small, several merged with the New England Company or other groups, and many fizzled. Among the more interesting unsuccessful groups were the Vegetarian and Octagon Settlement Companies. Chartered in 1855, Henry S. Clubb recruited antislavery vegetarians to settle in two large planned communities, in the shapes of octagons, in Allen and Woodson Counties. Enthusiastic settlers traveled to Kansas in 1856 and laid out their claims, but in short order the communities failed, mostly because the sponsor, Mr. Clubb, promised far more infrastructure improvements than he could deliver.[48]

The relatively quick settlement of places such as Lawrence and Manhattan by antislavery emigrants was a surprise to many, especially to those who assumed that Kansas would become a slave state. Pro-slavery emigrants were settling in Kansas, but mostly as individuals rather than as part of organized groups. To try to compete, the "Law and Order Party of Kansas Territory" was created in 1856 for the primary purpose of appealing to the "Friends in the South, and the Law-Abiding People of the Union." In the group's publication, *The Voice of Kansas*, the organizers railed against the antislavery organizations saturating Kansas with settlers, and issued the appeal for Southerners to "send us men and means. We must have your help."[49]

The pro- and antislavery sides were jockeying for position, but they were doing so under the legal framework of the Kansas Territorial Government. Soon after establishment of the territory, President Franklin Pierce appointed a Democrat, Andrew Reeder of Pennsylvania, as territorial governor in July 1854. Reeder arrived at Fort Leavenworth on October 7 and immediately began a tour of his new domain. In November, he called for a census to count the number of residents, and, in particular, the number of eligible male voters for the upcoming elections for the territorial legislature. The territory was divided into seventeen districts, and census takers asked the names of the males twenty-one years or older, where they were from, their occupations, the number of people in

Andrew W. Reeder. Kansas State Historical Society.

their households, if they were United States citizens or intended
to become citizens, if they had any enslaved people and if so how
many. Finally, the most important question was if they planned to
remain as permanent residents of Kansas. The census also counted
free blacks, but excluded Indians and members of the military stationed in Kansas territory.

The census was conducted in January and February 1855. It
counted 8,521 total residents, of which 5,138 were males and 3,383
were females. Many males were dependents because only 2,378
of them were eligible to vote. Breaking the numbers down a little
further, of the eligible voters, 128 were from Massachusetts, with
another 50 from other New England states. There were 1,358 from
Missouri and another 235 from other slaveholding states. Midwest
states, not including Missouri, produced 607 residents. Finally,
the census takers identified 211 enslaved people, owned by 166

individuals, with the highest concentration living near the Missouri border.[50]

District 1, including Lawrence, was populated with 87 people from Massachusetts and 20 from other New England states. Another 101 were from Midwestern states, excluding Missouri—58 from there—from which no enslaved people were counted in this district. Scattered throughout the territory were families from other countries, of which the highest concentration was in District 16, in which 62 foreign families, many from Germany, were counted.[51]

The presence of so many residents from Missouri and other slave states did not mean that Kansas would automatically become a slave state. If the census takers would have added a question such as "why did you decide to settle in Kansas?" to their list, a large majority from free or slave states likely would have answered something such as: "I came here looking for a better life for myself and my family."

3 I Shall Build a Cabin for Myself Forthwith

BEFORE THE NEW RESIDENTS OF Lawrence could slay the pro-slavery dragons, they first had to provide for the spiritual, economic, and physical needs of their community. B. R. Knapp, one of the first Emigrant Aid Company pioneers, documented the beginnings of the settlement, recording and then mailing his notes to a Boston newspaper on August 9, 1854. He reported that it cost thirty dollars to build a log cabin, thus placing carpenters and laborers in high demand. "I shall build a cabin for myself forthwith," he wrote, "and have already commenced log-cutting." It was hard work "for a green hand," but he hoped he "would soon get used to it." Knapp also reported that each member of the party was developing his own claim.[52]

Ferdinand Fuller, another pioneer, added to Knapp's description. He reported that as soon as the first party arrived on August 1, 1854, at about noon, they ate their meal on the ridge where the state university eventually would stand, and which they called Mount Oread, in honor of the school established by Eli Thayer. They held a meeting in which Mr. Fuller was elected president of the community. The first order of business was to decide if the site was appropriate to establish the town—it was—and so they stayed and started laying out their town and their claims.[53]

Dr. Doy, reported that when the second party arrived, he was forced to take down his temporary log house. He and his pioneer party colleagues thought they would be granted more land, since they were the first ones to arrive. Instead, Doy reported that they were granted "only one lot apiece extra." He was upset but undaunted; he "went out and selected a beautiful farm of one hundred and sixty acres, with a stream, timbered on each side, running through it, about a mile and a half from Lawrence[.] There I built my second log-house. . . ." In October 1854, he wrote: "my family [arrived], consisting of my wife and nine children—six sons and three daughters— the eldest then about twenty-one, and the youngest two years old."[54]

Joseph Savage, a member of the second party, recorded his reminiscences several years later in weekly installments in the *Western Home Journal,* published in Lawrence. He reported that the Emigrant Aid Company had planned well. The journey took seven days from Boston to Kansas City, and when they arrived in Kansas City, the society had tents for them and a pleasant area in which to camp. On the steamship journey from St. Louis to Kansas City they had several "sharp discussions" with slavery men, who backed off when they saw James Sawyer's Sharps rifle in action. When he arrived, Savage reported that a Mr. Stearns had a log cabin, and that he asserted his squatter rights to 160 acres under the Preemption Act, which became the heart of the community. The Emigrant Aid Company bought him out for five hundred dollars, and thus took possession and clear title to most of the town site.

It seems that the early settlers were given to appointing committees for almost everything. Ferdinand Fuller reported that his committee was in charge of setting up tents and taking a vote that decided Lawrence would be their home. When the second party arrived, a new committee replaced the first one, with Charles Robinson as its head. Of the myriad committees, one was formed to make a recommendation about religious affiliations—or lack thereof—in the new community. Some of the more liberal residents thought it would make sense to not worry about denominational differences, but instead pool the community resources, build one big nondenominational church, and invite a prominent, well-known minister to shepherd the collective flock. The committee did not reach an agreement, and apparently strayed somewhat from its charge into theological issues. A majority focused on orthodox Christian dogma, arguing that the dead would rise from their graves upon the second coming of Jesus. The minority, on the other hand, argued that the resurrection of the dead was physiologically impossible since, with decomposition, bodies turned into something else. Thus, the idea of one unified church was stillborn.[55]

Although the residents dropped the concept of one big, ecumenical church, they did organize a church, and the first service was held on October 1, 1854. An unnamed source reported a detailed account of the service: "Last Sabbath was my first *prairie Sabbath*. Sabbath our parties had assembled for the 'hearing of the word.' Rev. Mr. Lum, sent us by the American Home Missionary Society, preached very acceptably. The place of meeting was one of the large receiving and boarding houses. We have two nearly adjoining each other, each of them about 20 by 48 feet, covered and thatched with

Straw houses, the first structures built in Lawrence. Sketch by J. E. Rice c. 1854–55. Kansas State Historical Society.

prairie grass, very warm and very good. We had a large and attentive audience."[56]

From this first service, two weeks later the Congregational Church was organized on October 15, 1854. The members drew up a creed and constitution, based on the model of Mount Vernon Church of Boston, and named their church Plymouth Church, drawing a similarity to the Pilgrims who had also settled a new land two centuries earlier. Plymouth Congregational Church is still in existence. The first church structure was a small brick building. The second—still used today—was completed in 1870, designed by architect John Haskell. The church celebrated its sesquicentennial in 2004, and remains an important fixture in Lawrence.[57]

One member of the church/theology committee and a gentleman whose name popped up frequently in early Lawrence was Franklin Haskell, the father of the architect who later would design the new Plymouth Church. He was listed on the manifest for the second group as a farmer from North Brookfield, Massachusetts, and was selected as one of the surveyors to lay out the town plan. His wife and thirteen-year-old son joined him in 1855. Haskell died suddenly in January 1857, and his two older sons came to Kansas to care for their mother and younger brother. Franklin, but for his early death, would likely have been one of the leading individuals in the state. His sons, though, would have made him proud. John was the leading architect in early Kansas. Another son, Dudley, later was elected to the US House of Representatives from Lawrence.

For the most part, the Emigrant Aid Company settlers purchased the land claimed by settlers without much difficulty. But several other squatters were not so easy to deal with. John Baldwin had selected a claim in the future site of Lawrence, but he was not willing to sell. Under the Preemption Act of 1841, individuals could "squat" on up to 160 acres, provided they actively resided on and continually improved the land and did not allow it to sit idle for six months or longer. They could then purchase the land from the government for not less than $1.25 per acre before it was made available to the general public.

John Baldwin had staked out his preemption claim, then left Kansas. He returned when he heard that the Emigrant Aid Company intended to settle in Lawrence. He set up a tent in the middle of the community and refused to sell or relinquish his claim. Baldwin was a pro-slavery man from Missouri. Dr. Robinson set up a tent as well on the land Baldwin claimed. On October 6, 1854, Baldwin brought in a wagonload of pro-slavery Missourians armed to the teeth, and threatened to go to war if Robinson did not remove his tent from the disputed land. Baldwin sent a note to Robinson, saying that if he did not remove his tent within one-half hour, "we shall take the trouble to move the same." Robinson responded to Baldwin that "if you molest our property, you do it at your peril."

The half hour passed, then another quarter hour, with both sides wondering what would happen next. Neither side, it seemed, wanted bloodshed. After some saber rattling, both sides dispersed, and the first salvo in what would later be called "Bleeding Kansas" was averted. Several months later, Baldwin brought his case before a panel headed by Governor Reeder. The panel divided the town into 220 shares. Baldwin and his associates would hold 100 shares, the Lawrence Association would own 110 shares, the Emigrant Aid Company would hold 10 shares, and 2 would be held in trust for a college that would be built in the future. The antislavery residents of Lawrence were not happy with the decision, but as a local newspaper editor wrote, it did remove a cloud that "hung like an incubus over the city for several months."

The newspaper reporting on the land issue was the Kansas *Herald of Freedom*, published by George Washington Brown. Brown had practiced law, and then became the editor of a newspaper in Conneautville, Pennsylvania. He was drawn to the Emigrant Aid Company and agreed that he would go to Kansas and start an anti-slavery newspaper, with financial backing from the company. He claimed to have the first newspaper in Lawrence, publishing the

George Washington Brown. Kansas State Historical Society.

first edition of the *Herald* on October 21, 1854, in his offices in Pennsylvania, then shipping the papers to Lawrence. In this first edition, Brown printed a letter from Eli Thayer, asking him to "represent our [the Emigrant Aid Company's] interests" in Kansas. Thayer went on to request the *Herald* print truthful news about individuals and the community, share news provided by Emigrant Aid Company agents, and publish news shared by emigrants to Kansas.[58] Brown moved to Lawrence in December 1854 and set up his newspaper office.

In the first edition printed in Lawrence, Brown announced that he had enough paper and ink on hand to last for several months. He reported that a minister from a New Jersey church planned to lead his entire congregation of some forty families to Kansas. He also reported that a group of Quakers from North Carolina inquired about land in Kansas—its fertility and availability—and asked if there was a Quaker community in the territory. Brown asked for volunteers to answer numerous similar inquiries. In this first Kansas edition, a doctor, a dentist, four lawyers, a produce and meat store, and several other businesses placed advertisements. Dr. John Doy advertised that he had opened a practice in "hydropathic medicine." Brown wrote that he would also be more than happy to print just about anything anybody wanted. He continued publishing his paper for the next five years.[59]

Although George Washington Brown claimed to have the first newspaper in Lawrence, it was not the only paper. In a letter Charles Robinson wrote to Amos Lawrence in December 1854, he mentioned plans for two new ventures, "making three antislavery newspapers in Lawrence."[60]

John Speer established the *Democratic Whig* newspaper in Medina, Ohio, in 1843, which he operated until 1854. After the passage of the Kansas-Nebraska Act, John and his brother Joseph came to Lawrence. They started the Lawrence *Kansas Pioneer,* an antislavery newspaper, in 1855, but the first issues were printed from Medina. They later changed the name to the *Kansas Tribune* and eventually moved the newspaper to Topeka. John Speer later returned to Lawrence and revived his newspaper there. He remained active throughout the troubled territorial years of Kansas,

John Speer. Kansas State Historical Society.

denouncing slavery, attending the Topeka constitutional convention of 1855, and serving in the first free-state legislature in 1857.

Of Lawrence's earliest newspaper editors, Josiah Miller had, by far, the most interesting background. He was from South Carolina. His family members were strong antislavery advocates. His father was nearly beaten to death by pro-slavery men when he defended his minister, who had been tarred and feathered for preaching an antislavery message from the pulpit. Having observed the cruelties inflicted on his father and other antislavery individuals in South Carolina, Josiah adopted his parents' views on slavery. He attended Indiana University and later studied law. With the passage of the Kansas-Nebraska Act, he was among the early Emigrant Aid Company immigrants, arriving in Kansas in August 1854. His newspaper, the *Kansas Free State*, which he published with R. G. Elliott, was the first printed in Lawrence on January 3, 1855. Miller reported that its newspaper office had neither "floor, ceiling, nor window sash." The pro-slavery faction in Kansas considered Miller a serious threat due to his abolitionist connections, so in the summer of 1856, he was seized by pro-slavery men and charged with treason

Josiah Miller. Kansas State Historical Society.

against the State of South Carolina. He was nearly transported back to his native state for trial, but when cooler heads prevailed, he was released from prison after a few weeks.[61]

In the first run of the *Free State*, Josiah Miller and his partner described the primitive office from which the paper was produced. Many structures in early Lawrence were similar. When the first parties arrived, they stayed in the tents provided by the Emigrant Aid Company, but these were temporary and not suitable for winter. The company also promised a sawmill, but it had not yet arrived. Timber was scarce, and the trees that grew along the streams and rivers were quickly used up. There was one framed lumber house built for the minister of the Plymouth Church, but that was the only one in town.

As a temporary measure, the new residents built their houses and other buildings with straw. They set two rows of poles together, attached them at the top in an A-frame, and then filled in the gaps between the poles with straw.

The largest such structure, the Pioneer Boarding House, was twenty feet wide by forty-six feet long, and served as the boarding house, the temporary church, and the community gathering center. Fortunately, the first winter was relatively mild, and while these "straw tents" left a great deal to be desired, they provided adequate temporary shelter.

In its haste to encourage as many antislavery settlers to Kansas as possible, it soon became clear that the Emigrant Aid Company had not adequately planned for accommodating their needs. The lack of comfortable housing was one problem. Another was that when new groups arrived, there was nowhere to put them. The third Emigrant Aid–sponsored party left Boston on September 26, 1854. It started with ninety-six individuals, and by the time the party reached St. Louis, it had nearly doubled in size, picking up additional emigrants along the way. The trip took longer, the accommodations in Kansas City were inadequate for the size of the party, much of their luggage was lost or misplaced along the way, and the expenses incurred were much higher than the company had advertised. Each member had to find his or her own way from Kansas City to Lawrence, and upon arrival, each also discovered that he or she would not receive equal shares of land in the community.

A reporter for the *New York Times*, observing the plight of this third group, wrote on October 9: "the truth is, that the Boston Emigrant Aid Company has by no means fulfilled its pledges to the public, or its duty to its protégés. There seems a total lack of system in their operations, and of efficiency in their agents." Several members of the party expressed their frustrations in letters home. Charles Loomer wrote that "those who bring with them $500 or $1,000 to buy stock and implements for their farms, and are young, or have good constitutions, get along very well; but for men without capital, or whose health is none of the best, it were better for them to stay at home." Another young man reported to the Boston *Daily Evening Traveller* "that of the party of one hundred and sixty who left with him, at least ninety are on their way back to the Eastward, well satisfied that they are not fitted to settle a new and unbroken country, and quite disposed to pronounce the whole Kanzas scheme a grand humbug."[62]

The fourth party of 126 left Boston on October 17, and by the time it reached Kansas City, the number had swelled to 230. Their complaints were similar to those of the third party. George O. Willard, a member of the fourth party, wrote that "of our company, which numbered 230 when we landed, I do not think 100 can be found in the territory." He continued, writing that "few were dissatisfied with the country, but the cost of living was so much more than they had been told at the east [*sic*], that many became discouraged and returned. In fact, while we were coming out we met a number of the previous company [the third party] returning."

When the fourth party arrived in Lawrence, many decided to start a new community at Rock Creek, about seventy-five miles west of Lawrence. They expressed their dissatisfaction with the Emigrant Aid Company in a resolution they prepared on November 12, 1854. The document opened with their admiration for the "beautiful scenery, and . . . the healthfulness of its climate, and the fertility of its soil. . . . But in our candid opinion, the 'Emigrant Aid Company' [has] erred in failing to present the dark, as well as the bright side of the condition of things here." The group was particularly upset that the company had not made more of an effort "to select locations for parties arriving here, and that misrepresentations have been made respecting the price of provisions and the cost of living." They advised others to be careful and not to accept all of the pronouncements of the Emigrant Aid Company.

Recognizing that the complaints of the third and fourth parties were valid, when the fifth and sixth Emigrant Aid groups—both much smaller—arrived in November and December 1854, Charles Robinson encouraged many of the new arrivals to head further up the Kansas River to settle in the future site of Topeka. Although the members of these parties complained about the expenses they incurred, those who settled in Topeka were pleased with the site of the new town. They laid out a plan for the town, and by late December called their community "Topeka," an Indian name for the wild potatoes growing along the riverbanks.[63] Before long, Topeka would equal Lawrence as a hotbed of antislavery advocates. It also would become the capital of the free-state movement, and later the capital of the new state.

4 You Might as Well Read Bibles to Buffaloes

THE EMIGRANT AID COMPANY CLEARLY had not prepared for the settlers it was encouraging to emigrate to Kansas. The goal of flood-
ing the territory with antislavery advocates as quickly as possible
was working, but these poor souls encountered numerous practical problems, as well as other problems, upon arrival. Although Eli
Thayer and other company members traveled throughout New England successfully recruiting new emigrants, they met with much less
success raising money.

Amos Lawrence, who continued to serve as treasurer, became
more and more exasperated with the fund-raising efforts and with
the promises Thayer and others were making to prospective Kansas
emigrants. In a letter to his friend, John Carter Brown, he shared his
frustrations. "There is a great deal of bluster in regard to the movements of this company," he wrote, "and statements to the magnitude
of our plans are untrue." He continued: "I am sorry to say the prospect under our present arrangement is very poor; some change must
be made. Meantime we are making large promises as to what we will
do for settlers which are certain to be broken, and which will entail
much dissatisfaction."[64]

Even with his frustrations, Lawrence remained devoted to the
cause of making Kansas a free state. He had already spent thousands
of his own money to scout the land, to purchase supplies and property, and to buy out squatters. As he had intimated to friends earlier,

he did not invest his money expecting a return, but he was becoming alarmed that the effort might drain more from his wallet than he could afford. One day, in his personal diary he wrote: "Kansas drafts came in; no money in the treasury and never have had, and no money of my own. So I transferred some manufacturing company's stock to be sold and pay them. If Kansas should not be a free State, I shall lay it to heart and to my pocket too."[65] Later in 1855, Lawrence wrote his friend Dr. Samuel Cabot complaining about the constant requests for more money, and in a note at the bottom of the letter marked "private," he wrote: "I am out of pocket $13,000 for Kansas by loan & gift within the last 12 months & think it time to hold up, since every cent of it is borrowed money."[66]

Finally, in September 1855, Lawrence seemed to have reached the end of his patience and submitted his resignation as treasurer of the Emigrant Aid Company.[67] When his friend, John Carter Brown, caught wind of Lawrence's resignation, he announced that he would resign as well. Lawrence obviously had a change of heart because he continued as treasurer without a lapse in service.

In addition to money, organizational, and planning problems, the Emigrant Aid Company experienced public relations problems as well. Pro-slavery advocates started spreading the rumor that the Emigrant Aid Company was paying the expenses of its settlers, and that its emigrants were radical abolitionists. In the 1850s, there was an important nuanced distinction between antislavery advocates and abolitionists. Neither liked the institution of slavery. Generally, abolitionists demanded that slavery in the United States should end immediately, no matter the cost, whereas antislavery advocates such as Lawrence wanted slavery to end but they begrudgingly were willing to accept slavery confined to the states where it already existed. The antislavery group was passionate, however, that slavery should not be introduced into new territories.

Lawrence attempted to deflect the bad publicity by writing to Thomas Hart Benton, who had just left his seat in the House of Representatives, and who had recently published a speech claiming that the Emigrant Aid settlers' expenses were being covered by the company. "I am the treasurer and a trustee of the only New England society which has sent out settlers," Lawrence wrote, "and know that all the money collected has been spent in erecting schoolhouses, temporary huts, steam saw and gristmills, . . . and for similar purposes, and for nothing else."

Regarding the claim that the company was only recruiting abolitionists as settlers, Lawrence, in another letter to President Franklin Pierce, wrote that he "had been pained often by seeing this association [the Emigrant Aid Company] called an affair of abolitionists." He continued, "some societies [claiming to send emigrants to Kansas] under this name have been formed by abolitionists, but have accomplished nothing."[68]

Even with bad publicity, funding and logistical problems, plus a drought, Emigrant Aid Company parties kept coming. The first 1855 party of about 200 set out from Boston on March 13, followed by a second party of about 170 leaving a week later, and the third party of about 100 leaving the following week. In all, some 900 settlers, almost all from New England, ventured to Kansas in 1855. They encountered the same problems faced by the late-1854 parties, namely that Lawrence was not ready for them, so the company had to scout adequate sites. Further, a drought that had gripped the region lowered the level of the Missouri River to the point where it was difficult, and later impossible, for steam vessels to navigate through the shallows. The cost of transportation rose accordingly. As was the case with many of the later emigrant parties in 1854, many arrived in Kansas, turned around, and returned to their home states.[69]

George Brown devoted considerable space in his newspaper to the problems, but also to the potential for Lawrence. By the spring of 1855, farmland within a twelve- to fifteen-mile radius was taken. There were, however, still plenty of lots available in town. To encourage development, a block of building sites was set aside at no cost, if the prospective owner committed to erecting buildings from $300 to $3,000 in value within eighteen months. If someone wanted to purchase property in prime business locations, the cost could reach as much as $3,000 per lot.

In several editions, Brown decried the lack of adequate lumber for construction, along with the need for many more sawmills. He continuously scoured newspapers and publications from the East for new construction techniques and alternative building materials. He found and described composition roofing materials, advertised as fireproof. He was particularly enamored with concrete houses, as described in O. S. Fowler's *A Home for All* (1854). Fowler provided guidance for building octagon-shaped houses made from concrete. He gave instructions for preparing the materials, erecting the forms, and pouring the concrete. The problem, of course, was that while there was plenty of lime, sand, and gravel readily available, the lack of lumber to form the walls was a major issue.[70]

At this early stage of the immigrants living in Lawrence, it mattered little whether houses were built of wood or concrete. What mattered most was whether or not Kansas would be a free state. On the other hand, pro-slavery advocates were just as determined that Kansas would enter the union as a slave state. The first test for the territory's future came with the first territorial elections in March 1855. The census taken in January and February 1855 identified 2,378 adult males qualified to vote in the upcoming election for a territorial legislature. In Lawrence, 369 men were eligible to vote. But when the election was held on March 30, 6,307 men cast ballots throughout the territory, and of that number, 1,034 voted in Lawrence. Granted, the census likely missed some residents and new settlers who arrived in Lawrence and elsewhere after the census, but neither of those factors accounted for the disparity. How did this happen?

The Reverend Richard Cordley described what happened in his *History of Lawrence, Kansas* (1895). Weeks before the election was scheduled, groups of pro-slavery Missourians organized and targeted areas in Kansas where they planned to vote, ensuring that their numbers would be substantial enough to outvote the free-soil settlers. Then, starting three days before Election Day, they crossed the border in organized bands and traveled to the areas they had targeted. According to Rev. Cordley, "the evening before, and the morning of the day of the election, about one thousand men arrived at Lawrence, and camped in a ravine a short distance from the town, and near the place of voting. They came, in wagons (of which there were over one hundred) or on horseback. . . . They were armed with guns, rifles, pistols and bowie [*sic*] knives; and had tents, music and flags with them. They [also] brought with them two pieces of artillery."

Election judges volunteered, and were on hand, to ensure that only eligible voters—residents of Kansas Territory—were allowed to cast ballots. Three election judges agreed to serve in Lawrence. One judge, N. B. Blanton, was absent, later reporting that Missourians threatened to hang him if he appeared. The Missourians replaced him with one of their own judges, a Mr. Cummins. Mr. Cameron, one of the three judges, did not object to allowing Missourians to

The Reverend Richard Cordley. Kansas State Historical Society.

vote. The third judge, James B. Abbott, did show up, but was out-voted by Cummins and Cameron on each voting challenge. Abbott resigned his post and left. He was replaced by a Mr. Benjamin.

The voting pattern started when Colonel Samuel Young, the leader of the Missourians, stepped up and "refused to take the oath prescribed by the governor, but said he was a resident of the territory." James Abbott objected, but he was overruled by the other election judges, and Young cast his ballot. The other Missourians did the same, with the oldest voting first. Very few votes were challenged, and most legal Lawrence voters were either so intimidated or so disgusted with the whole affair they did not vote. Some mustered enough courage to vote later in the day, but only about half of the eligible Lawrence residents cast ballots. After they voted, most Missourians left and returned home.[71]

The story of the election in Lawrence was repeated throughout the territory. In Leavenworth, five times the number of voters recorded in the census showed up to vote. As in Lawrence, a free-state judge was intimidated and resigned his post, replaced by one sympathetic to the Missourians. In Bloomington, the judges who were prepared to exclude the interlopers from voting were threatened with instant death if they did not resign. Not surprisingly, they left their posts. Missourians penetrated as far as Pawnee, some 120 miles west of the Missouri state line, to vote. Of the 6,307 men who voted throughout the territory on March 30, 5,427 voted for pro-slavery candidates.[72] Not surprisingly, the entire new territorial legislature was sympathetic to the pro-slavery cause.

Charles Robinson had just returned to Lawrence from leading the first 1855 Emigrant Aid Party from Boston when the election was held. Soon after the election, he dashed off a letter to Eli Thayer reporting what had happened, writing that an "election in Kansas Territory has passed [and it] was controlled entirely by Missourians." The violent nature of the vote, with Missourians threatening judges and voters, was making it clear that for Kansas to become a free state, antislavery forces might need to fight. To that end, he reported that "our people have now formed themselves into four military companies & will meet to drill till they have perfected themselves in the art. . . . Give us the weapons & every man from the north will be a soldier & die in his tracks if necessary to protect and defend our rights. It looks very much like war & I am ready for it & so are our people." He then asked Thayer if he could send at least two hundred Sharps rifles to Kansas.[73]

Shortly after Amos Lawrence heard the results of the territorial elections, he recorded in his diary that Kansas "may be saved, and be a free state, but the prospect is dark." Several days later, he noted that his stepmother accompanied his business partner, Robert M. Mason, to Washington to meet with her nephew, President Pierce. During their meeting, the president expressed his regret that her stepson Amos was "mixed up in the [Kansas] business." Lawrence's observation was that his position "was better than [Pierce's]," and that by "mixing up with Douglas and getting the Kanzas and Nebraska Bill passed has overturned him and his party."

Following the election, territorial governor Reeder was in a bind. Up to that point, he had conducted his responsibilities well. He called for a census to identify the eligible voters. He called for an election for the territorial legislature. He issued the proper instructions to the election judges. But the Missourians foiled his best intentions. Following the elections, six districts protested the results. The governor declared the results invalid and called for new elections for those districts on May 22, 1855. Before the special elections were held, however, Reeder headed for Washington to confer with President Franklin Pierce. He was seeking the support and assistance of the federal government to deal with the political turmoil in Kansas. Pierce offered neither, and likely had already decided to replace Reeder. While the governor was away, the special election in the six districts was conducted with little disturbance. Antislavery candidates won in the new elections, but the results made no difference because the pro-slavery faction held a solid majority in the new territorial legislature.[74]

Dr. Robinson was ready for battle, if necessary, to ensure that Kansas would become a free state. His wife, Sara, on the other hand, was more circumspect. As the territorial legislature was about to meet, she observed that it would "enact laws for the people of this territory. They, many of them residents of Missouri, and all of them elected by Missouri voters, ignorant and brutal men, having gained their election at the point of the bowie-knife [sic] intend to enact laws to govern enlightened and intelligent people." She continued, "The question is, shall the laws, whatever they may be, be boldly repudiated as no law for us?"[75]

The newly elected territorial legislature convened in Pawnee on July 2, 1855. Its first act was to expel the free-state legislators elected from the May 22 special election, replacing them with pro-slavery members. Its second act was to move the meeting place to Shawnee Mission, which was near the border of Missouri—a more convenient location—since these "lawmakers" were residents of Missouri. Governor Reeder had returned to the territory on June 23. He vetoed these first pieces of legislation. Reeder also vetoed a harsh slave code and new voting regulations that essentially allowed any adult male to vote, so long as he paid a one-dollar poll tax, and swore to uphold the federal Fugitive Slave Act of 1850. The governor went further to declare the territorial legislature illegal. For his actions, President Pierce removed Reeder from office on August 16, 1855, on trumped-up charges that he had illegally speculated on Kaw Indian lands.[76]

Even before Reeder's removal, the legislature had gained the upper hand. The law establishing Kansas Territory allowed the territorial legislature to override a territorial governor's veto, and the pro-slavery legislature wasted little time overturning Governor Reeder's vetoes. Of the laws it passed, the slave code was particularly heinous. Three sections carried the death penalty for anyone who attempted to incite a slave rebellion. Assisting a slave to escape carried a ten-year sentence. Anyone who deigned to "print, write, introduce into, publish or circulate, or cause to be brought into, printed, written, published or circulated," or anything to induce "slaves to escape from the service of their masters, or to resist their authority, . . . shall be guilty of felony, and be punished by imprisonment and hard labor for a term not less than five years." And, finally, "no person who is conscientiously opposed to holding slaves, or who does not admit the right to hold slaves in this territory, shall sit as a juror on the trial of any prosecution for any violation of any of the sections of this act."[77]

As the "bogus legislature"—the title contemporary antislavery residents tacked onto the pro-slavery territorial legislature—was in session, Charles Robinson called for a convention of free-state Kansans in Lawrence on June 8, 1855. This small gathering called for a larger convention on June 25, also in Lawrence, which was attended by representatives from nearly every community in the territory. They debated a course of action and passed resolutions, stating that they were in "favor of making Kansas a free territory, and as a consequence a free state." In one resolution, they voted to not meddle in the affairs of Missouri, but vowed that Missouri would not be allowed to participate in Kansas politics. The final resolution declared that since the territorial legislators owed "their election to a combined system of force and fraud, we do not feel bound to obey any law of their enacting."[78] While these resolutions held no legal authority, they served to meld the antislavery residents in the territory into a cohesive body.

Shortly after the June 25, 1855 convention, and while the "bogus legislature" was in session, the residents of Lawrence celebrated their first Fourth of July in Kansas. In many ways, the festivities did more to galvanize antislavery Kansans together than anything up to that time. According to Sara Robinson, everyone in Lawrence and the surrounding area was invited, including delegations from the Delaware and Shawnee Indian tribes (the Delaware Nation continued to occupy the land just north of the Kansas River from Lawrence). She estimated that between 1,500 and 2,000 attended. "After the reading of the Declaration of Independence, whose embodied truths seemed to have gained new vitality, new force, since we last listened to it," Sara Robinson wrote, next "came the oration," by her husband, Charles Robinson. He concluded his speech, saying: "Fellow-citizens, . . . shall we have freedom for all the people, and consequent prosperity, or slavery for a part, with the blight and mildew inseparable from it? Choose ye this day which you will serve, Slavery or Freedom. . . . If slavery is best for Kansas, then choose it; but, if liberty, then choose that."[79]

Charles Robinson was quickly expanding his role beyond the Kansas agent for the Emigrant Aid Company to the *de facto* leader of antislavery residents in the territory. In addition to his political efforts, marshaling the antislavery residents to oppose the "bogus legislature," it was becoming clear that violence was a real possibility. Again, Amos Lawrence came to the rescue. In his diary, he wrote that "I must trust Providence and try to do my duty," and clearly he saw his duty as taking a more aggressive position on supporting the antislavery efforts in Kansas. Later in the same diary entry, he reported that he "paid $4,000 for rifles for Kansas settlers." To ensure that the weapons safely reached the intended recipients in Kansas—without raising suspicion—he ordered the crates labeled for shipment to the "church of the pilgrims" in Lawrence.[80]

At the same time Lawrence purchased and shipped rifles to Kansas, James B. Abbott, a member of the third Emigrant Aid Company party, traveled to the East to acquire weapons. Abbott was a personal friend of the owner of the Sharps Rifle Manufacturing Company in Connecticut; he sold his property in Lawrence to fund his trip and left for Connecticut in July 1855. At that time, Sharps Rifles were considered superior to all other rifles available.

Years later, Abbott wrote about his adventure while he was the director of the Kansas Historical Society. He visited the Sharps Company and negotiated an excellent price for one hundred rifles since "they [the company owners] were good free-state men and would sell us arms on generous terms." He arrived in Boston on August 10 and "presented [his] credentials and letters to Mr. Eli

Thayer and Amos A. Lawrence. . . . After an hour's consultation with a few friends, Mr. Lawrence gave me an order on the Sharpe's [*sic*] Rifle Company for one hundred rifles—costing $2,600."[81]

From Boston, Abbot went to Providence, where he "collected between two and three hundred dollars, and thence to Hartford and arranged for the packing of the rifles in a manner not to excite the suspicions of our pro-slavery neighbors, as the packages should pass up the Missouri river." His next stop was New York, where he "called upon Horace Greeley, who gave his influence and zealous efforts to the raising of funds for our cause. At Mr. Greeley's suggestion, a meeting was called to be held at the Astor House," where "special invitations were given to over twenty of the active and wealthy opponents of slavery in New York." He concluded, writing that "my efforts in behalf of army organization in Kansas were successful. Sufficient money was collected to pay for 117 Sharpe's [*sic*] rifles, a twelve-pound brass howitzer, and quite a large quantity of fixed ammunition, and enough to pay the freight to Lawrence."

For fear that he would be recognized on the return journey, Abbott disguised himself with different clothing, such that even his friends did not recognize him. He directed that the rifles be shipped in pieces, marked as books, on the theory that no one would bother to open the crates, and even if someone did, most inspectors would not see that the crates contained rifle parts. As a further precaution, he traveled separately from the crates, for fear that even with the disguise, he might be recognized in connection with the shipment. When he returned to Lawrence, he found that the five crates, on which the bills of lading marked the contents as "books," had arrived safely, that the rifles and howitzer were properly assembled, and that the free-state army was well armed with the finest rifles then available.[82]

In time, more "books" arrived in Kansas. As more and more Emigrant Aid Company emigrants bought (or were given) Sharps rifles, they soon became known as "Beecher's Bibles." The Reverend Henry Ward Beecher was quoted as saying that he "believed that the Sharps Rifle was a truly moral agency, and that there was more moral power in one of those instruments, so far as the slaveholders of Kansas were concerned, than in a hundred Bibles. You might just as well . . . read the Bible to Buffaloes as to those fellows who follow Atchison; . . . but they have a supreme respect for the logic that is embodied in [the] Sharps rifle." To back up his words, Beecher donated and urged his congregation to donate funds for purchasing the rifles. Beecher's pronouncement was a sign of the times. If a minister of Christian principles would not only advocate an end to slavery, but would also admonish his flock to contribute to the purchase of guns for the residents of Kansas, little room is left to wonder at the strength of passions at that time.[83]

As Charles Robinson was beginning to organize the antislavery faction in Kansas to oppose the "bogus legislature," another political figure entered the scene. James Lane moved to Lawrence from Indiana in the spring of 1855. Lane had been active in Indiana politics, serving as lieutenant governor and as a member of the US

Henry Ward Beecher. Brady-Handy Collection, Library of Congress.

House of Representatives. At the end of his term in Congress, James Lane decided to seek his political fortunes in Kansas Territory. At first, it was unclear where Lane's political views would land. He had voted for the Kansas-Nebraska Act while serving in Congress, and he earlier had been quoted as saying that he "would as soon buy a negro as a mule," suggesting that he was sympathetic to the institution of slavery. When he arrived in Kansas, however, he underwent a transformation. He was an opportunist, and he quickly recognized that his best chances for political success lay with the antislavery faction, rather than with the pro-slavery side. So he threw his support behind the antislavery camp.[84]

James Lane had a gift, crucial to political success at the time—he was a spellbinding orator. He could modulate his voice from shrill to grave. One minute he had his audience rolling with laughter; in the next, they were in tears. Although Lane allied with the antislavery side by wholeheartedly opposing the introduction of slavery into Kansas, he just as strongly opposed admitting free blacks into the

James Henry Lane, Brady-Handy Collection, Library of Congress.

territory, believing that blacks were inferior to whites. Robinson and many New Englanders, on the other hand, believed that African Americans were equal to whites and had as much right to live in Kansas, with the same rights and privileges.

Lane was an opportunist. Years later, John J. Ingalls, a future US senator from Kansas, said of Lane that "to reach the goal of his ambition he had no conviction he would not sell, made no promise he would not break, and had no friend he would not betray."[85] Lane calculated that his political fortunes in Kansas were with the antislavery faction. He also observed that many Kansas immigrants opposed the institution of slavery but were prejudiced against free blacks as well. He calculated an opening and aspired to place himself at the head of that faction.

Charles Robinson continued to hold antislavery conventions in Lawrence. Each one drew larger crowds, culminating in the largest meeting to date in August 1855. At that meeting, there was a call for an even larger convention to be held in Big Springs, a small community between Topeka and Lawrence. Each community was authorized to elect a delegate. At the conclusion of the August meeting, James Lane announced that he would give a major speech on the issues of the day. He marshaled his oratorical skills, had his audience completely enraptured, and when Lawrence voted to send a delegate to the Big Springs convention—to the surprise of many—he was elected as the community's representative over Charles Robinson.

If Robinson was unhappy with his non-election as a delegate, he did not share this in his autobiography or any of his letters, nor did his wife reference this in her book. Instead, he continued to do everything in his power to ensure that Kansas would become a free state. He discussed the Big Springs Convention, held on September 5, and noted that former Governor Reeder had joined the antislavery forces and attended the convention. The convention passed resolutions to refute the "bogus legislature" and the officials it appointed, and called for free-state citizens to ignore or take whatever action was necessary to remove any power from that body. In other words, they were taking the very risky stance of saying that they would not obey the laws passed by the territorial legislature. For all intents and purposes, it declared that the Free-State Party, created by the convention, was the legal arm of the territory. It called for new elections, and placed Reeder in nomination as the territorial representative to Congress.

Robinson noted that the platform committee, chaired by James Lane, proposed planks that would ban free blacks from the territory and condemn radical abolitionists. It also proposed the non-interference of slavery where it existed and defended the Fugitive Slave Act of 1850. Further, it proposed that any slaveholders in the territory would be treated fairly, so that they would be protected from financial ruin if and when the territory became a free state. Robinson noted that there was one, and only one, dissenting vote in the convention—that of Charles Stearns—whom Robinson referred to as a Garrisonian. Stearns rebuked the convention for not going far enough. Kansas becoming a free state was but one effort; he wanted the convention platform written to also make a statement that slavery should be immediately abolished throughout the entire country.[86]

Robinson did not agree with much of the Big Springs platform. He and Eli Thayer saw the effort in Kansas as a wedge driven into the institution of slavery nationwide. As he continued the discussion of the convention, he wrote that the fight against slavery would end when all men were "free and abolitionists would disappear when there was no slavery to abolish." In other words, he believed that both moderates and radicals had the same goal—to end slavery. Several sentences later, Robinson noted another man who arrived in the territory about a month after the Big Springs Convention, who was as disgusted with the convention as Charles Stearns. This man was against the Free-State Party, and was particularly incensed with the provision that banned free blacks from the territory. His name was John Brown.[87]

All free-state residents, whether they were radical or moderate, were unified in their opposition to the "bogus legislature," and together they were waiting to see what was in store with the new territorial governor. They did not need to wait long. A week before President Pierce fired Governor Reeder, he appointed Wilson Shannon, a former governor of Ohio, a member of Congress, and a former minister to Mexico to the post. Shannon arrived in Kansas and assumed his duties on September 7, 1855. He had solid Democratic Party credentials, had voted for the Kansas-Nebraska Act as a congressman, and was known to have pro-slavery sentiments. Pro-slavery advocates in Kansas and western Missouri were pleased with the selection; free-staters were not happy, but they were willing to wait to see how Shannon would govern.

Shortly after Governor Shannon took office, the Territorial Legislature called for the election of the territorial representative to Congress on October 1, 1855. The Free-State Party members refused to participate in this election, and J. W. Whitfield, the already seated pro-slavery candidate, received 2,721 of the 2,738 votes cast. A week later, the Free-State Party held its own election, unanimously electing former governor Reeder with 2,849 votes. The party also elected delegates to a constitutional convention, scheduled for Topeka on October 23. Not to be outdone, the pro-slavery faction established the Law and Order Party, or States Rights Party, and called for a convention in Leavenworth for November 14.

In writing their constitution, the free-state delegates squabbled over a number of issues—such as admitting free blacks into the state—but ultimately left many contentious issues alone. They opted instead for a document that made slavery illegal, along with provisions that made it virtually impossible to amend the document. The Law and Order Party convention elected Governor Shannon as its chair, thus proclaiming which side he was on. It passed resolutions calling every action by the Free-State Party treasonous; it condemned the election of Reeder as delegate to Congress, and it called for the strict enforcement of all laws passed by the pro-slavery Territorial Legislature.[88]

Josiah Miller, editor of the *Kansas Free State* newspaper, wrote his parents in South Carolina on October 15, 1855, saying that the arrival of Governor Shannon and his alignment with the pro-slavery legislature and the territorial officials would be pitted "against the [free-state] people" in a "tug of war" for dominance. He went on, "this is an awful crisis in our affairs at present. How it will go we know not."[89]

Indeed, no one could predict the outcome in Kansas in the fall of 1855. Pro-slavery forces believed they were in control of the territory's destiny, holding all seats in the territorial legislature, all territorial appointed positions, and having a new governor who, by all indications, was sympathetic to their side. And they were the legally constituted political body in territorial Kansas. Antislavery residents, on the other hand, had written a constitution, elected their own delegate to Congress, and openly rebuked, ignored, or simply disobeyed legislation repugnant to them. But they had no legal authority for anything they had done. By late fall, it seemed that the smallest provocation could set off a firestorm.

PART II
THE CONFLICT

5 The Almost Bloodless Wakarusa War

HORACE GREELEY, EDITOR OF THE *New York Tribune* and a strong antislavery advocate, is credited with coining the term that describes this era and has stuck for over 150 years—"Bleeding Kansas." Bleeding Kansas evokes images of daily violence and blood running in the streets. But how bloody was Kansas during this period?

Contemporaries created and perpetuated the image of uncontrolled violence, such as this description by Thomas H. Gladstone, an Englishman who recorded his observations in *The Englishman in Kansas: Or, Squatter Life and Border Warfare in 1857*: "Murder and coldblooded assassination were of almost daily occurrence at the time of my visit."[90] A more educated guess was offered by the congressionally appointed Hoagland Claims Commission in 1859, which concluded that the number of deaths that could be attributed to political violence between November 1855 and the end of 1856—the period most often cited as the period of Bleeding Kansas—was something like two hundred.[91] Robert W. Richmond, state archivist and assistant director of the Kansas State Historical Society, looked at the numbers of political deaths in his *Kansas: A Land of Contrasts* (1974) and concluded that the numbers were much lower—closer to fifty.[92] Then, in a 1995 article in *Kansas History*, appropriately titled, "How Bloody Was Bleeding Kansas?," Dale E. Watts painstakingly searched records from the territorial period and concluded that in the period from 1854 until statehood in 1861, fifty-six

political killings occurred in Kansas, with the highest concentration—thirty-eight—in 1856. In other words, Kansas, during this
period, was not very bloody after all. Watts did find that there were
a total of 157 violent deaths in Kansas during this time frame, from
brawls, domestic violence, fights over land claims, and lynchings
for cattle rustling. But through his impressive research that found
only fifty-six political killings, the term "Bleeding Kansas" seems an
exaggeration.[93]

With pro-slavery and antislavery factions fighting over political
control of the territory, it did not take much of a spark to touch
off the first battle. The spark was a dispute that escalated into a
killing. A recent free-state arrival from Indiana, Charles W. Dow,
was invited to stay and work on a land claim belonging to another
Hoosier, Jacob Branson, several miles south of Lawrence. Franklin
N. Coleman, a pro-slavery man, had a claim next to Branson, and
the two men were disputing the exact boundary between their prop-
erties. Coleman came to the territory as a radical abolitionist, but
in a short time turned to the pro-slavery side.[94] On November 21,
1855, Coleman and several of his pro-slavery colleagues got into a
heated argument with Dow. Exactly what the dispute was about was
never clear. A few minutes later, Coleman shot Dow, probably in
cold blood, although Coleman later claimed it was in self-defense.
Hours later, Branson discovered Dow's body, but in the meantime
Coleman fled to Missouri, where he sought refuge with Samuel J.
Jones, the pro-slavery sheriff of Douglas County, Kansas—Jones,
like many territorial officials, lived across the border. At that point,
the story got fuzzy. Somehow Coleman placed the blame on Branson, and Sheriff Jones led a posse to arrest Branson on the night of
November 26, 1855.

That same night, one hundred free-state men met and debated
what they should do in light of Dow's murder. Several hotheads
broke into Coleman's house and set the straw from his bed on fire,
intending to burn his house down, but others extinguished the fire,
saying that free-state men should not resort to the tactics of the

pro-slavery thugs. As the men were heading back to Lawrence, they heard that a posse had arrested Branson.

Samuel N. Wood later described what happened next. He separated the one hundred men into three groups to locate the posse. After stumbling around for several hours in the dark, Wood and his party intercepted Sheriff Jones and his posse. In the ensuing conversation, both sides threatened to shoot each other. Wood recalled that he said: "gentlemen, shoot, and not a man of you shall leave alive." Both sides cocked and aimed their weapons, but neither side fired. Branson came over to the free-state side, and Sheriff Jones followed and said he had a warrant for Branson's arrest. Wood replied that he was Branson's attorney and asked to see the warrant to determine if it was legal. Jones refused to produce the warrant, and after several more threats, both parties went their separate ways without either side firing a shot. Wood and his party went to Lawrence. They arrived at about 4:00 a.m. and went straight to Charles Robinson's house.[95]

Robinson recognized that Branson's rescue likely was all the provocation Governor Shannon needed to call for volunteers from the pro-slavery faction to retaliate. The Missourians were anxious to have any excuse to burn Lawrence to the ground, confiscate the Sharps rifles, and run the free-state settlers out of the territory. Robinson later wrote that at this point, he hoped he could "thwart, baffle, and circumvent" the bogus territorial government. But he hoped to do so by avoiding violence.[96]

For his part, Sheriff Jones sent a message to Governor Shannon stating that a force of free-state vigilantes attacked his posse and took his prisoner. And as Robinson predicted, Shannon called for volunteers to assemble and deal with the renegades in Lawrence. He sent a note to Colonel Edwin Sumner, commander of the US Army in Kansas, asking for support, and another to President Pierce, stating that this lawless band of free-state men was attempting to overthrow the legal government of Kansas Territory. His message was simple. If he, as governor, did not enforce the laws against the free-state faction, he would be forced "to submit to their lawless dominion."[97]

This whole affair presented an interesting legal dilemma. On the one hand, Wilson Shannon was the legally appointed governor of Kansas Territory. True, the territorial legislature was elected by Missouri voters, who were only interested in making Kansas a slave state. They had no intention of living there. But the legislative body was the legal governing body for the territory. On the other hand, the free-state residents were clearly incensed about the political situation, but they had no recourse through the legal realm to change things. President Pierce supported the governor and the pro-slavery legislature. Congress was not interested in intervening. The United States Supreme Court was not an option either, since the majority were pro-slavery southerners. Free-state settlers had tried to circumvent the legal process by holding meetings, by drafting a constitution, and by selecting a delegate to Congress. They also did everything in their power to repudiate or simply ignore the laws passed by the "bogus legislature" they found repugnant.

When Branson's rescuers came to Lawrence, Charles Robinson asked Samuel Wood and the others to state that they rescued Branson on their own accord, and that their actions were not sanctioned by the citizens of Lawrence. They agreed to do so. Robinson called the Committee of Safety into action. He and his committee were not sure what would happen, but in case the pro-slavery Missourians were up to something, he wanted to be prepared. He assumed command of the town's defenses and appointed James Lane as his assistant. Free-state men swarmed to Lawrence from Leavenworth, Topeka, and elsewhere. Defensive breastworks were thrown up at strategic locations in and around Lawrence, and the townspeople were ready for battle. The free-staters had a regiment—about one thousand men—ready on hand that could be divided into smaller companies with assignments to defend different areas of the town at a moment's notice. They held several advantages. With the Sharps rifles, they had superior firepower. They had been training for several months and were ready for nearly any contingency. Further, if actual shooting started, they had excellent defensive positions.[98]

By December 1, 1855, the Missourians started gathering several miles outside Lawrence on the Wakarusa River bottom. Robinson reported that the Missourians were "bold and blustering, threatening the direst vengeance against the hated town of Lawrence and all abolitionists." The residents of Lawrence went about their daily business, and Sheriff Jones and other pro-slavery men were even allowed to enter the town undisturbed. On the other side, the Missourians attempted to keep Lawrence residents pinned in the town, and keep outside free-state supporters from entering. The Missourians, however, were not aware that free-state women in Lawrence were acting as soldiers too. Samuel Wood's wife Margaret and Lois Brown (newspaper editor George Washington Brown's wife) passed freely through the Missourians' lines. On their outgoing trip, they went to a hidden ammunition cache just outside of town. They loaded two kegs of powder under their wagon seat. They also hid bullet molds, cartridges, lead bars, and caps under their dresses. To dispel any suspicions, they left a basket of knitting, a book, and a container of milk in plain sight. On their return trip, they were allowed to pass through without any trouble.[99]

On December 6, the Missourians stopped three free-state men who were heading home from Lawrence. Following an argument, one of the travelers, Thomas Barber, was shot and killed by a Missourian. Now the war had escalated from a standoff to an actual killing.

Three days before Thomas Barber was killed, on December 3, Sheriff Jones wrote to Governor Shannon, saying that if he did not do something soon, no Missourians would be left to fight the "Wakarusa War." Volunteers were leaving in droves. The next day, Shannon agreed to meet with members from the Lawrence Committee of Safety. The two men, Camri Babcock and Grosvenor Lowry, said the people of Lawrence wanted peace, but if necessary, they would fight to the death to protect their land and their rights. Shannon responded that he would consider peace if the citizens agreed to surrender their Sharps rifles. Babcock and Lowry made it clear that no one in Lawrence would be willing to do so. Further, if the governor did attack and kill the residents of Lawrence, the word would spread, and the entire country would consider him a murderer.

Governor Shannon was in a bind, and looking for a way to save face. His "army," called together to teach the people of Lawrence a lesson, would likely dwindle to nothing in a few days. So, on December 7, he went to Lawrence to meet with Charles Robinson and James Lane to begin serious negotiations to end the conflict. The governor expressed regrets that a hotheaded Missourian had killed Thomas Barber. He implied that he had been wrong to call in the pro-slavery militia, and he made it clear he wanted peace. The next day, both sides negotiated a treaty to end the conflict, and on December 9, it was read to the public. Each party assumed some responsibility, but Robinson insisted on including a sentence at the end stating "that we wish it understood that we do not herein express any opinion as to the validity of the enactments of the Territorial Legislature."[100]

Following the announcement of peace, the citizens of Lawrence and free-state supporters from the region—an estimated eight hundred in all—celebrated the victory at the Free State Hotel. Although still under construction, this was the largest building in Lawrence. They even invited Sheriff Jones to attend; he did, and he impressed the women with his courtliness. To almost anyone who was paying attention, the free-state residents of Kansas had won a clear victory. Even southern, pro-slavery sympathizers grudgingly conceded that the antislavery forces had won. Round one in "Bleeding Kansas" went to the free-state side.

On December 16, the community gathered to bury Thomas Barber. Charles Robinson gave the eulogy and John Greenleaf Whittier composed a poem to honor Barber. Even with the honors paid to Thomas Barber as an innocent martyr for the free-state cause, and even with the euphoria over the victory, Governor Shannon, the pro-slavery territorial legislature, and the territorial appointed officials were still in power. The eyes of the country were on Kansas, and many wondered what would happen next.[101]

The warmth of the victory in the Wakarusa War was blunted by the bitterly cold weather that gripped Lawrence and Kansas in late December 1855. Sara Robinson reported that on December 22, the weather was warm and pleasant, but later in the day, the temperature started plummeting and it started to snow. By the 24th, it had dropped to –17 degrees, and on Christmas Day, the temperature dropped further to between –20 and –30 degrees. Everything froze solid and had to be thawed on the stove. Writing was impossible because the ink froze. She was concerned that some of the poorer folks in and around Lawrence whose houses had thin walls and dirt floors would suffer or freeze.[102]

As the year 1855 drew to a close, Lawrence could look back at its short history and see tremendous progress. The town continued to grow. New businesses were springing up almost everywhere. They had stared down the Missourians and had won the Wakarusa War. Maybe now the future of Lawrence would be secure, with no more threats from the pro-slavery forces.

6 The Fabian Policy is the True One

FOLLOWING THE WAKARUSA WAR, IN part because of the bitterly cold weather, and in part because the pro-slavery faction was licking its wounds and regrouping, things were quiet in Lawrence for a couple of months. Charles Robinson would later reflect on the situation: "As the 'smoke of battle' cleared away," he wrote, "an opportunity was offered to take a calm and unbiased survey of the field and ascertain the gain or loss to respective fields. One item on the side of gain [for the free-state Kansans]" was that Governor Shannon could now more realistically gauge the situation. Up until this point, Shannon had viewed the free-state side as "a set of anarchists, made up of the off-scouring of the land, ready to overthrow any and all government that might stand in their way." On the other hand, his view of the pro-slavery side was that they "were but little, if any, lower than the angels." After the Wakarusa War, the governor now understood that the free-state "men were under complete control, and that no outrage . . . [could] drive them to take a false or untenable position. On the contrary, the pro-slavery men were desperate and ungovernable characters, determined to accomplish their purposes though the Government and heavens should fall."[103]

In late December 1855, Sheriff Jones returned to Lawrence to arrest Samuel Wood and Samuel Tappan for their involvement in rescuing Mr. Branson. They were arraigned, released, and returned to Lawrence.[104] Also on December 15, 1855, residents were offered the opportunity to vote on the Free-State Party's Topeka Constitution. Since neither the territorial governor nor the territorial legislature sanctioned the constitution, or even the Free-State Party, this action was illegal. Undaunted, the Free-State Party went ahead with the vote and asked the populace two questions. On the question of whether the territory should adopt the constitution, the vote was 1,731 for and 46 against. On the second question, proposed and pushed by James Lane in the constitutional convention, on whether or not to allow free blacks to live in Kansas, the people voted 1,287 against the admission of blacks to 453 who voted to allow their admission. This was a bitter pill for Charles Robinson since he not only favored welcoming free blacks into Kansas, he also advocated that blacks and women should be allowed to vote in future elections. He was a politician, though, and could see that this might damage Lane's future political ambitions.[105]

Later in December, the Free-State Party held a nominating convention for "state" offices. As with the vote on the Topeka Constitution, this action of the Free-State Party was illegal. James Lane told two potential candidates he planned to throw his support to them, but instead he threw his own hat into the ring for governor. He was nominated, as was Charles Robinson. Lane could feel the tide shifting toward stronger abolitionist waters, and, according to Robinson, became "the most radical of radicals," which compelled the real radicals "to put on the brakes to prevent a political wreck." For his part, Robinson later said he was not interested in seeking the governorship, but since Lane's name was on the ballot, he wanted to defeat him.

At the end of 1855 and the beginning of 1856, the residents of Lawrence had reasons to feel optimistic about the future. They had won the Wakarusa War, and for the time being, at least, there were no threats from the pro-slavery side. George Brown reflected optimism that Lawrence's recent troubles were over in his *Herald of Freedom*. He moved his offices and his newspaper and printing operations into a new building. In a little over a year, Lawrence had one thousand residents. Businesses, such as a carriage shop, a tailor, a barber, several doctors, dentists, and lawyers, as well as several construction companies, were doing well. Advertisements in the *Herald* had grown,[106] including the one for Mr. Hutchinson's new Emporium, which offered merchandise comparable to that found in the finest stores on Broadway in New York, at prices only a fraction higher. Mr. Faxon had recently opened a new meat market. Mail service was expanded from Lawrence to Westport, Missouri, and Mr. Emory, the new contract mail carrier, would be carrying mail in new stagecoaches that were comfortable and pulled by young, healthy horses. The service would expand to Leavenworth later that year. Finally, Child, Pratt, and Company, the largest hardware and cutlery company in the West, based in St. Louis, wanted to expand its business in Kansas, offering quick delivery of its goods to the residents of Lawrence.[107]

George Brown also reflected on Lawrence's cultural and spiritual progress. Residents had established an athenaeum, filled with books donated by Amos Lawrence and others as a cultural center; there were two schools, supported by the community using the finest educational materials then available; and land was reserved for a college. In addition to Plymouth Church, people in the community could worship in a Methodist, a Baptist, or a Unitarian church.[108]

Sara Robinson also marveled at the progress of construction in the town. "Many houses are going up," she wrote. "Men are digging at the quarries above us, and teams continually going up and down both sides of [our] house for buildings in town. . . . Large stone buildings, which would be an ornament to any place, are fast being erected," she continued, "while buildings of humble pretensions, of wood and stone, are springing up with a rapidity almost equaling the wonderful genius of Aladdin. We can count already fifty dwellings erected since we came; and the little city . . . will, in intelligence, refinement, and moral worth, compare most favorably with many New England towns of six times its number of inhabitants."[109] Sara was particularly pleased that her "house [was] at last complete. . . . [It was built] is entirely of black walnut; the finish, doors, window-casings, and mantels, of the same, all nicely polished. The paper of white satin, with a neat flower, in one room, while pretty wood-colors, in rosebuds and leaves, cover other walls, and give the whole a pleasing contrast."[110]

The Emigrant Aid Company had promised investments in the town's infrastructure, and late in 1854, Samuel Pomeroy arranged for the purchase of a used steam-powered sawmill for Lawrence. It was disassembled from Westport, Missouri, transported to Lawrence, reassembled, and in operation by December. Joseph Savage, one of the early settlers, noted that the mill was "well-nigh worn out," was "a rickety, leaky old thing" that required constant maintenance. He thought it was a terrible investment, but it was better than nothing.[111]

Even if it were in great shape, the mill would not have been able to meet the needs of the residents because the Emigrant Aid Company had committed two-thirds of all the lumber produced toward the construction of the Free State Hotel. By June 1855, two additional mills were nearly operational, but with the building boom, the *Herald* and the *Kansas Free State* both reported that the town needed many more mills to meet the demand.[112] Lumber was readily available and substantially cheaper from numerous mills in Kansas City and other towns on the Missouri River. The problem was transportation. Lawrence's founders located their town on the Kansas River, thinking that for the foreseeable future, this waterway would be sufficient for transporting goods to and from their community. They soon realized that under the very best of circumstances, the Kansas River was not navigable during much of the year, and under drought conditions, it was unnavigable year-round. Lawrence was experiencing a building boom, but structures could have been erected more quickly and more efficiently if lumber was more readily available at more reasonable prices.[113]

Several Lawrence residents purchased and erected prefabricated houses. Hinkle, Guld, and Company of Cincinnati introduced ready-made houses in the West, and advertised that they would cost 30 percent less than other construction. The first prefabricated house appeared in Lawrence in May 1855 and others followed. But again, the problem was transportation. The first house was shipped to Lawrence on board the *Hartford*, a river steamer. It grounded, however, and never made a return trip.

By far the largest and most important building project in Lawrence was the Free State Hotel. The Emigrant Aid Company had committed to building the hotel, which would serve as temporary housing for new residents as well as a gathering place for the community. It was large, fifty by seventy feet at its base, and three and a half stories in height. Construction began in November 1854, stopped and started again, and finally was scheduled for completion by May 1, 1856. As the project was underway, several features—a parapet at the top and loopholes in the walls for firing at attackers—were added, so it would also serve as a fortress. It was built of concrete, with fireproof roofing materials, and thus built to last.[114]

While calm prevailed, the Free-State Party elections were held on January 22, 1856, and Robinson was elected governor by a nearly three-to-one margin. A free-state territorial legislature and other executive officers, such as attorney general, were elected as well. For the most part, these elections were peaceful. The exception was the election in the Leavenworth region, where pro-slavery Kickapoo Rangers did all they could to disrupt the elections. There were several pro- and antislavery skirmishes and one fatality. Pro-slavery ruffians captured a free-state man, R. P. Brown, brutally beat him, put him in a wagon, and delivered him to his house, where he died. The free-state side had another martyr.

The free-state election was clearly illegal. The legal process for creating a new territory, and ultimately a new state, generally had been an orderly process during the previous seventy-five years. The Northwest Ordinance of 1787 established a three-stage process for the admission of new states, which continued as the formula with minor modifications. In the first phase, the president would appoint a governor, secretary, and judges to rule the territory, confirmed by the Senate. In the next phase, the territory could elect its own legislative assembly. Finally, as the population grew, the citizens could draft a constitution and apply for admission to the Union.

The Kansas-Nebraska Act essentially followed the framework of the Northwest Ordinance. The major variation was that the citizens could decide whether or not they wanted slavery. Another difference was that the governor could veto laws passed by the territorial legislature, and the legislature could override those vetoes. The governor and other territorial officials served at the pleasure of the president; thus, President Pierce's removal of Governor Reeder was perfectly legal. On the other hand, the election of the territorial legislature, under the requirements of the Kansas-Nebraska Act, specified that only "actual residents of said Territory" could vote.[115] The pro-slavery legislature was elected by Missourians who had no intention of permanently residing in Kansas, so, in a strictly legal sense, the members were serving illegally, but for the time being, they held the power.

The political situation in Kansas did not escape Amos Lawrence. He was particularly concerned about the free-state elections. He wrote several letters to Charles Robinson at the beginning of 1856,[116] focusing on the sovereignty of the federal government. He was worried that Robinson and others might cross a fine line that might put the Emigrant Aid Company's efforts in Kansas in jeopardy. In a letter dated January 31, 1856, Lawrence implored Robinson to "not under any circumstances resist any legal representative of the U[nited] States, nor allow our people to do it." He continued, "the Fabian policy is the true one. . . . This you must adopt, or rather you have only to keep on as you have done. You must gain time, & so strength." While Lawrence was concerned that Robinson and others were on the precipice of going too far in defying the territorial government, he also assured Robinson that he would continue writing to his half-cousin, President Pierce. Even so, he had "small hopes of [it] doing any good." Because he was convinced that the president was "struck [in his own] blindness."[117]

Lawrence warned Robinson and others not to challenge the federal government, but he recognized that the free-state citizens in Kansas needed the means to defend themselves. To that end, he continued to dip into his own pocket to supply Kansans with weapons. He and his fellow board members were careful to keep the weapon funds and the operating funds for the Emigrant Aid Company separate. Dr. Samuel Cabot was placed in charge of buying rifles and other armaments for Kansas. Not only did Amos Lawrence continue to spend a significant amount of his own money on the venture, he encouraged his brothers, James and William, to contribute as well. Dr. Cabot arranged to ship guns and ammunition to Kansas, but he also made it as easy as possible for new emigrants to purchase Sharps rifles at significant discounts. He negotiated a price of $26 a piece from the company, which was $4 less than the wholesale price the government paid. Dr. Cabot also was flexible with the terms of purchase. If an emigrant did not have the full $26, he would take partial payment, and in other cases, Cabot would simply provide the weapon with a promise to pay later, with the understanding that payment was not absolutely mandatory.[118]

Lawrence redirected his money to weapons because the financial picture of the Emigrant Aid Company was improving. News spread that the free-state residents of Lawrence had successfully stared down the Border Ruffians in the Wakarusa War. "Border Ruffians" was a contemporary term used by both the pro-slavery Missourians and the free-state Kansas to describe the pro-slavery paramilitary faction, who had no qualms against using violence to make Kansas a slave state. With the news that the free-state side seemed be gaining the upper hand in Kansas, in the early months of 1856, money started pouring into the company's coffers. The account stood at $45,835 in November 1855, but by May 1856 it jumped to $98,940. This did not include the weapon fund nor a new relief fund created to help Emigrant Aid Company Kansas residents who were victims of the Wakarusa War.[119]

In part to heed Amos Lawrence's concerns about going too far with Free-State Party politics, and mostly as a smart strategic move, Charles Robinson and the Free-State Party hired Mark W. Delahay as its representative to Washington. Delahay's job was to test the winds in Washington to determine what might happen next. On February 16, 1856, he wrote to Robinson and Lane, reporting that Governor Shannon had just left Washington for Kansas after meeting with President Pierce. His understanding was that "he [Governor Shannon] is directed to arrest and punish all who may take part in the making and [the enforcing of] any law in opposition to the Territorial laws now upon the Statute Book." Delahay further advised Robinson to not call the free-state legislature into session. There were some rumblings that Congress would take some action on the status of the territory that might benefit the free-staters. But even if Congress acted, and if the Free-State Party continued its activities, Delahay understood that "the Gov[ernmen]t has private orders to command the regular troops & to arrest any and all persons that may take part in the organization of the Independent State Gov[ernmen]t."[120]

By the time Delahay sent his report to Robinson and Lane, President Pierce had already issued a proclamation warning free-state Kansans to behave themselves. On February 11, 1856, he wrote that "all persons engaged in unlawful combinations against the constituted authority of the Territory of Kansas" could expect to face the local militia or "any available force of the United States." The main target of his message was the Free-State Party, but he also warned the pro-slavery residents of Missouri to not use force in Kansas. His proclamation also included a veiled threat for the Emigrant Aid Company, saying that if "agencies of emissaries" interfered in the territory, such actions "will constitute the fact of insurrection."[121] The president wanted to remove any possible doubt as to whether Governor Shannon, other territorial officers, the territorial legislature, and the army made up the legally sanctioned government in Kansas. Any circumvention of that federal authority would not be tolerated.

Charles Robinson chose to ignore Delahay's warning and the president's proclamation, and went ahead and called the Free-State

Party's elected legislature into session on March 4, 1856, in Topeka. Free-state Kansans continued to call the official pro-slavery Kansas territorial legislature "bogus," although it was the official, legal entity. In fact, the free-state legislature really was the "bogus" body because it had no authority to do business. The "legislators" elected former governor Reeder and James Lane as future US senators. They sent Lane to Washington to deliver a copy of the Topeka Constitution written and approved months earlier, along with message seeking admission to the Union. When Lane arrived in Washington, he convinced Galusha A. Grow, an antislavery Congressman from Pennsylvania, to submit the Topeka Constitution along with a bill for Kansas's admission to the US House of Representatives. It passed the House by a vote of ninety-nine to ninety-seven on July 3, 1856, but it was defeated in the Senate.

Although the bill for Kansas's admission failed, the US House of Representatives wanted to find out more about what was happening in Kansas and it appointed a special committee to investigate. William Howard, a Republican from Michigan, was the chair. John Sherman, a Republican from Ohio was the other majority member, and Mordecai Oliver, a Democrat from Missouri, was the minority member. They arrived in Kansas on April 18, 1856, and started taking testimony. Their findings were published in the Howard Report, which provided the most detailed firsthand account of the events in Kansas up to that time. It was published in 1856 and ran to over 1,200 pages of testimony.

At the end of their investigations, Representatives Howard and Sherman concluded that the elections held under the "organic or alleged Territorial law" were illegal, in that citizens from outside the territory voted, and prevented many legal citizens from voting. Since in their opinions, the elections were illegal, the "alleged Territorial legislature was an illegally constituted body," thus all laws and enactments it passed were "null and void." Further, the elections of both delegates to Congress, John W. Whitfield, elected under the authority of the Territorial legislature, and Andrew H. Reeder, elected under the auspices of the Free-State Party, were illegal, and thus neither should be seated as delegate to Congress. They recommended a new census for the territory, followed by new elections, to be held under the supervision of the United States military at each polling place. They noted that while the Topeka Constitution created by the Free-State Party at its convention was voted on by citizens in Kansas and embodied "the will of a majority of the people," they did not believe they had the authority to declare that it should be the basis for admission to the Union. They concluded that while they were in sympathy with the free-state residents, they were not "in a position to suggest remedies for the existing troubles in the Territory of Kansas."

For his part, the minority member of the committee, Congressman Oliver from Missouri, offered a very different view of the situation in Kansas. He concluded that the elections under the organic act to establish the Territory of Kansas were perfectly legal, and thus all laws established by the territorial legislature were valid. Further, the election of John W. Whitfield as the territory's delegate to Congress was legal as well; whereas the election of Andrew H. Reeder was illegal.[122]

Lawrence remained calm in early 1856. Sara Robinson reported that even though there appeared to be no imminent threat of violence, the town's citizens were on daily alert for possible attacks. To prepare for that eventuality, they reinforced the barricades they had erected for the Wakarusa War. She also reported that the cold spell continued. When the free-state legislature convened in Topeka, she noted that attention turned to its activities. On March 31, she noted that the town was "still all quiet."

The calm that had settled over Lawrence for the past several months, however, was about to end. On April 19, 1856, Sheriff Jones returned to Lawrence to arrest Samuel Wood, the leader of the Branson rescue mission. Sheriff Jones, probably at the behest of Governor Shannon, was exerting the increased authority given to the territorial government by President Pierce. Wood and the free-state party who had rescued Branson months earlier could not be allowed to snub territorial authority.

Wood had traveled to Ohio, where he spoke to numerous groups, raised money, and recruited about one hundred new emigrants to settle in Kansas. When Wood returned to Lawrence, Sheriff Jones succeeded in arresting him, but Wood managed to escape. The sheriff returned the next day and tried to recruit a posse from the town's residents—no one volunteered—and when he could not find Wood, he instead tried to arrest Samuel Tappan, a coconspirator in the Branson rescue. But Tappan punched the sheriff in the face and escaped as well. Then, on April 23, Sheriff Jones again appeared in town, but this time he brought along a squadron of soldiers, requisitioned under the new powers granted by President Pierce. In addition to the warrants to arrest Wood and Tappan, he carried warrants for the citizens who had refused to join his posse. The sheriff planned to spend the night in Lawrence, but while walking the streets, he was shot in the back by an unknown assailant.[123] Jones survived the shooting. In an attempt to maintain the peace, the citizens on Lawrence quickly offered a $500 reward for the arrest and conviction of the would-be assassin.[124]

With the additional powers granted to the official territorial government and the military by President Pierce, and with the assassination attempt on Sheriff Jones, the situation for free-state leaders quickly became more precarious. During the first week of May, a pro-slavery grand jury convened in Lecompton in the US District (territorial) Court and issued indictments for treason against Charles Robinson, Andrew Reeder, James Lane, Samuel Wood, and others for establishing a government outside the legal territorial government. The promise of peace and quiet that ushered in 1856 in Lawrence was short-lived. It did not take long for things to heat up again.

7 It Was the Grossest Outrage Ever Perpetrated

IN EARLY 1856, THE SENSE of unease in Lawrence was palpable. Because of the constant concern for the town's and citizens' safety, church services and classes often were canceled or postponed, sometimes for weeks. At times, church services were interrupted when men were called out to defend the town. One church minister later recalled that "all the public buildings [were] turned into barracks, the preaching hall with the rest, and nothing [was] thought of but the best means of defense."[125]

The unease in Lawrence reached a crescendo when the indictments for "high treason in levying war against the United States" were issued for Charles Robinson, Andrew Reeder, James Lane, Samuel Wood, George Brown, George Deitzler, George Smith, and Gaius Jenkins on May 20, 1856. George Brown had just published his *Herald of Freedom* three days earlier on May 17. He was arrested the same day the indictment was issued. Gaius Jenkins and George W. Smith were arrested one day later. George Smith was an early settler in Kansas who moved to Lawrence from Pennsylvania as an attorney. He quickly became involved in free-state politics and served as chair of the Big Springs convention. Gaius Jenkins was a native of New York, who moved Lawrence in 1854 and settled on a farm. He later became a colonel in the Free-State Militia. George Deitzler came to Lawrence in 1855 and built one of the town's sawmills. He also was a commander of Lawrence's defenses during the Wakarusa War.[126]

Former Governor Reeder claimed immunity as the elected Free-State Party delegate to Congress, but since the "legal" territorial government recognized neither his appointment nor the Free-State Government, his claim of immunity was ignored. He escaped from the territory disguised as an Irish woodcutter. James Lane fled the territory and avoided arrest as well. Charles Robinson and his wife tried to escape, but Charles was taken off a river steamer in Lexington, Missouri, arrested, and returned to Kansas on May 26. In Leavenworth, he was nearly lynched by a pro-slavery mob, but he was protected and hustled off to Lecompton, where he was imprisoned along with the other accused free-state men. Sara Robinson was allowed to continue on her journey.[127]

Sara Robinson chronicled the early settlement of Lawrence and Kansas in her *Kansas: Its Interior and Exterior Life* (1856). Beyond her literary talents, Sara was a woman to be reckoned with. Southern sympathizers called her a Spartan woman, which was anything but a compliment. In describing her reaction to her husband's arrest, one pro-slavery account said she pulled a dagger and a gun from her bosom, fell on her knees, and begged her husband to defend himself to the death, rather than surrender to his arrest. This story was untrue, but it added to Sara's Amazon-like image.[128]

Sara was the most well known of Lawrence's antislavery women, and from her writings, she made it clear that living on the frontier of Kansas was a difficult life. But she also was passionate about her mission and partnership with her husband to rid the nation of slavery, and above all to make Kansas a free state. In the introduction for her Kansas book, she noted the important contributions of women in the American Revolution. Now, she implored women to rise up again to ensure that Kansas was not "thrown open to the foul inroads of slavery."[129]

Margaret Wood was another committed female abolitionist. She was the wife of Samuel Wood, who had an arrest warrant for treason with Charles Robinson and the others but managed to elude capture and head to Ohio. The abolitionist cause was not new to Margaret. She formed a lifelong partnership with her future husband—a fellow Quaker—when he delivered a wagonload of escaped slaves to her father's house in Ohio. Their shared passion to rid the nation of slavery led the couple to Kansas, where they continued their Underground Railroad activities. While Samuel was in Ohio, Margaret sent letters providing news on the pro-slavery activities in Kansas, which Samuel reported to antislavery sympathizers in Ohio to stir up support for the antislavery cause in Kansas.[130]

After the arrest of her husband, Sara Robinson traveled to Illinois, where she met Abraham Lincoln; Joseph Medill, who had recently become editor of the Chicago *Tribune*; Owen Lovejoy, a leading abolitionist; and others. As she continued on her journey, she met with Salmon P. Chase, the recently elected antislavery governor of Ohio, then on to Boston and New York. Unfortunately, with the passage of time, we do not know the substance of her meetings, but it is safe to say that she was passionate in her support for the free-state movement in Kansas, as well as for the release of her husband and the others from their imprisonment. What we do know for sure is that Charles Robinson would later write that her mission did more for the Kansas free-state cause than he could have accomplished—had he been allowed to leave the territory.[131]

Since Robinson and the others were actively defying the legally constituted territorial government, the territorial grand jury was acting within its authority to have the men arrested for actively defying the territorial government. But the indictment also declared that the *Herald of Freedom* and the *Kansas Free State* newspapers were "inflammatory and seditious [in] character denying the legality of the Territorial authorities, and advising and 'commanding' forcible resistance to the same." Further, the Free State Hotel was built as a "strong hold of resistance to law, . . . encouraging rebellion and sedition." Because there was no way to arrest the newspapers or the hotel, the pro-slavery faction read the grand jury declarations as licenses to enter Lawrence and destroy these "nuisances." The charges gave Sheriff Jones, who had recovered from the assassination attempt, the justification to seek his revenge against the town in which he was shot.[132] Just days after the free-state "traitors" were imprisoned, Sheriff Jones, US Army troops furnished by Governor Shannon, and a large contingent of pro-slavery volunteers—some six hundred to eight hundred total—started arriving and camping on the outskirts of Lawrence. For several days, the Border Ruffians harassed and robbed some of the Lawrence residents.

Then, on May 21, 1856, the Missourians invaded Lawrence in what has since been called the Sack of Lawrence. Oscar E. Learnard, a lawyer and recent arrival to Lawrence from Vermont, described what happened in a letter to his friends back home. He wrote that May 21 would be "remembered in years to come, as the scene of the grossest outrage ever perpetrated under the cover of war." He wrote that the citizens of Lawrence did not offer any "resistance to the US authorities, and thus give the lie to the base slanders of our disloyalty. . . . Sheriff Jones was in command . . . and demanded a surrender of all the arms public and private in town. Not waiting for a reply, he ordered all the forces [to march] into town." He continued: "Four cannons were planted in the principal street and the 'sack' commenced. The Free State Hotel and the printing presses having been 'indicted as nuisances' by Judge Lecompte were made the first objects of their vengeance." The Free State Hotel "was first battered with the guns failing an attempt to 'Blow it up. . . .' It was then [set on fire]. It cost twenty thousand dollars and was just finished." The newspaper presses "were thrown into the Kansas river. Every house in town was plundered and the women and children driven off." He concluded that "we do not dispair [sic] of success, indeed, we are more confident than ever."[133]

The *Herald of Freedom* and the *Free State* presses were destroyed in the raid. The competition for readers ended because Josiah Miller did not attempt to restart his *Free State* newspaper. The other antislavery

The Sacking of Lawrence. Destruction of Free State Hotel. From Sara T. L. Robinson, *Kansas: Its Interior and Exterior Life, Including a Full View of Its Settlement, Political History, Social Life, Climate, Soil, Productions, Scenery, Etc.* (1856).

newspaper, the *Kansas Tribune*, started by the Speer brothers in 1855, had folded in October 1855. So for several months, until November, when George Brown reopened his printing shop, there was no source of news in Lawrence.

Just before the Border Ruffians began what became known as the Sack of Lawrence, David Atchison, former US senator from Missouri, and the most powerful advocate for Kansas becoming a slave state, gave a rousing, inflammatory speech to the attackers. He opened with, "Gentlemen, Officers & Soldiers! This is the most glorious day of my life! . . . Men of the South, I greet you as border-ruffian brothers." At the end, he said he knew his men were up for the task. "Yes, I know you will [destroy Lawrence and its inhabitants] the South has always proved itself ready for honorable fight, & you, who are noble sons of noble sires, I know you will never fail, but will burn, sack & destroy, until every vistage [*sic*] of these Norther[n] Abolitionists is wiped out."[134]

Across the country, as the Border Ruffians were preparing to sack Lawrence, the halls of Congress were lit up in quite a different manner. Senator Charles Sumner from Massachusetts gave a speech that lasted over two days, May 19 and 20, 1856, in which he lambasted the slave states and Senators Stephen A. Douglas from Illinois and Andrew Butler from South Carolina for what he called the "Crime Against Kansas." "Not in any common lust for power did this uncommon tragedy have its origin," he said. "It is the rape of a virgin Territory, compelling it to the hateful embrace of slavery; and it may be clearly traced to a depraved desire for a new Slave State, . . . in the hope of adding to the power of slavery in the National Government." Then he lashed out particularly at Senator Butler, "the senator from South Carolina." He "has read many books of chivalry, and believes himself a chivalrous knight with sentiments of honor and courage. Of course he has chosen a mistress to whom he has made his vows, and who, though ugly to others, is always lovely to him; though polluted in the sight of the world, is chaste in his sight—I mean the harlot, slavery."[135]

Senator Douglas, who listened to Sumner's tirade in the Senate, was reported to have said to a colleague that "this damn fool Sumner is going to get himself shot by some other damn fool." His prediction was not far from what actually happened. On May 22, two days after the speech, Preston Brooks, a member of the House of Representatives from South Carolina, and Senator Butler's nephew, entered the Senate chamber and attacked Sumner with a gutta-percha cane with a heavy gold head. Brooks beat him so severely, he broke his cane and knocked Sumner unconscious. The speech and beating further polarized an already divided country. Sumner became a hero in the North for attacking slavery, and Brooks became a hero in the South for attacking Sumner.

Back in Kansas, the free-state population was recovering from the Sack of Lawrence, but as Oscar Learnard wrote to his friends, and his words probably captured the sentiments of many that he was "more confident than ever," the efforts to make Kansas into a free state would soon become a reality. Although the Emigrant Aid Company settlers took the nonviolent approach—and for the most part, this gained them the respect and sympathy of many, particularly in the North—it came at a very high monetary price. The Emigrant Aid Company had invested over $20,000 to build the Free State Hotel, and although contributions to the company were on the rise, this was a huge loss. The destruction of the newspaper presses and other buildings and houses were tough pills to swallow as well.

One abolitionist who did not share the passive philosophy was John Brown. Brown followed several of his sons and settled in the free-state community of Osawatomie in 1855. Before Brown left for Kansas, he contacted Amos Lawrence, to whom he had sold wool in 1843. He asked Lawrence for a letter of introduction to Charles Robinson, which Lawrence provided, and after writing the letter, Lawrence noted in his private diary that Brown "had the look of a determined man."[136] Although Lawrence did not approve of Brown's radical methods, he continued to meet and correspond with him over the next several years.

The only speech Brown was known to have made while in Kansas was in a public meeting in Osawatomie, in which he condemned the Free-State Topeka Constitution for not being radical enough. He and his sons went to Lawrence and were ready to fight in the Wakarusa War, but by the time they arrived, negotiations to end the conflict were underway and their services were not needed.[137] Since his arrival in Kansas, Brown had remained mostly in the background. His son, John Jr., participated in the Free-State Party meetings and even sought an office in the free-state legislature. John Jr. also organized a militia band, called the "Pottawatomie Rifles," which he led to Lawrence.

John Brown Sr. came to Kansas and drew his inspiration on how to attack slavery from the Old Testament—"an eye for an eye, and a tooth for a tooth."[138] Brown Sr. was becoming more and more frustrated with the Emigrant Aid Company leaders like Charles

Robinson, who tried to avoid violent conflict with the pro-slavery side. The Sack of Lawrence pushed Brown to the boiling point, and when he learned of Senator Sumner's caning in Washington, DC, according to witnesses, "Brown went crazy—*crazy!*" He decided to take revenge. For some reason, he had it in his mind that pro-slavery men had killed five abolitionists, so, on the night of May 24, 1856, he led four of his sons and three others on a rampage through the pro-slavery community near Pottawatomie Creek. Brown's marauders first went to the home of James Doyle. They dragged Doyle and his two oldest sons outside where they murdered them with guns and broad swords. They then continued to the houses of Allen Wilkinson and William Sherman, and brutally murdered them in the same manner. According to later reports, John Brown Sr. did not participate in the killings, but he approved of them and probably watched. All five victims were pro-slavery supporters, but none owned slaves.[139]

With John Brown's raid, the cork was now out of the bottle. The efforts of Charles Robinson and others to go to extreme lengths to avoid bloodshed were of no avail. Now blood was on the hands of the abolitionists, and the result was a guerrilla war that lasted for almost a year.

8 The Latest Edition of the Herald of Freedom

IT DID NOT TAKE LONG for the pro-slavery ruffians to seek revenge. Upon hearing of the Pottawatomie Massacre, Captain H. C. Pate, a deputy US Marshal and commander of a territorial militia unit, moved quickly to capture Brown and his followers. He captured two of Brown's sons, burning John Jr.'s cabin, and was poised to lead a full-scale assault on Brown and his comrades. John Brown Sr., however, learned of the planned attack and instead attacked Pate and his militia near the small community of Black Jack. Although outnumbered, Brown fooled Pate into thinking that he was surrounded; Pate and his men surrendered, and he would later say the he "went to take Brown—and he took me."

The Battle of Black Jack on June 2, 1856, and other skirmishes around the territory made it clear to Governor Shannon that he had a serious problem on his hands. Still smarting from the Wakarusa War, and probably with little confidence that he could control the situation that very easily could have erupted into a full-scale civil war, he called on the US Army to send forces to potential hot spots in the territory to try to maintain the peace. The army, under Colonel Edwin Sumner, a future Civil War general, would disperse pro- and antislavery militias, but almost as quickly they would just regroup somewhere else and go at it again. By the end of June, Shannon left the territory for official business in St. Louis, leaving the territorial secretary Daniel Woodson in charge. Whereas Shannon tried to balance the tables between pro- and antislavery factions, Woodson was clearly on the pro-slavery side. When he got wind of the Free-State Party calling for a convention in Topeka on July 4, he ordered Colonel Sumner to disperse the gathering. Colonel Sumner was a cousin of Senator Charles Sumner. He had little taste for dispersing the Free-State Party delegates, but he was a good soldier and followed his orders. Violence was avoided, in part, because Charles Robinson, who was still imprisoned for treason, sent messages from Lecompton, entreating the free-state residents to avoid violence and allow Sumner to do his job. Sumner brought six hundred dragoons to Topeka, and the convention disbanded peacefully. The army maintained a semblance of order through July, but the relative peace was temporary.[140]

With the events and national attention drawn to Kansas, antislavery emigrants from the North, and even a few from the South, started pouring into the territory. Rev. Cordley reported that many college students and graduates "turned their back on the literary life they had chosen, or the professional life to which they were looking, and went to Kansas at the call of freedom. . . . It was no uncommon thing to find college graduates driving an ox team through the streets of Lawrence, or cutting timber by the river, or living in some lonely shanty or dug-out. . . . They did not come as adventurers to see how they would like it. . . . [They] came with honest intent to make Kansas a free state."

With the flood of new antislavery settlers, Missourians posted militias on all roads through Missouri and met all steamships on their way to Kansas, threatening violence if the emigrants continued on their journeys through the state. Undaunted, antislavery travelers bypassed Missouri and the Missouri River altogether, finding new routes through Iowa and Nebraska.[141]

To the people of Lawrence, the influx of antislavery immigrants provided a desperately needed boost to morale. Before long, they started rebuilding—after the Sack of Lawrence—determined that they would not allow the Border Ruffians to have their way in the future. The men formed into armed companies, with names such as the "Lawrence Stubbs" and the "Bloomington Guards." They trained, and they established fortifications in and around the town. The most immediate threats came from three manned pro-slavery fortresses surrounding Lawrence. Franklin, just four miles east; Fort Saunders, twelve miles to the southwest; and Fort Titus near Lecompton to the northwest were Border Ruffian strongholds, well supplied with food and ammunition, with strategically placed loopholes for firing at any attackers. From these forts, the ruffians harassed travelers, raided free-state farms, and posed constant threats to the citizens of Lawrence.

Up until that time, Dr. John Doy probably captured the sentiments of many when he wrote that "we were quiet, peaceful, and industrious citizens, and wished to remain so, but we would not consent to bring up our children on a land cursed by the toil of slaves." With the sacking of Lawrence and constant threats to him and his family, Doy wrote that "we could endure the present state of things no longer. We swore to treat the invaders as noxious vermin; we would drive them out or die."

He became a member of the "Lawrence Stubbs," and on August 12, 1856, he and the other members of the "Stubbs" went to Franklin to attack "a party of these marauding ruffians." They found the ruffians holed up in the well-fortified log structure. They attacked, but lost one man and several others were wounded. They then pushed a load of hay against the log building and set it on fire, driving the ruffians out. The "Lawrence Stubbs" recovered many of the arms, including a cannon that was taken from them during the sacking of Lawrence.[142] The cannon was the pride and joy of Captain Thomas Bickerton, a mechanic from Maine, who had joined an Emigrant Aid party when going to Lawrence in March 1855. As a commander of one of the Lawrence militia companies, he was more upset than anyone that the ruffians had confiscated the cannon several months earlier. He had arranged for purchasing the piece and had gone to great lengths to sneak it into Lawrence.

Bickerton took the responsibility of securing and transporting the artillery piece back to Lawrence. He found only five cannon balls in the Franklin fort, so when he returned to town, he cleverly enlisted the town's citizens to scour the Kansas River mud and the burned newspaper offices to gather up the lead type scattered from the raid months earlier, and molded the pieces of type into cannon balls. On August 15, 1856, the Lawrence armed companies moved on Fort Saunders—another Ruffian stronghold. Fearing that the Lawrence men would set the fort on fire and knowing that they now possessed a cannon, the ruffians fled without a fight.[143]

The third fortress, Fort Titus, was commanded by, and named for, Colonel Henry Titus, who was a scoundrel of monumental proportions. Fort Titus was the most formidable of the three forts, near Lecompton, the territorial capital. The presence of the pro-slavery territorial government and a company of US soldiers stationed nearby provided a degree of protection for the occupants of Fort Titus. Titus and his "desperados" would ravage the countryside; then, if they were chased by any free-state pursuers, they would rush back to the safety of their fortress. Rev. Cordley later wrote that "when pro-slavery men committed depredations, the authorities at Lecompton could never get any 'official' information in time to interfere. But whenever free-state men were moved to retaliate, the information came quickly and was always 'official.' Then a squad of troops would be ordered to go to the scene of disturbance and 'preserve order.'" Although the military was an arm of the "legal" pro-slavery government, and commanders followed the orders given by its governor, Titus was a particularly nasty brute, generally despised by the military. He and many of his men participated in the Sack of Lawrence, and he bragged that if he ever returned to Lawrence, he would kill every abolitionist there. Titus had a special hatred for Samuel Walker, a free-state man who lived close to Fort Titus. He printed a large handbill offering $500 for Samuel Walker's head, "on or off his shoulders."

It seemed only fitting that Walker, the commander of the "Bloomington Guards," led the attack against Fort Titus on August

16, 1856. Titus thought he could rely on the US Army to come to his rescue, but Major John Sedgwick, who would later be one of the finest generals in the Union Army during the Civil War, was the officer commanding the contingent near Lecompton. He was disgusted with Titus and his bluster, and was equally unhappy that he was frequently ordered to side with pro-slavery militias. Several days before the attack, he quietly told Captain Walker that if "they wanted to gobble up old Titus and would do it quickly, he did not think he should be able to get over in time to hinder him."[144]

Captain Walker and his army moved quickly and attacked Fort Titus. Captain Henry J. Shombre, who had raised a company of soldiers from Indiana, led the first cavalry charge but was shot from his horse, mortally wounded. His company retreated, waiting for the main force. When the rest of the free-state men arrived, they started firing their rifles at the fort, with little effect. But then Captain Bickerton brought up and started firing several well-placed lead balls into the fort from his cannon, announcing that they were the latest "edition of the *Herald of Freedom*." The free-state companies were deployed surrounding the fort on all sides, closing off any route for escape. After several salvos from Bickerton's cannon, Titus raised a white flag in surrender. Titus and several men were wounded, and two were killed. Titus, who had terrorized residents in and around Lawrence, was a blubbering, pitiful coward in surrender, begging for his life. When Captain Walker and the free-state men entered Fort Titus, they carried away four hundred muskets, knives, thirteen horses, several wagons, a large stock of household provisions, farm equipment, and $10,000 in gold and bank drafts. They also discovered several slaves owned by Titus, whom they set free and instructed to go to Topeka, where they would be cared for. Then Walker and his men burned the fort to the ground.[145]

Titus and thirty-four survivors were marched to Lawrence, where they were held as prisoners of war. The next day, Governor Shannon and Major Sedgwick traveled to Lawrence to meet with the town leaders. Charles Robinson and the others were still in custody, so

Captain Walker and the other militia captains negotiated for the town. Both sides agreed to surrender prisoners. Titus and his men were surrendered to Major Sedgwick, and members of the Lawrence militia held at Lecompton were surrendered to the town. Walker and the other captains agreed to turn over some of the arms they had captured to the army as well.

At the end of the negotiations, Governor Shannon asked if he could address the town. His tenure as territorial governor was nearly over, and, as one reporter wrote, "he wanted to leave the territory with the people feeling better towards him, and in a quiet state, to his successor." When Governor Shannon rose to speak, he was greeted with jeers and catcalls, but Captain Walker stood before the crowd and asked for quiet out of respect for the governor. He was interrupted several times, but he concluded with: "Fellow citizens of Lawrence, before leaving you I desire to express my earnest desire for your health, happiness, and prosperity. Farewell." Shannon left Kansas several weeks later, no doubt hoping never to return. Not long after, however, he did return to Kansas and practiced law in, of all places, Lawrence, where he was well respected until he died in 1877. Several visitors to his office reported that when asked about his experience as territorial governor, he would say: "govern Kansas in 1855 and '56! You might as well attempt to govern the devil in hell."[146]

Wilson Shannon was replaced by John Geary, a veteran of the Mexican War and a former mayor of San Francisco. He was an imposing figure, both with his ability as a political leader and with his stature—he stood six feet six and weighed in at 260 pounds. President Pierce chose Geary as territorial governor in the hope that this mountain of a man could bring order to the chaos reigning in Kansas. Pierce knew he would not have a second term as president, because the Democratic Party Convention held in Cincinnati in June nominated James Buchanan as the party's standard bearer.

Geary arrived at the territorial capital in Lecompton on September 10. In his first speech, he made it clear that he would not

John W. Geary, Library of Congress.

side with either the pro- or antislavery factions. He immediately disbanded the existing territorial militias and created a new militia, but he decided early on that he would mostly rely on the US Army to keep the peace. Geary's neutrality rankled the Border Ruffians, who for the most part had been able to coerce Shannon to support their positions; the free-state advocates were not pleased either because they had hoped the new governor would see things their way.[147] Charles Robinson was certainly willing to give him the benefit of the doubt, writing that he hoped both sides—pro- and antislavery—would agree that when the "new Governor [Geary] takes his seat, [it would be good to] give a chance for justice & peace to reign if he wills it."[148]

On the day Geary arrived in Kansas, Charles Robinson and the others were released from their confinement. Amos Lawrence and Sara Robinson had roles in their release. After Sara was forced to leave her husband when he was charged with treason, she ended up in Boston, where she met with Amos Lawrence, who started a letter writing campaign to gain support for Kansas and to seek the release of Charles Robinson and the others from their imprisonment. He wrote to President Pierce and several members of Congress, to no avail. Then, Lawrence cleverly offered a draft of a letter for Mrs. Robinson to edit and rewrite in her own hand to send to Mrs. Pierce, along with a letter written by his stepmother, seeking her husband's release. The letter to Mrs. Pierce had the desired effect, for Lawrence wrote to Sara that "not long since the President wrote to my brother that he had given such instructions [presumably to release her husband from his confinement] as would gratify him [his brother] and his friends here, especially my mother, whose good opinion he valued more than that of all the politicians."[149]

Charles Robinson and the other prisoners were released on bail on September 10, 1856. Before they were released, and before Geary arrived, however, territorial secretary Woodson had one more chance to work his mischief on the free-state residents of Kansas. On August 25, 1856, as acting governor, Woodson issued a proclamation declaring that the territory was in "an open state of insurrection and rebellion," and that "all law-abiding citizens" should rally to support the "territory and its laws." To the Border Ruffians this was a blank check to raid and pillage. So, on August 30, a band of some three hundred ruffians attacked the community of Osawatomie, John Brown's stronghold. This time the ruffians prevailed; they killed several abolitionists, including John Brown's son Frederick, and burned the town to the ground. Of the communities reviled by the Missourians, Osawatomie was only a notch below Lawrence.

With the successful attack on Osawatomie, the pro-slavery militia felt emboldened to again attack Lawrence, with the goal of annihilating the entire town. The militia planned its attack for September 1856. In short order, an army of nearly three thousand Border Ruffians started gathering near Lawrence on September 14. The town was still recovering from its sacking in May, and many members of its militia companies, such as the "Stubbs," were away. Mustering every able-bodied man available, the town could only count three hundred defenders. On the fourteenth, there was a brief skirmish outside of town, but the Missourians were waiting for their forces to arrive. What the ruffians did not count on, however, was that Governor Geary intended to end the violence in Kansas and would not tolerate any independent militias.

The situation in Lawrence was Geary's first test. Would he maintain a neutral course or side with the pro-slavery or the antislavery factions? On September 14, as more and more Missourians poured into the area, the town sent a messenger to Geary, apprising him of the situation. Geary immediately sent Colonel Johnson and a force of artillery and cavalry, which arrived during the night. The next morning, Geary himself arrived and went to the ruffians' camp and informed them that they were disobeying his order, and if they did not disband immediately, he would unleash the full force of the US Army on them. They grumbled, but quickly realized that they were no match for the army, so they turned tail and headed back to Missouri.

The "Stubbs" were away from Lawrence on September 14, attacking a pro-slavery stronghold at Hickory Point, several miles from Lawrence. They were victorious, but killed one pro-slavery man, and several on both sides were wounded. By attacking a pro-slavery target, the Stubbs were just as guilty of breaking Governor Geary's orders as were the pro-slavery force lined up against Lawrence. So, as they were returning to Lawrence, they encountered the US Army. They were placed under arrest, taken to Lecompton, and charged with murder. Geary wanted to make it clear that he would not tolerate militias from either side. The Lawrence militiamen were confined for several months, then released.[150]

Geary achieved what his predecessors had not. By taking charge immediately, and initially refusing to take sides, he brought temporary peace to Kansas. Both the pro- and antislavery factions were wary of him. The Border Ruffians were outraged that he had thwarted their attack on Lawrence. On the other hand, the free-state side was equally angry with his order to arrest the Stubbs following the raid on Hickory Point. Charles Robinson met with Geary, and wrote to his wife that he feared that Geary would "turn out a worse man than Shannon knew how to be."[151]

While he was imprisoned, Charles Robinson decided to relinquish his position with the Emigrant Aid Company in favor of devoting his attention to the political situation in Kansas. Amos Lawrence agreed with his decision, but asked him not to sever all ties with the company, and further requested that he not submit his resignation until after the November presidential election. Lawrence also went to the Emigrant Aid Company board and asked that Robinson continue to receive a salary for six months after his resignation took effect. The board agreed, and Robinson threw himself into the political maelstrom.[152]

When George Brown returned to Lawrence after his incarceration, he found that his printing presses and lead type were destroyed, and that the paper stock was burned as well. The ruffians had tried to burn his printing office to the ground, but the citizens extinguished the fire and saved the building. It took some time to acquire new presses, lead type, and a supply of paper, but the *Herald of Freedom* resumed publication on November 1, 1856. Not surprisingly, Brown devoted a great deal of attention to Kansas politics. The advertisement section was much smaller, but he was back in business and, for the time being, without any competition.[153]

At about the same time Brown and Robinson were released and Governor Geary arrived in the territory, the Reverend Thomas Wentworth Higginson led a group of emigrants to Kansas. He arrived in Topeka on September 25 and was immediately discouraged, meeting other parties who were leaving the territory. The consensus among those departing and the settlers who were staying was that Governor Geary was a tyrant much worse than his predecessors.[154] He heard more of the same when he arrived in Lawrence three days later. Within a few days, he met Governor Geary and developed his own opinion of the man. "He impressed me as a man who intends to do the right thing," wrote Higginson, "and is profoundly convinced that he has the full ability to do it." However, Higginson also observed that Geary neither had "the mental ability to understand the condition of Kanzas nor the moral power to carry out any systematic plan for its [the territory's] benefit."[155]

While Higginson was concerned about the political situation in Kansas, he was buoyed with the steadfast resolve of Lawrence's residents to ensure that the territory would become a free state. "A single day in Kanzas makes the American Revolution more intelligible" than almost anything else. He went on to say that "in Kanzas, nobody talks of courage, for everyone is expected to exhibit it."[156]

Higginson spent about two weeks in Kansas, and when he returned to Massachusetts, he wrote down his observations about the situation in the territory. In his opinion, the greatest threat to the antislavery residents was not the bullying of the Border Ruffians, but rather the "bogus laws" passed by and enforced by the "official" territorial government. Further, in his opinion, Governor Geary, who was trying to placate both sides, would ultimately fail because although he was attempting to make both sides equal, he was not taking any steps toward ending the armed conflict. Higginson feared that if John C. Frémont, the Republican Party candidate for president, was elected in November, the Pierce Administration would make a last desperate attempt to quickly push for the admission of Kansas as a slave state. Frémont, who rose to fame for his explorations in the West and for his participation in the Mexican War, was the first presidential candidate for the new Republican Party in the 1856 elections. Higginson concluded by saying that before he went to Kansas, he "feared that her children would gradually scatter and flee, rather than meet the final desperate struggle. I stand corrected," he wrote. "They will stay and meet it. They will meet it, if need be, unaided."[157]

9 Will Buchanan See That Justice is Done?

THE PRESIDENTIAL ELECTION OF 1856 dominated discussions in Kansas and the rest of the country. The fate of Kansas was the central topic of many of these discussions. The Whig Party, which had elected a president in 1848 and had nominated Mexican War hero General Winfield Scott as its candidate in 1852, was all but dead in 1856. The Whigs joined forces with the American Party, also known as the "Know Nothing" Party, whose main platform was to use whatever means necessary to keep emigrants—mostly Irish Catholics and Germans—out of the country. Some Whigs shared these nativist views. Most, however, had almost nothing in common with the Know Nothings but hoped that by joining forces they would have a chance for a showing in the upcoming election. The American Party rallied around former President Millard Fillmore as their standard bearer along with Andrew Jackson Donelson, who, as his name implied, was Andrew Jackson's nephew, as his running mate.[158]

Franklin Pierce had been one of the darkest of dark-horse candidates of the Democratic Party in 1852, but because the Whig Party was nearly dead, he won the election that year in a landslide. But his handling of Kansas, among other missteps, caused the Democratic Party leaders to abandon him and turn instead to James Buchanan from Pennsylvania in its convention. Buchanan had been a member of the House of Representatives and the Senate. He had served as minister to Russia and Secretary of State, and during much of the Pierce Administration, he had served as minister to England. Based on his credentials, Buchanan might very well have been—at least on paper—the most qualified candidate for president in our nation's history. Further, because he was out of the country during the Kansas conflict, Democratic Convention delegates thought he would be a safe candidate.

The Republican Party did not even exist in 1852, and so the 1856 election was its first entry on the national political scene. Some party optimists believed their candidate for president, John C. Frémont, would win in 1856; most, however, hoped that whoever was nominated for president would at least make a decent showing. Voters knew that he had explored the American West, was a hero in the Mexican War, and was the son-in-law of the venerable Democrat, Thomas Hart Benton. Politically, his supporters knew that he held strong antislavery views and supported the party's platform plank to keep slavery out of new territories.

Since Kansas was still a territory, the residents were not allowed to vote for president in 1856. Most northern antislavery advocates and nearly all Emigrant Aid Company officers enthusiastically supported Frémont with the notable exception of Amos Lawrence. Lawrence supported Millard Fillmore, not so much because he was in tune with the American Party platform, but because he was an old and very dear friend. Buchanan won with 45.3 percent of the vote, with Frémont second at 33.1 percent, and Fillmore third with 21.6 percent. The vote in the Electoral College was 174 for Buchanan and 114 for Frémont, who carried New York and Ohio, the largest and third largest states.

In a brief article in the *Herald of Freedom* on November 15, George Brown reported the preliminary results from the election. And although the Electoral College votes were weeks away, he noted that Buchanan was an almost certain winner. He wondered if the territory would have "to submit to another four years of mob violence," or "will Buchanan see that justice is done to the American citizens in Kansas?"[159] Perhaps Brown buried the results of the presidential election in the recesses of his paper because he and the citizens of Lawrence understood that their world could change dramatically between the election and the inauguration.[160] Their immediate concern was how they would be treated by their current territorial governor, John Geary.

Geary continued with his policy of not favoring either the free-state or the pro-slavery sides. After several months as governor, however, he became more and more disgusted with the pro-slavery side. In November 1856, he ordered the arrest of Charles Hays, a member of the notorious pro-slavery Kickapoo Rangers, for the murder of a free-state man. Before his case could be brought before the grand jury, however, Judge Lecompte released Hays on bail. Geary ordered Hays's rearrest, but while he was away from the territorial capital, Lecompte again released Hays on a writ of habeas corpus. Geary was livid at this blatant breach of justice and vented his anger toward Lecompte in a letter to President Pierce, which also asked for the judge's removal. Pierce agreed, but the Senate would not confirm a successor, so Lecompte remained on the bench.[161]

Judge Lecompte was only one source of Geary's growing anger with the pro-slavery faction. The territorial legislature passed several bills overriding Geary's vetoes. One bill would have bypassed a referendum of the citizens for a new state constitution, sending it directly to Congress. At some point near the end of 1856, Geary gave up completely on balancing his actions between the pro- and anti-slavery sides and threw his lot with the free-state leaders. He hoped he might remain in Kansas and become its governor. As Geary moved to the free-state side, Charles Robinson later wrote that he would have been happy with Geary as governor, but, by taking sides, his days as territorial governor were numbered.[162] Geary resigned at the end of President Pierce's term. While his governorship was short, Geary did manage to keep the peace, which was no small accomplishment.

James Buchanan was inaugurated as the fifteenth president on March 4, 1857. In his inaugural address, he announced that the issue of slavery in the territories would soon, and "happily, [be] a matter of but little practical importance." This was so, because he believed that it "is a judicial question, which legitimately belongs to the Supreme Court of the United States, before whom it is now pending, and will, it is understood, be speedily and finally settled." Buchanan was referring to a case that had been wending its way through the court system, *Dred Scott v. Sandford*, which would become one of the most infamous decisions by any Supreme Court. "To their decision," the president said, "in common with all good citizens, I shall cheerfully submit, whatever this may be." He went on to address the situation in Kansas, saying that "though it has ever been my individual opinion that under the Nebraska-Kansas act [*sic*] the appropriate period will be when the number of actual residents in the Territory shall justify the formation of a constitution with a view to its admission as a State into the Union. . . ."[163] He intended for his administration to move quickly to admit Kansas to the Union, but what was left unsaid was that he intended for Kansas to be admitted as a slave state.

President Buchanan appointed Robert J. Walker from Mississippi as territorial governor and Frederick P. Stanton from Washington, DC, as territorial secretary. Walker had served as a US senator and as secretary of the treasury in the Polk Administration. Stanton had been a congressman from Tennessee, and most recently was a successful attorney in Washington. Stanton arrived first in the territory as acting governor and Walker came later. Both made it clear that they wanted to maintain the peace that Governor Geary had established, but they made it equally clear that they intended to do whatever was necessary to ensure that the territorial laws passed by the pro-slavery territorial legislature would be enforced.[164]

Peace keeping in the territory was not difficult. Whether from having their noses bloodied in battles and skirmishes with free-state forces the year before, or whether they thought they again had the upper hand with the new territorial administrators, the pro-slavery faction concluded that violence would not serve it well.

The free-state side was happy for the tranquility, too. The army had successfully disbanded the non-authorized militias on both sides. Further, the Missourians again opened their borders, so emigrants had an easier time coming to Kansas, no doubt believing that no matter how many antislavery settlers entered the territory, they still had the political clout needed to make Kansas a slave state.

There probably was, however, some trepidation on the pro-slavery side about the actual numbers of new residents coming to Kansas in the spring of 1857. The *Herald of Freedom* reported that between 1,500 and 2,000 emigrants were arriving daily, and nineteen out of twenty new arrivals favored Kansas's admission as a free state. Rev. Cordley reported similar numbers of new settlers arriving, and he added that many came from southern states but were against slavery. He estimated that three out of four were against slavery.[165]

While hordes of new emigrants were arriving in Kansas, only a trickle came under the auspices of the Emigrant Aid Company, and for that matter, only relatively small numbers came from New England. A year or so earlier, the Company had shifted much of its focus to providing relief to its immigrants who had suffered from the harsh winter of 1855–56, and to the residents of Lawrence who had lived through the Wakarusa War, the sacking of their town, and the general privations resulting from Bleeding Kansas. The destruction of its Free State Hotel and other company property was a devastating financial loss as well, which prompted its creditors to clamor for payment of debts owed. The role of the company and its officers was evolving, and Amos Lawrence captured the company's changing role in his resignation letter as treasurer. "The main object for which the association was formed," he wrote, "the incitement of free emigration to Kansas, has been successfully accomplished. The corporation must hereafter be considered a land company."[166]

Even with the shift in focus, the Emigrant Aid Company and Amos Lawrence remained committed to the cause. The members continued doing everything in their power to ensure that Kansas would be admitted as a free state. For his part, Lawrence authorized a substantial donation of $12,696.14 to be placed in trust "for the advancement of religious and intellectual education of the young in Kansas." Part of the money would come from a fund he had established for Lawrence University in Appleton, Wisconsin, and the rest from shares he held in the Emigrant Aid Company. He intended for the money to accrue interest, with the eventual dispersal of about half for Sunday schools throughout the future state, and half for educating the young. He stipulated one caveat: that should Kansas become a slave state, the money would be returned to him or his heirs.[167]

It is difficult to translate 1857 dollars to twenty-first century dollars, but an amount over $12,000 was a great deal of money at that time. As a comparison, a house in a city such as Chicago at that time cost about $500. A skilled craftsman such as a blacksmith earned, on average, $500 a year, and an unskilled laborer earned about $300 a year. Added to the substantial money he had already invested in Kansas, Lawrence had truly put his money where his mouth was.

Peace continued in Lawrence into the spring of 1857, and the town was prospering. Many emigrants came through Lawrence either to stay, or more likely as a passing point to other areas in the territory. If they chose to stay in Lawrence, land was becoming quite pricey. A 1,500-square-foot lot at the corner of Massachusetts and Winthrop sold for $1,250 in cash in May 1857. It had been purchased for $250 eighteen months earlier. As quickly as anyone could build a hotel or lodging house, it was filled. A one-hundred-pound sack of corn fetched the astonishing price of $4; a one-hundred-pound sack of flour went for $5.50. Unskilled laborers demanded and received $2 a day, and that was if anyone could find a laborer who would work for any amount of money.

After enjoying a few months of a newspaper monopoly, George Brown once again had competition. On May 28, 1857, T. D. Thatcher and Norman Allen published the first issue of the *Lawrence Republican*. At the head of the first page, the publishers quoted from the Declaration of Independence, then went on to state that their sole purpose was to ensure that all citizens in Kansas—black and white—would be equal. It did not take long for the newspapers to start slinging mud at each other. On June 25, Thatcher and Allen asked if "the *Herald of Freedom* at all times sustained the position and policy of the Free-State Party in Kansas." The question was rhetorical, and they answered that "the *Herald of Freedom* can pursue its own course and its own language . . . but it must not attempt longer to palm itself off as sustaining the position and policy of the Free-State Party." Two days later, Brown asked his subscribers to renew the subscriptions and sought new readers because "a partisan press for partisan purposes are laboring to crush it [the *Herald*]." He continued: "[The *Herald of Freedom*] has been stricken down, but it has risen, and will rise again and again, if necessary, until freedom triumphs, and every occupant of Kansas is truly free."[168]

Although Lawrence was growing and—again—beginning to prosper, remnants of the sacking remained. Many residents had lost their crops the previous summer; others had lost their houses and were not able to rebuild. Groups from New Hampshire and New York, hearing of their plight, raised relief money that was distributed to those most in need. On the brighter side, many of the buildings damaged or destroyed a year earlier were repaired or replaced. The sawmill owned by the Emigrant Aid Company was repaired and back in business. The Free State Hotel was still in ruins, but a Mr. Eldridge and a partner purchased the site—which still had a solid foundation and basement—from the Emigrant Aid Company for $5,000. They would soon begin rebuilding a larger and more elegant hotel.[169]

In addition to rebuilding their town, the residents of Lawrence began looking forward to the elections scheduled later in 1857 for the territorial legislature. But before those elections, the sitting pro-slavery territorial legislature called for elections in the spring for delegates to a convention to draft a Kansas constitution. An article in the *Herald of Freedom* on May 2, 1857, noted that the free-state men of Kansas had decided to boycott the convention election. For one thing, they were convinced that the convention would produce a constitution that made slavery legal. Further, territorial Governor Walker promised that any constitution would be submitted to voters for approval before it was submitted to Congress. Since a substantial majority of Kansans opposed slavery, Charles Robinson and other antislavery leaders believed they were safe in advising free-state residents to boycott the election for the constitutional convention.[170]

Robinson and nearly all free-state men indeed did boycott the constitutional convention election, which was held on June 15, 1857. The polls did not attract much interest from the pro-slavery faction either, in that only about 20 percent of eligible voters cast ballots. The areas with the highest turnout were along the Missouri River, but unlike the vote to elect the territorial legislature two years earlier, few Missourians crossed the border to vote.

Sixty delegates were chosen to write the new constitution. But before they began their work, it was clear that a great many were interested in their proceedings, including President Buchanan.[171] The president had hoped that the *Dred Scott* Supreme Court decision would settle the question of slavery in the territory once and for all. Instead, it unleashed a firestorm of protest in the North, with no end in sight. Dred Scott, an enslaved man, sued for his freedom because his owner had taken him to Illinois, a free state, and to Wisconsin, a free territory. The court could have simply said Dred Scott was a slave and left it at that, but it went much further. It said that because Scott was an African American man, he had no rights as a citizen, and thus had no standing. In a more far-reaching ruling, however, the court also said that Congress could not restrict slavery in the territories, tying the ownership of slaves to the property rights clause of the Fifth Amendment of the Constitution.[172]

Since the *Dred Scott* decision further inflamed the North, President Buchanan turned his attention to Kansas, naively hoping that the constitutional convention would produce a pro-slavery constitution that would be acceptable to the residents of Kansas, and would pass both houses of Congress. He thought the South would be pleased to have another slave state in its fold. He hoped the North would accept Kansas as a slave state to maintain peace. He was wrong again.

The pro-slavery territorial legislature had the power to call for a constitutional convention, but it could not delay the call for an election for the territorial legislature. The election was scheduled for October 1857. The free-state men debated whether or not they should bother to vote, fearing that no matter what the numbers showed, the pro-slavery folks would somehow find a way to rig the election. On the other hand, Governor Walker—of whom both sides still were wary—very much wanted the free-state residents to vote, and promised that he would ensure that the election would be fair. Ultimately, Dr. Robinson and the others concluded that it was in their interest to vote for the territorial legislature. Free-State Party members met in Grasshopper Falls on August 26 to debate this issue, and all in attendance agreed to vote.[173] The election took place on October 5, 1857, and true to his word, Governor Walker stationed troops at all polling places in which it was suspected that there might be trouble. The election went off without a hitch, or at least that was how it seemed.

The citizens of Lawrence were jubilant. Eligible voters turned out in force, and it appeared that they had finally elected their people to the territorial legislature. But, up to their old tricks, the sitting territorial legislature had linked Douglas County, where Lawrence was located, with neighboring pro-slavery Johnson County in the election, allowing eight legislators to be elected from the combined district. On the day of the election, Douglas County reported 1,638 votes for the free-state side and 187 for the pro-slavery side. Johnson County was much smaller, and although more residents there voted in a pro-slavery block, there were nowhere near enough votes to tip the balance in their favor. Miraculously, however, two days after the election, the tiny precinct of Oxford in Johnson County reported an additional 1,547 proslavery votes, which would have thrown the election to the pro-slavery side.

The result was miraculous in that on the first day of voting, only ninety-one men had voted in the Oxford precinct. It was later discovered that the instigators took names from the city directory of Cincinnati, Ohio, cast votes in their names, and had them certified. True to his word, Governor Walker threw out the rigged ballots, giving the election to the free-state candidates.[174] Across the territory, the free-state candidates won by a wide margin, ensuring that the new legislature would be under their control.

Because the free-state faction won a territorial election, residents of Lawrence and elsewhere paid little attention to the constitutional convention, believing that no matter what it produced, if it included a provision for slavery, it would easily be defeated when submitted to the people for approval. George Brown noted in his *Herald of Freedom* that the convention met on September 7 and recessed until October 19. There also was a rumor that no money was available to pay the delegates, and that the convention likely might not reconvene.[175]

The people of Lawrence were overly optimistic that the constitutional convention meeting in Lecompton would come to nothing. It reconvened on October 19, 1857, and wrote a state constitution that—not surprisingly—included a provision allowing slavery in the new state. Section 1 of Article VII stated that "the right of property is before and higher than any constitutional sanction, and the right of the owner of a slave to such slave and its increase is the same and as inviolable as the right of the owner of any property whatever."[176] The delegates concluded their business and submitted the new constitution directly to Kansas residents for a vote on December 21, 1857, bypassing the territorial legislature.

Rather than a vote on the entire document, however, residents were only allowed to vote on one of two options: namely, if they voted for the constitution "with slavery," they were endorsing the unlimited growth of the institution in the new state. On the other hand, if they voted for the constitution "without slavery," they were not voting to outlaw slavery, but rather to limit the number of slave owners to the number already in Kansas when admitted to the Union. Slaves already in Kansas would remain slaves, but no new slaves would be imported into the state. In other words, either option made slavery legal. But the language followed the requirement of the Kansas-Nebraska Act that the people of Kansas would request admission as a state "with" or "without" slavery.

Free-state Kansans boycotted the constitutional vote, and in their absence, the pro-slavery faction approved the constitution "with slavery," by a vote of 6,226 to 569. They then submitted it to Congress for admission. Although it probably was not necessary, since the free-state side stayed away from the polls, the pro-slavery side intimidated anyone it thought might vote against the constitution. Missourians also crossed the border and voted with the pro-slavery side. Governor Walker was temporarily away from the territory, and Territorial Secretary Frederick P. Stanton, who was acting as territorial governor at the time, was concerned with the irregularities of the vote. Stanton also understood that any vote for the pro-slavery Lecompton Constitution or, for that matter, any constitution, required the territorial legislature to initiate the process. So he called the territorial legislature into a special session and asked the members to pass a law submitting the Lecompton Constitution to a vote of the people. The legislature complied and scheduled a new election to be held on January 4, 1858. The result was 138 for and 10,266 votes against the Lecompton Constitution.[177]

Nevertheless, the pro-slavery side went ahead and submitted the Lecompton Constitution, based on the December 21 vote, to Congress through President Buchanan. The president saw this constitution as a gift. Nothing in his first year in office had gone well. In addition to the slavery issues, the nation was in the throes of the Panic of 1857, the most devastating economic downturn in the nation up to that point in its history. Buchanan was not concerned that there were problems with the way the Lecompton Constitution was presented to the people of Kansas; he went ahead and submitted it to Congress. To blunt the potential argument that the free-state faction boycotted the December 21 vote, he argued that they had the opportunity to vote but chose not to, and thus "suffered the election to pass by default." He further made the case that the January 4 vote was not legal since the December 21 vote had already taken place.[178]

As he had miscalculated on the *Dred Scott* decision, Buchanan misjudged how Northern Democrats would view the Lecompton Constitution. Many, including Senator Stephen A. Douglas, who had pushed through the Kansas-Nebraska Bill, were incensed that the president would even consider presenting the document to Congress. Buchanan tried to strong-arm Democrats to support the constitution, and was successful with the Senate but not the House. The two houses eventually came up with a compromise in which the Lecompton Constitution would be resubmitted to Kansans for an up or down vote. But, as part of the compromise, Congressman William Hayden English, a Democrat from Indiana, proposed a desperation measure to sweeten the pot for Kansas residents to support the constitution. In what was called the English Bill, Kansas would receive an additional 3.5 million acres in federal land if it approved the constitution; nothing if it did not. On the third vote, on August 2, 1858, by a vote of 1,926 for to 11,812 against, Kansas buried the Lecompton Constitution. With the defeat, the issue of whether or not Kansas would become a slave state was decided as well. It would take two and a half more years, but Kansas would enter the Union in 1861 as a free state.

10 Glorious Intelligence! Kansas in the Union!

A FEW WEEKS AFTER THE legislative elections, the newly elected "Free State" territorial legislature began its deliberations. The body convened in Lecompton, but immediately moved to Lawrence, where it met on January 4, 1858—coincidentally, the same day as the second vote on the Lecompton Constitution. The first order of business was to repeal the pro-slavery laws that were so repugnant to nearly all Kansans. That part was easy. The part that was more difficult was drafting new laws. Under the pro-slavery legislature, the members essentially borrowed the legal code from Missouri, substituted "the Territory of Kansas" in place of the "State of Missouri" where appropriate, and that, for all intents and purposes, became the legal code. The exception was the slave code, which was much harsher. It would take several sessions for the new legislature to tear down the old, then build up a new set of laws.

One early piece of legislation was a city charter for Lawrence. Although the town, since its creation, had functioned as if it were incorporated, it was not allowed to legally do so until 1858. The town could not collect its own taxes, although the citizens voluntarily contributed to fund the schools and provide all necessary services—but without elected officials to oversee the management of the town. So, in many ways, incorporating the town was a formality, but now the citizens could officially elect city council and school board members and the town marshal, as well as a clerk and a treasurer.[179]

Stereo View of Lawrence 1859. Kansas State Historical Society.

Almost as quickly as the new legislature convened, Charles Robinson and James Lane started jockeying for position. They clearly did not care for each other, but Robinson was much more vocal in his dislike for Lane. He described Lane at his heart as a timid man, who with his "arbitrary power" was "cruel and blood-thirsty."[180] Again, according to Robinson, Lane's modus operandi was that—depending on the situation—he advocated bloodshed or peace if he thought one or the other would gain him political support. Lane's detractors focused on what they saw as his faults, and there were plenty. But he had a positive side as well. Like many politicians, he loved attention, but in at least one situation, he made a major contribution to the antislavery cause, and neither sought nor received much attention for what he did. He charted and marked a trail through Kansas with "chimneys"—called the Lane Trail—to guide abolitionists sneaking slaves out of Missouri, as part of the Underground Railroad.[181]

While Lane's views were often tied to how the political winds blew, one man who did not deviate in any way from the radical abolitionist path was John Brown. Brown returned to the East after the incidents of Bleeding Kansas to raise money and support. When he came back to Kansas, his new crusade was to encourage and help Missouri slaves escape to freedom.[182] On December 20–21, 1858, Brown and his followers successfully stole and led twelve Missouri slaves to freedom, and in the process, killed one slave owner. They successfully spirited their charges through Kansas on the Lane Trail and, about two and a half months later, into Canada.[183]

As noted earlier in this study, John Brown had sold wool to Amos Lawrence years earlier, and Lawrence provided a letter of introduction for Brown when he went to Kansas. The relationship these two men shared was interesting. In many ways, they could not have been more different. Lawrence was wealthy; Brown, through nearly his entire life, was hard-pressed to eke out a living. Brown was a radical, fanatic abolitionist; Lawrence was opposed to slavery, and even though he poured much of his fortune into creating a free Kansas, he generally was a moderate. Yet Lawrence was fascinated with and had a great deal of admiration for Brown. The two men met while Brown was in the East in early 1857. Brown asked Lawrence for money for his Kansas causes. Lawrence declined, explaining that he had just sent a substantial sum to Kansas to establish educational programs there. But when Brown pleaded with Lawrence to help support his wife and family, should he lose his life due to his abolitionist activities, Lawrence readily agreed to help—which, later, he did.

When Brown again visited Amos Lawrence in the spring of 1859, Brown had grown a long beard, and Lawrence observed that Brown and his companion were both ill, which he thought was "righteous visitation for their fanaticism." Lawrence was not shocked when he later heard the news of Brown's raid at Harpers Ferry, nor was he surprised when he learned that "Old Brown of Osawatomie" would be hanged for his crime. He realized that the old man would "die as a martyr [due] to his hatred of slavery," which would hasten the end of slavery in Virginia.[184] When, years later, one of Brown's compatriots in the Pottawatomie massacre confessed to the crime and described in some detail Brown's involvement, Lawrence's view was confirmed that Brown was a "monomaniac."[185]

One man who shared Brown's abolitionist passion and part-nered with the old man on several slave-stealing missions was Dr. John Doy. He successfully helped slaves escape from Missouri on the Lane Trail to Canada. Ironically, though, when he and his son were caught for supposedly helping slaves escape, they were assisting free blacks in leaving Kansas. In the winter of 1858–59, slave catch-ers came into Lawrence under the guise of the Fugitive Slave Act of 1850, and successfully kidnapped several free blacks. Fearing for their safety, a number of free blacks asked the citizens of Lawrence for assistance. The townspeople asked Dr. Doy if he would take on the mission. He agreed, and on January 25, 1859, he, his son, and a colleague left with fifteen free African Americans in two wagons from Lawrence. To ensure that it would not appear that they were attempting to help fugitives escape, Doy asked each of his charges to carry the proper papers, attesting to his or her free status.

When the party had traveled about twelve miles from Lawrence, "at the bottom of the hill," he wrote, "came a body of some twenty, or maybe more, armed and mounted men. Eleven of them approached us with leveled rifles and ordered us to halt." After some discussion and a great deal of bluster and posturing on both sides, Dr. Doy sur-rendered, recognizing that he and his party had no chance against the assailants. Their captors transported them first by land, then by ferry to Weston, Missouri, where they "were pushed and mauled, struck, and insulted with every indignity that can be conceived." The next day at a hearing, Dr. Doy and his son Charles were bound over for trial at Platte City, Missouri, on the charge of abducting slaves. They were confined from January 28 to March 24 and not allowed to leave their cell except to testify before the grand jury. Their white companion was allowed to return to Lawrence.

During their second day of confinement, Dr. Doy and his son learned the fate of the free African Americans they were escorting. The three men, Wilson George Hays, Charles Smith, and William Riley, were asked to pick who they wanted as masters. When they refused to do so, the Border Ruffians severely beat the three men to try to make them confess that they were slaves. They still refused, and next thing Doy heard was that they were sold at auction at Independence, Missouri, for $1,000 apiece. He observed that these poor men "though free, had but a small chance to assert their rights in a slave state."

As for Dr. Doy, he and Charles were moved to St. Joseph to await their trial. Doy's wife and daughter visited while they were still in Platte City. The trial centered on the charge that Dr. Doy and his son had enticed Dick, a slave who belonged to the mayor of Weston, Missouri, to escape his bondage. Dick was a musician who had been allowed to go into Kansas with his fiddle but had failed to return. Doy would later say that he and his son were well represented by their defense team, who made a strong case that Doy had no way of knowing that Dick was an enslaved man. But he also noted that the prosecuting attorneys were very capable as well. At the end of the trial, which lasted several days, the jury could not reach a verdict, and Charles Doy was released. Dr. Doy was held over for a new trial and jailed again since he was not able to pay the $5,000 bond, having spent his assets on his defense.

Doy's second trial started on June 20, 1859, with the same charge that he had induced the enslaved man Dick to escape. Again, Dr. Doy believed he made a strong case that he did, indeed, know Dick in Lawrence, but had no way of knowing that he was enslaved. In this second trial, however, the judge allowed the prosecution to enter into evidence a journal and map taken from Doy that the prosecutor claimed was the route for the Underground Railroad through Kansas. The judge instructed the jury that it would be allowed to "infer guilt from the circumstances," which meant that the members could view the map and journal as proof that Doy was trying to help Dick escape. This time, the jury convicted Dr. Doy, and the judge sentenced him to five years of hard labor in the state penitentiary.

Dr. Doy was held in the St. Joseph jail for thirty days awaiting transport to the state penitentiary to serve his sentence. When the thirty days were nearly up, Doy recognized several men walking by the jail; one of these men "made a familiar sign known to Kansas Free-State men." On July 23, in the late afternoon, a young man was escorted into Doy's cell who informed him that he had recently seen the prisoner's wife and family. He distracted the attention of the jailer for a moment, at which time, Doy, suspecting something, "saw a small slip of paper in the hand which he held behind him, which I took." The paper said: "be ready at midnight."

Dr. Doy gathered everything he could think of and went to bed with his clothes on. At midnight, there was a banging on the jailhouse door, and the jailor went to answer. Two men, holding a third, claimed that the man they had was a notorious horse thief, and they wanted him put in jail overnight. The jailor—Mr. Brown, who Doy said treated him like a gentleman—argued with the men that it was not his job to lock someone up who had not been officially charged with a crime. Eventually, the jailor relented and allowed the men to escort the "horse thief" back to the jail cells. When Jailor Brown opened Dr. Doy's cell, the men informed him that they "had not come to put a man in prison, but to take out of it one who is unjustly confined." Other prisoners wanted to join in the escape, but Doy's rescuers forced them back into their cells, saying they had come for only one prisoner.

Ten radical Kansas abolitionists made up the Dr. Doy's rescue party. Their rescue became legendary in the annals of Kansas history and gave them the distinction as the "Immortal Ten." They spirited Doy out of town to the Missouri River and to a small boat waiting to take him across to Kansas. When the boat reached the far bank, the doctor was placed in a covered wagon under a pile of hay and driven to safety. A day and a half later, Dr. Doy was escorted into Lawrence, where "the noble ten were cheered and welcomed, as [they] brought to a successful issue the boldest attempt at rescue ever planned and carried into effect, and as having effaced the stain of at least one of the insults offered to Kansas offered by her more powerful neighbor."[186]

Dr. John Doy's adventure makes a wonderful story. But it also brought to light the plight of free African Americans in Kansas. At

John Doy Rescuers. Kansas State Historical Society.

the beginning of his narrative, Doy explained that he was happy to guide the free blacks away from Lawrence because he had witnessed, firsthand, the dangers they faced. He described the plight of Charles Fisher, a free black barber, who was kidnapped but escaped. Rev. Ephraim Nute, minister of the Lawrence Unitarian Church, filled the rest of the saga of Charles (Charley) Fisher. Two men broke into his barber shop in Leavenworth, kidnapped and handcuffed him, and spirited him to an island in the Missouri River. While his captors were asleep, Fisher escaped and went back to Leavenworth, where he had a friend file off the handcuffs.[187] Rev. Nute wrote that Fisher "came to our house [in Lawrence] in a coach from Leavenworth disguised in female attire. We kept him 2 days. . . . [We] moved [him] on from house to house." He concluded by writing that Fisher would "be started in the small hours tomorrow morning for Canada." The tragedy was that Fisher was a free man, who should have been allowed to go about his business undisturbed, but for his own safety, he wanted to get as far away from Kansas as possible.[188] Doy also described another free African American, William Riley, who was also kidnapped and able to escape from the room in which he was held, several miles outside of Lawrence.[189]

Free African American Kansans' lives and safety were precarious no matter where they lived. Under the Fugitive Slave Act of 1850, they were theoretically protected as free people, but they were in constant fear that a slave owner could claim him or her as property, and a federal magistrate could find for the owner and send him or her into bondage on meager evidence. If there was a haven for free African Americans, or for that matter escaped slaves, that place was Lawrence, which was a major station on the Underground Railroad. The people of Lawrence "hated human slavery and believed in every man's right to freedom."[190] But people like the Reverend Cordley were conflicted. On the one hand, they believed—and believed strongly—that human bondage was wrong; on the other hand, they knew that helping enslaved people escape was against the laws of their country. They knew also that if they were caught aiding fugitives, they faced stiff fines and prison sentences.

Rev. Cordley expressed the thought processes of many when given the opportunity to become a "conductor" on the Underground Railroad. As a student at Andover Theological Seminary, Cordley was incensed when he learned of the passage of the Fugitive Slave Act in 1850, calling it the "outrage of outrages" and the "sum of all villainies." He promised himself that if he ever had the opportunity, he would do whatever he could to shelter or assist any fugitive slave. Yet once he was in Kansas, he found "it [was] easy to be brave a thousand miles away," but when confronted with the chance to put motion to his thoughts, knowing full well the potential consequences of breaking the law, he realized "there was only one thing to do." So when one of his congregants, Mr. Monteith, asked if he would help shelter Lizzie, a young fugitive woman who had run away from her master and was trying to escape to Canada, he and his wife accepted without hesitation. The Cordleys kept Lizzie as if she were part of the family for months.[191]

Because of the secret nature of the Underground Railroad, a great deal about the operation has been lost over the years. Most who did record their experience, like Rev. Cordley, did so much later. Some who wrote about the railroad at the time often did so in code. So in January 1858, when Samuel Tappan wrote to Thomas Wentworth Higginson hoping to raise money to support the cause, he wrote "that a certain Rail Road has been in full blast. Several persons have taken full advantage of it to visit their friends. Only one or two accidents have happened." It's not difficult to decode the message. The "Rail Road" was the Underground Railroad. Persons visiting friends refers to escaping slaves staying at various stations. And the "accidents" occurred when slaves were captured.

One of the "conductors" on the railroad was Robert Miller, the father of Josiah Miller, one of the early residents of Lawrence. Josiah had asked his parents to leave South Carolina and come to Lawrence, which they did in 1858. We do not know a great deal about Miller's role in the operation, except that the smokehouse on the Miller farmstead was one of the major "stations" in Lawrence. Miller family descendants report that their ancestors' role in the Underground Railroad is an important part of their family lore.[192]

Other Underground Railroad "conductors" did little to hide their activities. Such was the case with John E. Stewart, whose nickname was the "Fighting Preacher" since he had been a Methodist minister. In a letter to Thaddeus Hyatt, a wealthy benefactor in New York, he reported that he "brought away from [Missouri] fourteen [slaves], including one unbroken family, of which I feel rather proud." Stewart's strategy was to visit plantations disguised as a peddler. When he had the chance, he pretended to sell the enslaved people small trinkets. Instead, he told them of the opportunity to escape to Canada with his assistance. Before long, the planters in Missouri raised $1,000 for Stewart's capture.

Because so little was written or survived about the Underground Railroad in Lawrence, it is difficult to put a number on the escapees. John Stewart was reported to have personally assisted at least sixty-eight to freedom. Another active "conductor" reported that he personally knew of at least three hundred slaves who escaped through Lawrence. So at least five hundred, probably more, maybe even as high as one thousand former slaves found their way to freedom through Lawrence.[193]

In many ways, John Stewart, Robert Miller, John Doy, Rev. Cordley, and others had the easy part. They risked arrest, possible fines, and maybe even jail terms for aiding slaves in their escape, but the chances slaves took to escape, and the punishments if they were caught, were much harsher. But the benefits if they did indeed make it to freedom made the potential dangers worth the risks. Lizzie, the young slave woman for whom Rev. Cordley provided refuge, escaped to Lawrence. Cordley did not offer any circumstances of her escape, but he noted that her owner knew she was in Lawrence and sent US Marshals to find her and return her to captivity. The Lawrence Underground Railroad network was able to move her around from safe house to safe house and eventually to a permanent home in Canada.[194]

Rev. Ephraim Nute, minister of the Unitarian Church in Lawrence, reported the story of a fugitive slave who was captured and placed in the jail in Platte City, Missouri, until he could be recovered by his owner. "He broke jail by burning out the bars from the window; he walked 10 miles to the Missouri river & crossed on the floating cakes of ice," Rev. Nute reported. Then he got "on to an island or sand-bar in the middle of the river where he spent two days & nights hid in the young cottonwoods; thence again over the running ice to the Kansas side. . . . [He] walked the 35 or 40 miles to this place [Lawrence]." The day after he arrived in Lawrence, the Underground Railroad moved him "30 miles to another depot," then on to Canada.[195]

For the residents of Lawrence and Kansas, whether they were involved in the Underground Railroad or any other business, a high priority was to gain admission to the Union. And for that, the new legislature needed to take the lead to write and submit a new constitution. Neither the Topeka Constitution of 1855 nor the Lecompton Constitution, just voted down, was suitable for resurrection. The Kansas Territorial Legislature called for the election of delegates to a new constitutional convention on March 9, 1858, to be held at Minneola, Kansas. The delegates assembled on March 23, organized, and elected James Lane as president and Samuel F. Tappan as clerk. A day later, the convention voted to adjourn to meet at Leavenworth on March 25. After appointing the committees, Lane resigned as president and Martin F. Conway took his place. Lane did not give a reason for stepping down, but Charles Robinson, who was his bitter enemy, speculated that Lane wanted assurances from the delegates that he would become the first US senator from Kansas. He did not get what he wanted and bowed out.[196]

As the delegates to the Lecompton Convention were decidedly from the pro-slavery camp, delegates to the Leavenworth convention were just as decidedly from the more radical wing of the antislavery camp. The new Leavenworth Constitution granted full citizenship and voting rights to African Americans, and it empowered the new state legislature to draft legislation for universal suffrage. It provided for public and higher education for the future state's children. And it allowed married women to own property independent of their husbands.[197] The convention adjourned on April 3 and submitted the constitution to the citizens for ratification on May 18, 1858. Kansas residents approved the new document, submitted it to Congress, where, because of its radical provisions, it had no chance for approval.

The Kansas Territorial Legislature probably recognized that the Leavenworth Constitution would never pass muster in Congress, so in its 1859 session, it called for yet another constitutional convention to be held at Wyandotte in July of that year. One author made the astute observation that the first three Kansas constitutions were written to frame issues, whereas the fourth, the Wyandotte Constitution, was written to form a state.[198] Delegates were elected on June 17; they gathered in Wyandotte on July 5. Thirty-five Republicans and seventeen Democrats, with an average age of thirty-five, attended the convention. There were eighteen lawyers, sixteen farmers, eight merchants, three manufacturers, three physicians, one mechanic, one land agent, one printer, and one surveyor.[199] For various reasons, the warhorses from the free-state faction of Bleeding Kansas, such as Charles Robinson, James Lane, and others, did not participate.

Because the makeup of the convention included liberal, moderate, and conservative factions, the debates were often contentious. Not open to debate, however, was the issue of slavery, so Section 6 read: "there shall be no slavery in this State, and no involuntary servitude, except for the punishment of crime, whereof the party shall have been duly convicted." But other issues were not as easy to resolve. Conservative delegates wanted to exclude free blacks and mulattoes from the new state and limit the rights for white women. As a compromise, the constitution read that "every white male person, of twenty-one years and upward" was granted the full rights of citizenship, which, of course, meant women, African Americans, and Indians were denied these rights.

The site of the future capital entered the discussions as well. Several towns vied for the honor. It was clear from the outset that Lecompton had too many unpleasant memories and thus would not become the seat of government. Of the eight communities in competition, three were finalists—Topeka, Lawrence, and Atchison. Topeka put the most effort into its candidacy and won the straw poll, followed by Lawrence and Atchison. Although the convention's vote was nonbinding, on November 5, 1861, in a statewide election, Topeka was selected as the new state capital.

On October 4, 1859, by a vote of 10,421 to 5,530, the citizens of Kansas voted to adopt the Wyandotte Constitution. Although the Wyandotte Constitution was much more balanced than the first three, and although Kansas met the criteria established to enter the union as a state, it would take a year and a half until it was admitted.

A few weeks after Kansans voted to approve their new constitution, a politician who had begun his rise to recognition a year earlier, with his debates for the US senator's seat in Illinois, spent a week in eastern Kansas. Abraham Lincoln crossed the Missouri River from

St. Joseph to Elwood, Kansas, on November 30. He visited Troy, Atchison, and Leavenworth, received warm receptions—although the outside temperature was bitterly cold—and gave speeches at each stop. Most Kansans at the time were staunch supporters of William Seward for president, and they didn't take Lincoln's possible candidacy for the nation's highest office very seriously. One person who did take him seriously, however, was James Lane. Lane met Lincoln during his Kansas tour, instantly became one of his strongest supporters, and campaigned for him in 1860.[200]

Two weeks after Abraham Lincoln's visit, on December 17, 1859, an institution of the earliest years of Kansas, the *Herald of Freedom,* printed its last edition. George Brown mentioned—in passing—that he was having a difficult time buying paper for his newspaper, thus the next edition or so might not be published; he gave his readers no indication that this was the end of his newspaper. For the past two and a half years, the *Herald* had been losing readers and advertisers to the *Lawrence Republican.* The editors for both papers had been carping at each other frequently, and Brown lost the battle.[201] Brown's paper probably lost readership because his message was not in tune with the readers in Lawrence. He was a moderate antislavery advocate, whereas the people of Lawrence were becoming more radical in their opposition to slavery.

The Wyandotte Constitution was submitted to Congress, and in April 1860, the United States House of Representatives voted 134 to 73 to admit Kansas. But it was tabled in the Senate. In the meantime, the country was in the midst of the greatest crisis in its history. Abraham Lincoln, the Republican Party candidate, was elected as president. The one plank in the Republican platform that was unacceptable to the South stated that a Republican Administration would do all within its power to permanently prohibit the expansion of slavery into the territories. Although there was no legal mechanism to do so, shortly after Lincoln's victory, South Carolina seceded from the Union in December, followed by Mississippi, Florida, Alabama, and Georgia by the middle of January 1861. South Carolina, and the other southern states that left the Union, did so by calling for a convention to determine whether the state wanted to remain in the Union or leave. With the absence of the senators from these states, however, the way was now clear for Kansas's admission to the Union. Thus, on January 21, 1861, the Senate voted to admit Kansas. President Buchanan, who had stubbornly tried everything in his power to make Kansas a slave state, signed the admission bill on January 29, 1861, making Kansas the thirty-fourth state.[202]

The *Lawrence Republican* reported the news two days later. "Glorious Intelligence! Kansas in the Union! We have received the glorious news that Kansas is admitted into the Union." The writer continued, "we hear the jubilant news vocally heralded in the streets, and the sounds of the 'spirit-stirring drum' admonish us that the 'immortal [Lawrence] Stubbs' are glorifying the event. All hail! We are citizens of the United States once more, partners in 'Hail Columbia,' 'Yankee Doodle,' the stars and stripes, the Declaration of Independence, and the Fourth of July!"[203]

The people of Lawrence and Kansas were jubilant with statehood. But the future looked ominous. By the date of Kansas's admission, six southern states had already seceded from the Union. What would happen? Would the South be allowed to go its separate way, or would the North be willing to wage war to reunite the Union? These and other questions were unanswered when Kansas was admitted as the thirty-fourth state.

PART III

THE WAR

11 My Life Belongs to My Country, But My Heart Belongs to You

LAWRENCE, KANSAS, WAS NEVER FAR from the thoughts of Amos Lawrence, and he was delighted when Kansas finally became a free state. But his namesake town was not his only interest. He agreed to serve as treasurer for Harvard, and he led the fund-raising effort to build a major natural history museum at the behest of faculty member Louis Agassiz. As regional tensions increased, however, he did everything in his power to try to keep the nation together. He and several other "representatives of the conservative elements of Massachusetts" traveled to Washington with a petition containing fifteen thousand signatures, urging Congress to pass the Crittenden Amendment. In December 1860, Kentucky Senator John Crittenden had proposed a constitutional amendment that, among other provisions, would permanently protect slavery by forbidding the passage of any amendment or action of Congress that would interfere with the institution of slavery in any way. As the year 1860 drew to a close, Lawrence recorded in his diary that December 31 brought "a sad ending of one year in the history of my country; I fear the last year of our happy union."

Lawrence had good reason for discouragement about his country. The recent presidential election had clearly demonstrated the nation's deep political divisions. He had thrown himself—in partnership with other former Whigs—into creating and supporting the Constitutional Union Party, with John Bell from Tennessee as its standard bearer for president. Lawrence reluctantly agreed to run as the party's candidate for the governorship of Massachusetts. He lost, but was not unhappy with the results. Edward Everett, who had represented Massachusetts in numerous political offices and had served as the former president of Harvard, was the vice presidential candidate. The party was silent on the issue of slavery, but instead campaigned on the single issue of keeping the Union intact.[204]

The Constitutional Union Party (some referred to it as the National Union Party) was one of four parties with candidates in the presidential race of 1860. Abraham Lincoln was the choice of the new Republican Party, which promised to do everything in its power to keep slavery out of the territories. Stephen A. Douglas, the candidate for the Democratic Party, ran on the platform he had been espousing for years of allowing the people of the territories to decide whether they wanted slavery or not under the concept of popular sovereignty. Finally, the southern faction of the Democratic Party split from Douglas and nominated John Breckenridge from Kentucky to run on a separate ticket on the platform of protecting slave owners' rights to take and hold their human property in the territories without restrictions.

Abraham Lincoln won with one of the smallest popular vote totals in history at 39.6 percent, and won in the Electoral College with 180 of 303 votes. Between the election in November 1860 and Lincoln's inauguration on March 4, 1861, seven states, starting with South Carolina, had seceded from the Union, and four others would follow to establish the Confederate States of America. The delicate balance between slave and free states, which started with the Constitutional Convention and continued with compromises that held the nation together for decades, crumbled with Lincoln's election. The Republican promise that slavery would be prohibited in the territories was the final nail in the coffin of national unity. Slave owners believed their institution was dynamic and could expand into the territories within the continental United States and even into future territories in the Caribbean and other parts of the Americas.[205]

President Lincoln promised that he would not interfere with slavery in the areas where it existed in 1861. But the slaveholding South was fearful that closing the territories to slavery was the first step toward abolishing slavery throughout the country. They saw this action as a threat to their current and future livelihoods, and for good reason. In 1860, there were nearly four million slaves in the United States. About 385,000 white families, roughly 30 percent, in slave states owned slaves, and of that number, 12 percent owned twenty or more slaves. About 30 percent of the nation's population lived in the South, but 60 percent of the wealthiest individuals were concentrated in the South. Further, the per capita income in the South was nearly double that in the North. The value of slaves in the United States—again in 1860—was more than three billion dollars, which was greater than the combined value of railroads, factories, and banks in the entire country, or on another scale, greater than all land, cotton, buildings, and goods in the South.

Amos Lawrence, of course, did not own slaves, but he was as wealthy as most of the largest slave owners in the South. Unlike most of them, he did all he could to try to hold the country together. But once the nation split in two, Lawrence devoted his considerable energies and fortune to the Union war effort. He offered his services either to lead a regiment or to use his business skills to support the North. In 1862, he almost single-handedly raised the 2nd Massachusetts Volunteer Cavalry Unit, commanded by Harvard graduate Charles Russell Lowell. Many members of the regiment were Harvard graduates from many of the leading Massachusetts families. To fill out the ranks, Lawrence offered between $100 and $200—from his own pocket—as an inducement to any man who would volunteer to join.[206]

While Amos Lawrence was busy supporting the war effort in the East, residents of Lawrence, Kansas, reveled in their new statehood status—but only for a couple of weeks before the opening salvos of the Civil War erupted with the Confederates firing on Fort Sumter in the harbor of Charleston, South Carolina. In many ways, the new crisis was not that different from the old one. If Missouri opted to join other slave states and secede from the Union, Kansas would be isolated from other loyal states; but even if Missouri remained in the Union, the slave owners along the Kansas border would almost certainly support the rebel cause. For better or worse, no matter what her neighbor did, from their years of struggle to create their free state, the people of Lawrence and the rest of Kansas were probably better prepared for battle than any citizens of any other state.

In the days following the capture of Fort Sumter, President Lincoln called for seventy-five thousand volunteers to put down the rebellion. Charles Robinson was elected as the state's first governor, and one of his first actions was to issue the call for recruits. The men of Lawrence immediately answered the call. George W. Deitzler, an early resident, and one of the six free-state men imprisoned for treason in 1856, agreed to serve as the commander of the 1st Kansas Infantry Regiment; O. E. Learnard, another early resident and veteran of the Border War, was second in command. Samuel Walker, nemesis of the Border Ruffians for his leadership in the successful attacks against Fort Titus and other pro-slavery strongholds, joined the 1st Kansas and was selected captain of Company A. Frank B. Swift, leader of the "Lawrence Stubbs" in the border conflict, joined and became the captain of another company. Samuel Wood, another veteran of the Border War, was selected as commander of Company I, 2nd Kansas.

Other early Lawrence residents volunteered as well. Civic leaders such as Caleb S. Pratt, the city clerk, joined. The Haskell brothers—Frank, who would later become the leading architect in Kansas, and Dudley, who would later be elected to the US House of Representatives—were among the earliest recruits. Not to be left out, four of Lawrence's clergymen volunteered as chaplains to various regiments during the war.[207]

Volunteers were instructed to make their way to Leavenworth—where the 1st Kansas reported—and to Lawrence, where the 2nd Kansas organized. From the muster records of the 1st Kansas Infantry

Regiment, we are can draw a fairly complete picture of its makeup. Nearly 50 percent of the recruits came from the town or surrounding area of Leavenworth, followed by Lawrence, providing 12 percent; Atchison with 9 percent; and the rest from other towns across the state. Altogether, twenty-eight communities from around Kansas were represented. Not surprisingly, only one soldier listed Kansas as his place of birth—since most had arrived only a few years earlier. Nearly 50 percent of the regiment noted that they were foreign born, with the largest number listed as natives of Germany. Looking at the roster of Company G of the 1st Kansas, we can also glimpse a representative sample of professions. Of the 110 enlistees, about 10 percent would be classified as professionals, including artists, a professor, and a surveyor; about 47 percent were skilled craftsmen, such as blacksmiths, harness makers, printers, coach makers, cigar rollers, masons, and a confectioner; and the remaining 43 percent were laborers or farmers. Again, looking at Company G, the average age was identical to the national average age of twenty-six. There were twelve teenagers, sixty-seven in their twenties, twenty-seven in their thirties, three in their forties, and the oldest was fifty-one.[208]

The people of Lawrence welcomed the recruits for the 2nd Kansas with open arms. A soldier from Leavenworth, probably Sgt. John M. Mentzer, wrote to the Leavenworth *Daily Times* that "the people of Lawrence brim full of the Union spirit. The stars and stripes float from almost every corner of the streets, and [from] most of the public and private buildings. . . . Many of the little delicacies of life, to which a soldier is generally a stranger, find their way into our 'quarters,' accompanied by the well wishes of fair donors. The people here appreciate the worth of volunteers, and know how to treat them."[209]

From all indications, these new Kansas recruits or, for that matter, recruits from all over—North and South—were excited at the prospect of fighting the enemy. Although some Kansas soldiers had tasted battle during the Border War, even these veterans were not prepared for what lay ahead. All recruits, when they arrived in

Lawrence or Leavenworth, were immediately consumed with the rigors of training, and some learned very quickly—and in some cases, very forcefully—that their lives would be different. Several young soldiers in Captain Walker's Company A, training at Camp Lincoln near Leavenworth, decided it would be fun to go into town, break into a whiskey shop, roll out a barrel of liquor, and help themselves to its contents. They were caught, placed under guard, and their fate was turned over to Major Samuel D. Sturgis, who was in command of the regular army in Kansas at Fort Leavenworth. Sturgis ordered that each of the offenders be tied to a cannon and receive fifty lashes. A reporter for the *Lawrence Republican* was incensed with the barbarity of the punishment and offered the opinion that Sturgis should be "court-martialed" for his actions.[210] Sometimes, under the close living conditions, tempers flared. An argument broke out between two soldiers in Captain Stockton's Company G, and one stabbed and killed the other. The murderer was tried by his peers in a court-martial proceeding; he was convicted and sentenced to be shot by a firing squad. The sentence was carried out, and thirty soldiers, some with live cartridges, others with blanks, performed the deed.[211]

By the end of the war, over 22,000 Kansans in nineteen regiments and four artillery batteries fought for the Union. That represented 20 percent the state's population of just over 107,000 in 1860. Kansans also suffered one of the highest casualty rates, with 8,500, or a little more than 38 percent. [212]

Not only did the people of Lawrence welcome soldiers, they continued to roll out the welcome mat to fugitive slaves. The trickle of escapees seeking refuge before the war soon became a flood when the war started. While the principal aim for the Union at the beginning of the war was to reunite North and South, to the enslaved population the war had only one aim, and that was the end of slavery. Many had no intention of waiting to see what happened. They decided instead to use their own initiatives to seek freedom. Slave owners in Missouri and Arkansas quickly understood that the hold on their human property was tenuous, and many sold their enslaved people as quickly and for as much as possible. For their part, slaves just as quickly understood that if they were placed on the auction block, they would likely be sent to the Deep South with virtually no chance for freedom. Thus, their incentive to escape was stronger than ever, and they understood that if they could somehow make it to a free state, their freedom was almost ensured. If they could find their way to Lawrence, not only would they likely gain their freedom, but also the townsfolk would help them transition from slavery to freedom. They came to Lawrence in droves. John B. Wood wrote to his friend George L. Stearns in Boston that in early November 1861, "131 [fugitives] came into Lawrence in ten days, [and] yesterday [November 18] 27 had arrived by 2:00 p.m."[213] By 1865, there were 933 African Americans living in Lawrence and an additional 1,145 living in Douglas County, which made up a little more than 13 percent of the county's total population of 15,814.

When the fugitives arrived in Lawrence, most had only the clothes on their backs, and in many cases those were rags. "They were strong and industrious," Rev. Cordley wrote, "and by a little effort, work was found for them and very few, if any of them, became objects of charity." But while they were eager to make their new lives in freedom, they needed help translating their industriousness into livelihoods. Nearly all were illiterate because most slaveholding states had strict laws making it illegal to teach slaves to read or write. Fugitives arriving in Lawrence equated learning with liberty, so their thirst for education was overwhelming. But the town's fine educational system was not able to accommodate the number of eager new students.

Mr. S. N. Simpson, one of the town's 1855 pioneers, had started the first Sunday schools in town when he arrived, and he conceived a system of education for the fugitives based on his Sunday school model. Classes would be taught by volunteers in the evenings, and the curriculum would include basic reading, writing, and arithmetic, along with lectures designed to help them establish themselves in the community. The people of Lawrence were as excited to teach as their students were excited to learn, and enough volunteers were available to split the first class of about one hundred men and women into groups of six or eight.[214]

Josiah C. Trask, the editor of the *Lawrence State Journal*, spent an evening in January 1862 visiting the school and devoted an article to his observations. Eighty-three students, taught by twenty-seven teachers, met in the courthouse. "One young man who had been to the school only five nights," Trask wrote, "began with the alphabet, [and] now spells in words of two syllables." He observed that there was a class of little girls, "eager and restless," a class of grown men, "solemn and earnest," a class of "maidens in their teens," and "another of elderly women." Trask observed that the students were "straining forward with all their might, as if they could not learn fast enough." He concluded, observing that all eighty-three students came to class each evening "after working hard all day to earn their bread," while the twenty-seven teachers, "some of them our most cultivated and refined ladies and gentlemen," labored night after night, "voluntarily and without compensation." It was "a sight not often seen."[215]

Many in Lawrence were also concerned about the spiritual welfare of the new arrivals. Rev. Cordley, with his seminary training, was concerned that many black ministers of the fugitive community were illiterate, and thus did not have a solid grounding in the scriptures. In time, Rev. Cordley and others recognized that while the former slaves might not understand the nuances of the Bible, they were nonetheless solid in their Christian beliefs. Before long, black churches—most of them small, others larger—sprang up in the area. In March 1862, Rev. Cordley convinced his congregation to establish the African American Second Congregational Church in Lawrence, whose members were escaped slaves. Eventually, the members called themselves "Freedmen's Church." As Rev. Cordley was helping organize the church, one member joined for himself and his wife. When asked where his wife was, he replied that "his wife and children were sold down South before I got away." He hoped he would find his wife, and thus joined for her. Rev. Cordley's postscript to this story was: "we have seldom seen Slavery in so odious an aspect." The church grew from a handful of members, who were all escaped slaves, to nearly one hundred attendees in a couple of years. [216]

African American men were willing, able, and passionate to join the Union forces and fight. Their chance would come later. The volunteer soldiers training in Lawrence, on the other hand, were taught the basics of their new craft and were soon sent into Missouri to practice what they had just learned.

In Missouri, the political hierarchy of Governor Claiborne Fox Jackson, a strong pro-slavery Democrat, as well as a majority of the state legislators, strongly favored secession. On the other side, Congressman Francis P. Blair Jr., whose brother was the Postmaster General of the United States, and whose father was a close confidant of President Lincoln, determined to do everything in his power to keep Missouri in the Union. Blair succeeded in keeping Missouri in the Union because the mostly pro-Union delegates to the convention, who were to consider whether the state should remain in the Union or leave, voted to stay. But Governor Jackson and his colleagues were not willing to concede. Jackson recruited Sterling Price, a veteran of the Mexican War and a former governor, to lead the pro-Confederate militia forces in Missouri. On the Union side, Blair orchestrated the appointment of twenty-year military veteran and staunchly pro-Union Captain Nathaniel Lyon as overall commander of Union forces in Missouri. Thus, with the pro-Union and the pro-Confederacy sides jockeying for position and dominance, in the spring and summer of 1861, Missouri was one of the hottest battlegrounds in the country.

Lyon was promoted to the rank of brigadier general, and in June and early July, he and his forces drove Governor Jackson and the secessionist legislature out of the state capital, Jefferson City, and kept up the momentum, driving them into the southwest corner of the state. But Lyon's actions so incensed Missouri fence-sitters, many joined the Confederate side, so that Price's army eventually grew to about eight thousand Missourians. To shore up the Confederate side, Price was joined by Confederate Major General Ben McCulloch and his force of some five thousand Arkansans, Texans, and other southerners. As Lyon learned that the Confederate numbers were growing, dramatically outnumbering his small force of four thousand Missourians and regular army soldiers, he asked for help from anywhere, and the 1st and 2nd Kansas volunteers answered his call and marched to join him near Springfield, Missouri.

Lt. Levant L. Jones, a resident of Lawrence and an officer in Company F of the 1st Kansas, traced the journey of his regiment in letters home to his wife, Hattie, who was staying with her father in Olathe, Kansas. On June 8, he reported that the regiment stopped at a camp near Austin, Missouri. He was appointed judge advocate for his company, which included a bonus of $2 a day in extra pay. In his new role, he swore in sixty-four new recruits to his regiment. As Jones and his comrades continued on their journey to meet up with Brigadier General Lyon, he sensed that a battle would happen soon, but he was convinced that Union forces would "whip them, beyond any doubt." As the impending battle loomed, however, Lt. Jones recognized his own mortality: "if it shall be my fate to fall, to die in defense of my beloved country and of the noble principles which now find expression in the administration of its government, I can die contented so far as giving up my own life is concerned."

The 1st and 2nd Kansas finally joined up with Brigadier General Lyon and the rest of the Union Army, made up of four Missouri regiments and the First Iowa regiment, making a total of about six thousand men. Jones noted that Colonel Deitzler was named brigade commander over the 1st and 2nd Kansas, the First Iowa, and a small detachment of Illinois soldiers. By August 8, a major battle was imminent. Lieutenant Jones wrote his wife that the Union forces were outnumbered nearly two to one, but because his side was "drilled, disciplined, and well armed," he was confident of victory.

Still, he let his wife know that as he was "about to go into action, because I wish you to have my last words and thoughts—my life now belongs to my country, but my heart belongs to you." And he wanted to assure her that his brother would care for her if he fell in battle.

The next day, August 9, Lieutenant Jones was far more upbeat. He had just received a letter from Hattie which lifted his spirits immeasurably. "I shall not serve longer than October," he wrote, "and if the campaign is not then over, I shall resign, and come back to you, to home and to business." Later that night, Jones and the Union Army moved into position to attack the Confederate Army along a small stream about fifteen miles south of Springfield, Missouri, called Wilson's Creek.[217]

In the days before the battle, Brigadier General Lyon hoped the Confederate forces would attack his fortified position near Springfield. They did not, and Lyon became more and more concerned that the combined Confederate Army would continue to grow, and that he would be in an untenable position. So he decided to go on the offensive. He devised a plan that defied military logic, but almost worked. He split his forces, ordering Colonel Franz Sigel and his Second Brigade of about 1,200 men to attack from the south, or the rear of the enemy, while he led the remaining brigades from the north against the main force. For any chance of success, the attacks from both sides needed to be coordinated. Initially, Sigel overran the Confederate cavalry camps, and he started rolling up everyone in his front. Lyon had equal success overrunning the camps in his front and taking the high ground, which was later called "Bloody Hill."

But when Price and McCulloch finally put the Confederate troops in motion, they pushed Sigel back and eventually routed his forces. After attacks and counterattacks, in which Lyon was killed, the Union forces, then under command of Major Sturgis, finally withdrew from the field—they were dangerously low on ammunition. Since the Confederates held the field at the end of the day, it was a Confederate victory, but both sides were battered. Lyon was the first Union general killed in battle. The Union had 1,317 casualties, with

258 killed, 873 wounded, and 186 missing; for the Confederates, there were over 1,232 casualties, 277 killed, 945 wounded, and at least 10 missing.[218] While the tab for killed and wounded was not as high as Battle of Manassas (Bull Run) in Virginia a couple of weeks earlier, the results indicated that the war would be fought in multiple theaters, it would be bloody, and, although most did not realize it at the time, it would be a long, drawn-out affair.

Eight days after the battle, Edward R. Nash, the adjutant for the 1st Kansas, wrote a letter to Hattie Jones. It began as did many letters, written by many soldiers after many battles. Nash wrote: "it becomes my painful duty to inform you of the death of your husband, and my friend. He was killed in the battle of Wilson's Creek on the 10th instant." He continued: "he [Lieutenant Jones] suddenly said to Joe Gilliford, who was at his side, 'Joe I am shot.' Joe asked 'where?' Jones's answer was 'in my hip.' Just at that moment a ball came whizzing by Joe's ear—he turned his head quickly and saw Jones fall, shot again in the left breast in the region of the heart by a Minnie [*sic*] ball." Nash continued, saying that on the long journey

Lithograph of Battle of Wilson's Creek. Library of Congress.

from Kansas to Wilson's Creek, Lieutenant Jones, on numerous occasions, predicted his own death, but Jones asked Nash: "if I go under and you come out safe, I want you to write to Hattie and tell her my last thought was for her."[219]

Lieutenant Jones was one of seventy-seven members of the 1st Kansas killed in the battle. Another 255 were wounded. Six hundred and forty-four men and officers went into battle with the 1st Kansas, and 332, or over half of the regiment, were casualties.[220] The 1st Kansas was one of the lead regiments in the attack and caught the brunt of the Confederate counterattack. The 2nd Kansas was held in reserve, with the exception of Captain Wood's Company I, which was mounted infantry. In the heat of battle, the Second was called to the front, and according to an eyewitness, "stood firm, and met the enemy, handled him so roughly that he soon fell back in confusion." For the 2nd Kansas, the best estimates are that five were killed, fifty-nine were wounded, and six were missing, for a total of seventy casualties.[221]

Reports from the battle reached Lawrence two weeks later, and the *Lawrence Republican* published an article, "The Martyrs of Freedom," listing the casualties of the 1st Kansas. It drew particular attention to Lieutenant Jones's death, saying he "was a man of brilliant intellect and a good heart." The article also noted that Caleb B. Pratt, the city clerk, was killed, as was Lewis T. Litchfield, who left behind a wife and child. The article concluded by saying, "their names will be long remembered as heroes whose every pulsation was for the freedom and honor of their country."[222]

Levant Jones, Caleb Pratt, and Lewis Litchfield were all part of the regular Kansas militia. They readily volunteered to fight as part of the Union Army, with the primary purpose of reuniting the country. There was another Kansas military contingent that, in addition to bringing the nation back together, was equally passionate that the institution of slavery needed to be annihilated wherever it existed. Their name has become synonymous with Kansas over the years— the Jayhawkers.

12 Don't Turn Your Back on This Bird

SHORTLY AFTER THE SOON-TO-BE MEMBERS of Company G—the "Union Guards"—of the 2nd Kansas Volunteer Infantry Regiment arrived in Lawrence from Leavenworth, one of the members wrote that "Captain Jennison's mounted company of Jay Hawkers came up and greeted us with their cheers." He further noted that "Captain Jennison's company is about 120 strong, well mounted, and under good discipline for the short time they have been under drill." He went on to say that "they are strongly attached to the Captain, and say that should they fail to get into regular service, they will 'go on their own hook.'" Jennison and his men accompanied the regiment on the first leg of its journey to Kansas City as it traveled toward Wilson's Creek, but were not mustered in (included into the regiment) and returned home.

The Jayhawkers were a group of armed abolitionists who were willing to do anything to rid the country of the scourge of slavery. For years, they had operated as extra-legal vigilantes in southern Kansas, near the Missouri border, during the Bleeding Kansas period and they were absolutely devoted to their commander, Charles Jennison. At this early stage of the war, Union commanders did not know what to do with the Jayhawkers. The military hierarchy in Kansas was nervous about Jennison and his men for several reasons. First, they were concerned that the Jayhawkers were so devoted to their leader that they might follow his orders even if they were counter

Dr. Charles R. Jennison. Wikimedia Commons. Public domain.

to the Union war objectives. Second, Jennison's superiors feared that Jayhawkers' antislavery passions were so strong, they might go rogue—as guerrillas—and fight their own war against slave owners in Missouri, which at this early part of the conflict was at odds with the Union war aim of reuniting the nation.

Guerrilla warfare, in which small groups of combatants—throughout history—have used irregular military tactics, such as ambushes, sabotage, raids, and hit-and-run attacks to hit traditional military or other targets, was of great concern to Union commanders in the border area of Kansas and Missouri. It was critical to keep Missouri in the Union, and anything that could give the citizens reasons to secede, such as guerrilla attacks on pro-slavery targets by the Jayhawkers, could not be tolerated.

University of Kansas sports fans will immediately recognize that the name of their teams, the "Jayhawks," comes from Jennison and his men. But the origin of the name Jayhawkers is shrouded in mystery. Several explanations have been offered over the years. Some suggest the critter is a mythical bird, like the phoenix.[223] When Irish immigrant Pat Devlin was asked where he had acquired two fine horses on one of his adventures along the Kansas and Missouri border, Devlin replied that he "got them as the Jayhawk gets its birds in Ireland. . . . In Ireland a bird, which is called the Jayhawk, flies about after dark, seeking the roosts and nests of smaller birds, and not only robs nests of eggs, but frequently kills the birds."[224] The University of Kansas, long ago, abbreviated the name to Jayhawks as the teams' mascot. According to the school, "the name combines two birds—the blue jay, a noisy quarrelsome thing known to rob other nests, and the sparrow hawk, a stealthy hunter. The message here: don't turn your back on this bird."[225]

The origin of the term Jayhawker remains a mystery, but who the men were who rode under that name and what they did was not. Another reporter, writing in 1863, observed that "Jayhawkers, Red Legs, and Bushwhackers are everyday terms in Kansas and Western Missouri." He concluded that "they are all lawless and indiscriminate in their iniquities."[226]

Dr. Charles Jennison, who led the company of Jayhawkers into Lawrence, was born in Antwerp, New York, in 1834. When he was twelve, his family moved to Wisconsin, where, at the age of nineteen, he studied medicine. At age twenty, he married Mary Hopkins, and after spending some time in Minnesota, he moved to Osawatomie, Kansas, in 1857. In the fall of 1858, he settled permanently in Mound City, where he established a flourishing medical practice.[227] At some point, Jennison became a radical abolitionist, and not long after he arrived in Mound City, he met James Montgomery, whose hatred of slavery was equal to his.

James Montgomery was twenty years Jennison's senior. He was born in Ashtabula County, Ohio, and moved to West Liberty, Kentucky, in his early twenties, where he taught school and became a minister in the evangelical Disciples of Christ—often referred to as the "Campbellite"—denomination. His first wife died, after which he married the daughter of a slave owner. While in Kentucky, he purchased a large plot of timberland, then built and operated a sawmill on the Licking River until several floods washed out his operation.

James Montgomery. Kansas State Historical Society.

In 1851, he sold his timber business and moved his family to eastern Missouri. In 1854, shortly after the passage of the Kansas-Nebraska Act, he landed in Mound City, Kansas. By the time Montgomery arrived in Mound City, he was a radical abolitionist. He was constantly harassed by pro-slavery settlers, who burned his house when he refused to leave the area. He responded by building a new house that was nearly impregnable, which he dubbed "Fort Montgomery." Soon he became the leader of like-minded antislavery settlers called the "Self-Protective Company," who retaliated against the pro-slavery Border Ruffians.[228]

Of all the free-state military leaders, James Montgomery might well have been the most skilled and the most clever in guerrilla tactics. He never read nor heard of the ancient Chinese classic—Sun Tzu's *The Art of War*—which inspired twentieth-century guerrilla leaders like Mao Zedong and Ho Chi Minh, but he understood and practiced Sun Tzu's principles as if he carried a copy with him into his engagements. "Let your plans be dark and impenetrable as night," Sun Tzu wrote, "and when you move, fall like a thunderbolt." This was Montgomery's strategy, and his men followed him without question because he intuited another piece of Sun Tzu's advice to "treat your men as you would your own beloved sons. And they will follow you into the deepest valley."

Montgomery's tactics included harassing pro-slavery settlers on both sides of the border between Kansas and Missouri, ridding the area around Mound City of pro-slavery settlers, and seeking revenge for Border Ruffian incursions into southeastern Kansas. In 1856, the notorious pro-slavery leader, George W. Clarke, led some four hundred men on a sweep of Linn County—where Mound City was located—in which they "plundered, robbed, and burned out of house and home nearly every Free-state family in Linn County, while [Clarke's] hands were steeped in innocent blood, and the light of burning buildings marked his course."[229] To get even, Montgomery went into the area in Missouri purported to be Clarke's headquarters, claiming to be an unemployed teacher. He was hired for a teaching post, and from that position, he pieced together the names of twenty of Clarke's associates. After several weeks, Montgomery, the teacher, mysteriously disappeared, but then reappeared later as Colonel Montgomery, leading his Self-Protective Company. He and his men systematically visited each of the twenty Border Ruffians on his list and took each man's money, horses, cattle, weapons, and anything else of value, and rode back to Kansas.[230]

When "Doc" Jennison joined forces with Montgomery, it was—in many ways—like mixing oil with water. True, both men were passionate in their desire to eradicate the institution of slavery, but otherwise they were quite different. Montgomery was a teetotaler; Jennison drank heavily. Montgomery never swore, and chastised any of his men who did; Jennison often cursed a blue streak. Montgomery tried to restrain his men from excessive violence; Jennison often encouraged more violence. Not surprisingly, the two men eventually had a parting of the ways.

In November 1860, Jennison and his men captured Russell Hinds, a slave hunter operating in Missouri and Kansas. There was no question that Hinds made his living tracking down runaway slaves and returning them to their owners to make his living; there also was no question that what he was doing was not only legal, but sanctioned by the US Constitution and the Fugitive Slave Act of 1850. But Jennison wanted to use Hinds as an example to scare slave hunters out of Kansas, so the Jayhawkers tried Hinds in a kangaroo court, sentenced him to death, and hanged him. Montgomery probably disagreed with Jennison's way of dealing with Hinds, but he begrudgingly conceded that Hinds was "worth a great deal to hang but good for nothing else." Eventually the breach between Jennison and Montgomery was complete; in 1862, Montgomery said the doctor was "an unmitigated liar, black-leg and Robber."[231]

Although Montgomery and Jennison were most commonly associated with Jayhawkers, James Lane managed to have his name connected with them as well. Lane had kept a low profile for several years, settling into his law practice in Lawrence. After he was introduced to Abraham Lincoln during his visit to Kansas, however, Lane became a staunch supporter of the future president. Whether from his encounter with Mr. Lincoln, or whether the political bug bit him again, Lane soon re-entered the political arena, and when Kansas was admitted to the Union in 1861, he successfully campaigned and won the election in the new state legislature to the US Senate.[232]

When Lane arrived in Washington as a senator, he quickly ingratiated himself to the new administration by recruiting a security force called the "Frontier Guard" to protect the president and the Executive Mansion. For his efforts, Lane was authorized to raise and command two regiments in Kansas. He accepted the offer, but he did not officially accept the rank of brigadier general, with concerns that it might force him to resign from his Senate seat.[233]

In several speeches before the Senate, Lane made it clear how he intended to prosecute the war on the Kansas-Missouri border. In a speech before the Senate, he said "that the effect of marching an army on the soil of any slave State will be to instill into the slaves a determined purpose to free themselves." He continued, "I do not propose to make myself a slave catcher for traitors and return them to their masters."[234] Lane made it clear that freeing as many slaves as possible would constitute a significant part of his strategy and tactics.

When Senator Lane arrived back in Kansas with the commission to raise two regiments, he started recruiting volunteers who came to Fort Leavenworth for training. Enough men showed up—about two thousand—to form the 3rd, 4th, and 5th Kansas Volunteer Regiments. He moved his base to Fort Scott and decided that his strategy would be to harass Confederate forces and pro-slavery sympathizers in the border area. On September 2, 1861, Lane and a contingent of six hundred of his cavalry met Confederate Major General Sterling Price's and Brigadier General James S. Rains's substantially larger force near Fort Scott in an engagement near Big Dry Wood Creek. Although Lane and his men surprised the Confederates, the latter's numerical superiority soon determined the encounter's outcome. They forced Lane's men to retire and captured their mules.[235]

Next, Lane decided to move against Osceola, purported to be a Confederate stronghold, as well as the home of Waldo P. Johnson, a US senator from Missouri who would soon be expelled from his Senate seat for his support for the Confederates. Lane's brigade attacked Osceola on September 22–23, 1861. The attack, more appropriately called the Sacking of Osceola, was important—not because it was a major or significant strategic battle, but rather because of how it was later interpreted. There is no question that the Jayhawkers attacked Osceola, that they freed and took some slaves with them, that they burned parts of the town, that they inflicted some casualties, that they captured some military supplies stored there, and that they consumed, stole, and destroyed a certain amount of liquor, salt, bacon, and other commodities. These were the facts of the raid.

On the rumor side of the story, the Confederates reported that three hundred Jayhawkers were so drunk that they had to be carted out of town in wagons. Between one thousand and two thousand residents were driven out of town, and over one hundred buildings were burned. Lane and his men stole thousands of dollars in cash and valuables. James Lane alone was reported to have stolen a piano, silk dresses, and other valuables. The story seemed to get bigger and bolder with each telling. But the real significance that transcended the stories was that Osceola was a civilian—not a military—target, which played into the hands of secessionists and secessionist sympathizers. They condemned the attack as an act of barbarism. Osceola became a symbol and an excuse for Confederate soldiers and guerrillas to attack their military or nonmilitary targets in the border areas with brutality. Eventually, the attack on Osceola would have a direct impact on Lawrence. Two years later, when William Clarke Quantrill led his guerrilla band into Lawrence, he and his men were reported to have shouted "remember Osceola" as they ransacked the town. Their main objective was to find and kill James Lane.

Union leaders were upset by Lane's actions as well. Union Major General Henry Halleck wrote that "the course pursued by those under Lane and Jennison has turned against us many thousands who were formerly Union men. A few more such raids will make this State unanimous against us."[236]

Since Lane had received his military authority directly from the Lincoln Administration, he took this as a license to act independently, often to the consternation of Union commanders. Whereas Union generals had difficulty controlling Lane, they did their best to manage "Doc" Jennison and his Jayhawkers. He was given his opportunity when Kansas Governor Robinson recommended him to Major General John C. Frémont for a commission. Frémont was the Commander of the Department of the West. His abolitionist views were in line with Jennison's, so he appointed Jennison as commander of the 7th Kansas Cavalry. Daniel Anthony, Susan B.'s brother, and a member of the first Emigrant Aid party to Kansas, was second in command. John Brown Jr., who as the name implied was the eldest son of his namesake, joined the regiment and recruited a number of abolitionists from Ohio into the ranks.[237]

Jennison's Seventh Cavalry was assigned to protecting Union wagon trains in the border area. If Confederates attacked the wagons they were assigned to protect, Jennison and his men quickly retaliated. As with Lane's men at Osceola, they often attacked civilian rather than military targets. They burned the areas around Pleasant Hill, Dayton, and Columbus in Missouri, stole livestock, freed slaves, and generally wreaked havoc everywhere they went. President Harry S. Truman often told the story that Jayhawkers attacked his family's farm near Independence, Missouri, stole the family silver, killed and butchered the hogs, and burned the barn full of hay.[238] His mother, who suffered during the war as a Confederate sympathizer, was reported to have refused to sleep in the Lincoln Bedroom the first time she visited her son in the White House because it reminded her of the Yankee soldiers.

In part because the 7th Kansas stirred up so much resentment, the regiment was ordered into camp in Humboldt, Kansas, at the end of January 1862, and then to Lawrence at the end of March. At that point, Colonel Jennison chose to (or was forced to) resign as commander.[239] With Jennison's departure, Daniel Anthony was elevated to regimental commander. Because Jennison and his men had made such a nuisance of themselves and had stirred up so much resentment in western Missouri, the regiment was sent to Rienzi, Mississippi, where it arrived on July 23, 1862, to help shore up the Union forces near Corinth, Mississippi. On its journey south, and before the Seventh arrived in Mississippi, Colonel Anthony was removed as commander. While stationed in Tennessee on the way to Mississippi, Anthony issued an order that if any of his officers or men did anything to assist in the capture and return to slavery of any fugitive slave, he would be severely punished. Since he did not have the authority to issue that order, he was dismissed.[240] Stephen Z. Starr, author of *Jennison's Jayhawkers*, concluded that "no other regiment in the Union army had so bad a reputation" or "worked so diligently to deserve it" as Jennison's Jayhawkers.[241]

The Seventh remained in the Mississippi/Alabama/Tennessee region through most of the remainder of the war. Other volunteers from Kansas joined, including a seventeen-year-old who joined in 1863 as a teamster. He already had more adventures under his belt than most men of his era would experience in a lifetime—prospecting for gold in Idaho and riding for the Pony Express. This young man would remain in the Seventh for the remainder of the war and go on the great fame and fortune afterwards. His name was William—later Buffalo Bill—Cody.

The Jayhawkers were fierce fighters. But Union leaders faced the constant challenge of trying to control them. Major General Henry Halleck tried to implement a two-pronged strategy. On the one hand, he marshaled the forces under his control to rid Missouri of Confederate soldiers. Union Brigadier General Samuel R. Curtis successfully drove the Confederates out of Missouri. Then on March 6–8, 1862, he won an important victory at Pea Ridge in northwest Arkansas. Curtis and his troops were outnumbered, but they defeated the Confederates under the command of Major General Earl Van Dorn in this two-day battle. This part of Halleck's strategy worked well.

The second part of Halleck's plan was to do everything in his power to keep Missouri in the Union and to remove any reason for its fence-straddling citizens to side with the Confederate cause. This strategy was much more difficult to implement because he had such a difficult time keeping the Jayhawkers from raiding across the border into Missouri. Dealing with Lane's three regiments was complicated because of Lane's political clout. But while Lane was in Washington, fulfilling his senatorial duties, Halleck moved quickly and placed Major General David Hunter in charge of all Union forces on the border area, including Lane's three regiments. When he found out what Halleck had done, Lane returned to Kansas in January 1862 and tried to wrest control of his brigade from Hunter. He also offered to resign his Senate seat if he was granted the rank of major general and given command of a force of thirty thousand men to raid the South and free as many slaves as possible. He was neither given the command to execute his grandiose scheme nor was he able to regain control of his brigade. With Lane in check and with the 7th Kansas Cavalry out of the region, Halleck started making progress on the second part of his plan.

Halleck continued with his strategy, and in February 1862, he sent a letter to Hunter, asking him to "keep the Kansas troops out of Missouri." If Hunter did so, he (Halleck) promised "to keep the Missourians [meaning Confederates] out of Kansas."[242] To further emphasize his intentions, in March Halleck wrote to Secretary of War Edwin Stanton: "I will keep them [the Jayhawkers] out of Missouri, or have them shot."[243]

Foiled in his plan to lead a conquering army through the South, Lane returned to his Senate seat in Washington, DC, later in 1862. While there, John Speer, who was visiting at the time, reported that while walking down Pennsylvania Avenue, Lane casually mentioned that he had just received authorization to recruit three regiments of white and two regiments of colored soldiers. "When I asked in amazement to see the order to enlist colored troops," Speer reported, "he informed me that it was a verbal promise from the President, that he [Lane] would see that they were clothed and subsided until such time as they could be brought into line, armed and equipped for battle."[244] There is no way to know if, indeed, President Lincoln gave Lane any such directive. Lane was a clever operator, and with this new "authority," he enlisted James Montgomery to help, and he recruited former slaves who escaped to Kansas and slaves freed by the Jayhawker incursions into Missouri into a full regiment under the command of Captain James M. Williams. They were clothed and fed, and armed with Austrian and Prussian rifles and bayonets. Lane was careful to make sure everyone understood that his African American regiment was identified as a band of "laborers."

Very quickly, Lane's 1st Kansas Colored Volunteer Infantry was converted from "laborers" to soldiers. In October 1862, the 1st

Colored Regiment was sent into Missouri in search of a large contingent of pro-Confederate guerrillas that were reported operating in Bates County. The regiment was accompanied by the 5th Kansas Cavalry, serving as scouts. On October 29, they found the guerrillas in an area called Island Mound. The bushwhackers—a term used interchangeably with guerrillas—knew the African American soldiers were in the area and were itching for a fight. By most accounts, the guerrillas outnumbered the 1st Colored Regiment—400 to 240. In Civil War military parlance, the engagement was not large enough to be called a battle but rather a skirmish. It probably would have gone unnoticed except it was the first engagement between black Union troops and Confederates, and, more importantly, although outnumbered, the African American soldiers won the engagement.[245] Union casualties were minimal and the number of Confederate casualties

Flag of First Kansas Colored Troops. Kansas State Historical Society.

was not known. In the following days, the skirmish at Island Mound drew national media coverage.[246]

Through the remainder of the war, the 1st Kansas distinguished itself in several battles. On July 17, 1863, the regiment was involved in the Battle of Honey Springs in Oklahoma (Indian Territory), which was the largest and perhaps the only battle in which whites were in the minority on both sides. The 1st Kansas, along with several contingents of American Indian soldiers on the Union side, fought mostly American Indian regiments on the Confederate side. The 1st Kansas was instrumental in the Union victory. A year later, on April 18, 1864, the 1st Kansas was nearly annihilated in the Battle of Poison Spring in Arkansas. The Union Army had discovered and captured a supply of corn held by the Confederacy. As the Union soldiers were transporting the corn, loaded in about two hundred wagons, they were ambushed by the Confederates. Colonel Williams placed the 1st Kansas between the wagons and the Confederate attackers. The 1st Kansas successfully repulsed two Confederate charges, but ran short of ammunition and tried to retreat. Nearly half of the regiment—almost 250—was captured. Rather than taking the black soldiers as prisoners, the Confederates murdered, mutilated, scalped, and stripped all who surrendered.

Although technically not Jayhawkers, to James Montgomery and James Lane, African American soldiers were as important in winning a Union victory as any white soldiers. In December 1862, after Montgomery assisted Lane in recruiting black soldiers, he was offered an opportunity by David Hunter to relocate to South Carolina to recruit, train, and lead African American soldiers there. Hunter was reassigned to a command in the Department of the South, and he was anxious to recruit former slaves to fight for the Union cause.[247] Thomas Wentworth Higginson was given the command of the 1st South Carolina (African Descent) and Montgomery was placed in charge of the 2nd South Carolina regiment. Montgomery successfully recruited soldiers in Florida, Georgia, and South Carolina, but he was often criticized for his tactics, which not surprisingly resembled similar methods he had implemented with his Jayhawkers in Kansas.

In his most famous South Carolina exploit, he led an attack on Combahee Ferry, working hand-in-hand with Harriet Tubman, who had relocated to Beaufort, South Carolina. Tubman tended to wounded and sick soldiers and established an extensive spy network in the area. From her informants, Tubman learned and relayed to Montgomery that the plantations in and around the ferry were ripe for an attack. Montgomery led three boats up the river, and attacked and burned the plantations. Some seven hundred to eight hundred slaves seized the opportunity to escape; they ran and jumped on board the boats, bringing whatever they could carry.[248]

Montgomery remained in command of the 2nd South Carolina until he resigned his commission in 1864 and returned to Kansas. He led the 6th Kansas State Militia to defend the state against Sterling Price, who had organized a futile attack to attempt to regain Missouri for the Confederates. Montgomery's fellow Jayhawker—Doc Jennison—had re-entered the service as well, leading the 15th Kansas Cavalry.

Missourians despised the African American soldiers because many escaped from bondage from their state. Their resentment of Jayhawkers also knew few bounds. James Lane held a special place in Missourians' pantheon of villains both for commanding the Jayhawkers and for recruiting black soldiers. Because Lane lived in Lawrence, and because the town was the symbol of the abolitionist movement, and because it was the haven for escaped slaves, they despised this community as well. But Missourians did not just sit around and mope. They had bands of guerrillas of their own, who in time were more ruthless than their Kansas counterparts.

13 We Could Stand No More

WHEN THE WAR BEGAN, THE citizens of Lawrence were—justifiably—concerned that they would be in the crosshairs of attacks from Confederate sympathizers from Missouri. Why not? In the years leading up to statehood, Border Ruffians had attempted to annihilate the town three times, so what was to stop them now? Early in the war, troops trained on the outskirts of Lawrence, and other regiments came and went on their way to battle. Governor Charles Robinson did everything within his power to keep troops in or near the town as a further precaution. The citizens established their own defenses, taking turns watching the entrances into town, developing plans for defense on a moment's notice.

The year 1861 went by and nothing happened—the same with 1862. Alarms went off when the *Lawrence Journal* reported guerrilla raids into Aubry, Olathe, and Shawneetown, and the newspaper's editor declared, in September 1862, that the town's militia were "without arms, ammunition, and subsistence" because "the legislature did not appropriate a dime to provide for the public defense." The town was "powerless and [could] do nothing effectual for defense." The *Journal* cautioned its readers again in November 1862 that there had been "fugitive reports for some weeks that Quantrell [*sic*], the notorious predatory chieftain of the border rebels was making serious preparation to give Lawrence a call." But the editor went on to say that "our citizens have given all due heed to these rumors, . . ."

because the town had "13 companies of militia under the command of Col. Frank Swift, the hero of Wilson's Creek" ready for action.[249]

So, as the first two years of the war drew to a close, and since there were no attacks, and the citizens believed that the reports of guerrilla attacks near the Kansas/Missouri border did not concern them, they relaxed their defenses. It became more and more onerous for business people to conduct their daily affairs, and then be expected to stand on guard duty at night. Plus, the people were convinced that the distance between the guerrilla hideouts in Missouri and Lawrence would be so difficult, even the guerrillas would not attempt such a feat.

The town's complacency was a concern to George W. Collamore, who was elected mayor of Lawrence in the spring of 1863. Rev. Cordley wrote that Mayor Collamore "was a very active man . . . [who] realized as few others did the danger in which Lawrence stood, and he endeavored . . . to arouse the people to a sense of the situation." Rev. Cordley went on to write that Collamore "organized an effective military company and secured arms for them from the state. He also organized and armed companies in the country about Lawrence." But he believed "that the guns should be kept in the armory and not be carried home by the men," which turned out to be a disastrous decision when the town was attacked later that year. The mayor secured a small body of militia stationed in Lawrence, but on August 1, 1863, it was withdrawn.[250]

There was good reason for Collamore's concern, for just shortly after he took over as mayor, Dick Yeager, a lieutenant in a band of bushwhackers, led a raid into Kansas and attacked several people camped on the Santa Fe Trail near Willow Springs in Douglas County just a few miles south of Lawrence. The *Journal* reported the attack as "the Boldest Raid Yet!" But the report followed up that a large contingent of soldiers was formed to go after the gang in the hopes of picking up stragglers, so the immediate danger passed.[251]

Dick Yeager's commander, William Clarke Quantrill, was the leader of the largest and best-organized Confederate guerrilla force operating on the Kansas-Missouri border. Guerrillas for the Confederacy were different from their Union counterparts. Both fought with similar irregular military tactics, but the main difference was that in April 1862, the Confederate government legally sanctioned its guerrillas when it passed its Partisan Ranger Act. Guerrillas could form into military commands—companies and regiments—elect officers, receive pay and equipment from the government, and in nearly every way serve as regular soldiers, except they were irregulars. These ranger bands were scattered throughout the country. Some—like John Singleton Mosby in Virginia and John Hunt Morgan in the Upper South and Midwest, and Quantrill in the Kansas-Missouri border region—became legendary for their exploits, but as the war progressed, Confederate commanders became more and more uncomfortable with the undisciplined and brutal activities of the guerrillas, and they convinced the Confederate Congress to repeal the Ranger Act in 1864.

Of the Confederate guerrilla leaders, however, none were as famous to Southern sympathizers—or as infamous to Union supporters—as William Clarke Quantrill. Ironically, some Lawrence residents likely knew Quantrill. He briefly settled in town in 1860 and passed himself off as Charles or Charley Hart. When he arrived in Lawrence, he told a wild tale that when he and his brother arrived in Kansas, they were attacked by a gang of thirty-two Jayhawkers. His brother was killed and Quantrill was left for dead. He was rescued by an Indian, recovered, and then he hunted down and killed all thirty-two of his attackers. The story sounded good, and the men in his guerrilla army believed it, but it was a complete fabrication.[252] Telling tall tales fit nicely with Quantrill's shady profession in Lawrence. He captured fugitive slaves and returned them to their masters for the reward. He also stole horses. His tall tales came in handy as he expanded his operation, working with antislavery groups to kidnap slaves and help them escape. He then turned around and captured the slaves and returned them to their owners for the reward.

William Clarke Quantrill. Wikimedia Commons. Public domain.

On December 10, 1860, Quantrill led five young Quaker abolitionists from Lawrence on a slave-stealing raid into Jackson County, Missouri. Their plan was to steal the slaves belonging to Morgan Walker, who lived near Blue Springs and owned a 1,900-acre plantation. They arrived early in the morning. Quantrill told his companions to hide in the brush while he scouted out the situation. But instead of helping to steal slaves and selling them back to their owners, he decided to turn on his companions. He found one of Walker's sons and told him about the planned raid and the time it would happen and that he should warn his father. Quantrill returned to his abolitionist companions and laid out the plan for the night raid.

Morgan Walker enlisted several neighbors, and they were ready for the attack. They sprang their ambush, killing one Quaker and wounding two others. The other two escaped and made their way back to Lawrence. Quantrill conveniently stayed out of harm's way. Walker's men and Quantrill tracked down the two wounded Quakers and killed them. The Jackson County Sheriff arrested Quantrill and placed him in jail, but released him the next day when Quantrill convinced the sheriff that the Quakers were there to steal slaves.

Following this nasty business, Quantrill spent part of the winter in Jackson County and then traveled to Indian Territory, where he spent time in the Cherokee Nation. When war broke out, he joined the Confederate Army. The next time Quantrill visited Lawrence was in August 1863.[253]

How did Quantrill become such a ruthless individual? Early on, there was little indication of the person he would later become. He was born in Canal Dover (present-day Dover), Ohio, on July 31, 1837. He was the oldest of seven children. His father, a school superintendent and tinsmith, died when Quantrill was a teenager, which forced him to help his mother support the family. At age sixteen, he was hired to teach school, but to better his own circumstances and to help his mother, he left Ohio in 1855 and taught school in Illinois and Indiana. Numerous books have chronicled Quantrill's life, including one biographer who claimed that he showed sadistic tendencies as a child, which explained his later violent behavior.[254] His contemporaries, however, said that as a child, he was quiet, well behaved, and studious.

In 1857, Quantrill headed west with neighbors, hoping to cash in on the abundant land available in Kansas. They settled near Stanton, Kansas, on the banks of the Marais des Cygnes River. He corresponded with his mother, expressing hope that he would finally make it financially to better himself and provide more financial support for his family. When he first arrived in Kansas, his sympathies seemed to be with the free-state settlers, and he wrote to a friend that he thought James Lane was "as good a man as we have here."

Before long, Quantrill's neighbors in Stanton noticed that some of their property, such as blankets, clothing, and food had gone missing. They suspected that someone was stealing their belongings, and when Quantrill was caught red-handed, they asked him to leave the area. He did, and went to Fort Leavenworth where he signed on as a drover on a military wagon train headed for Utah. He stayed in Salt Lake City for a while, tried his hand at prospecting in the Pikes

Peak gold rush in Colorado, then returned to Kansas and settled in Lawrence as Charley Hart.

At the beginning of the Civil War, Quantrill joined the Confederate Army and participated in the Battle of Wilson's Creek. Toward the end of 1861, he either deserted or had permission to leave the Confederate Army, and he formed his guerrilla force to harass free-state Unionists in the border area. He joined up with Andrew Walker, the same young man he had warned about the planned Quaker raid on his father's plantation a year earlier. Quantrill and Walker heard of a Jayhawker attack nearby, so they, along with eight others, went in pursuit. After a brief engagement, they killed one Jayhawker and wounded several others.

Following this raid, Andrew Walker was the first to leave the band. His father, fearing Jayhawker attacks on his plantation, talked his son into staying home with a small private army to protect his property. But Quantrill had little trouble gaining new recruits. Before long, the number grew to about forty members, including two men: John Jarrett and his brother-in-law, Thomas Coleman Younger, who rode into Quantrill's camp in January 1862. Later in life, "Cole" Younger, as he was better known, wrote his reminiscences of his time with Quantrill. Younger came from a prominent and wealthy Missouri family. His father, Henry Washington Younger, owned several businesses, including the mail delivery contract for a five-hundred-mile radius, centered in Jackson County, Missouri, as well as a number of slaves. The elder Younger sympathized with the South but was opposed to secession. Yet because he owned slaves, and probably because of his business successes, he and his family were harassed by Union soldiers in the area. One officer, Captain Irvin Walley, had a particular dislike for the Younger family, and accused Cole of spying for Quantrill. So Cole decided that as long as he was accused of working with Quantrill, he might as well join up as a guerrilla.[255]

Cole Younger's autobiography provides valuable insights into Quantrill's guerrilla band. He wrote his reminiscences in 1903, after he was released from prison for his involvement in the famous Northfield, Minnesota, bank robbery. Beyond describing his exploits, Younger—probably inadvertently—helped to dispel one of the myths surrounding his guerrilla and later his outlaw band. The first part of the myth suggested that many of the guerrillas came from humble backgrounds. Far from coming from a poor family, Younger wrote that his father was worth nearly $100,000, a princely sum for that day. Frank James, who was with Younger as a member of Quantrill's guerrillas, and Frank's brother Jesse, who joined later, came from a well-to-do, slave-owning family as well. A recent study demonstrated that Quantrill's guerrillas were three times more likely to own slaves and possessed twice as much wealth as the average Missourian.

The other part of the myth said that Quantrill's, Younger's, the James brothers', and others' main purpose was to attack northern capitalism—in the form of the Union Army during the war, then by robbing banks and railroads afterwards. They were viewed as something akin to Robin Hood, who stole from the rich to feed the poor. Younger wanted his readers to believe there was a humanitarian side to the guerrillas in his descriptions of several raids. He implied that the men stole money and valuables for the widows and orphans in Missouri. The evidence, however, shows that they kept most of their spoils for themselves. Their motivations were not to rob the rich to give to the poor, but rather to perpetuate the institution of slavery and gain independence for the Confederacy during the war, and rob banks and trains after the war to enrich themselves.[256]

In late February 1862, not long after Younger became a guerrilla, Quantrill led fifteen men on a raid in Independence, Missouri, which supposedly was lightly defended. Instead, when they rode into town, they encountered an Ohio cavalry regiment. The guerrillas turned tail and rode away with the Ohioans in hot pursuit. Two of Quantrill's men were killed; Quantrill's horse was shot out from under him and he was wounded in the leg. They escaped and regrouped a day or two later, at which point Quantrill ordered his men to disperse. Scattering after a raid became a common practice for Quantrill and his men. Cole Younger wrote that "Captain Quantrill believed that it was harder to trail one man than a company." Younger went on to say that "every little while the company would break up, to rally again at a moment's notice."[257] As the band grew larger, members would splinter into small groups after a raid, which allowed them to escape capture.

Two weeks after the disaster in Independence, Quantrill decided to lead his first foray into Kansas. His target was the small town of Aubry, today called Stilwell, near the border. He led his hollering, cursing, and shooting forty bushwhackers into town, killing five men who happened to be in the way. While sitting on his horse, Quantrill glanced up at the local hotel and saw two men looking out the window. He pulled out his pistol and fired, hitting one of the men square in the forehead. He later found that Abraham Ellis, the man he had shot, miraculously was not killed. Even more amazingly,

Abraham "Bullet Hole" Ellis. Ellis was the school superintendent and Quantrill's former boss, whom he (Quantrill) shot in the forehead. Ellis survived and lived another twenty-two years. The bullet was removed several days later, but the bullet hole remained for the rest of his life. After he died, the bullet and twenty-seven pieces of his skull were sent to the Army/Navy Medical Museum in Washington, DC. Kansas State Historical Society.

he discovered that Ellis was the same Ellis who had hired him to teach school in Stanton several years earlier. Quantrill apologized profusely, tended to his former boss's wound, and said, "Ellis, I am damned sorry I shot you—you are one of the Kansas men I do not want to shoot!"[258]

In this early phase of Quantrill's guerrilla activities, he looked upon his role as that of an officer, practicing proper military etiquette. After each engagement with Union forces, he paroled his prisoners after taking their weapons, equipment, and horses and caring for their wounds. In military parlance, he gave his captives quarter, which literally meant he housed them in quarters or provided protection. He didn't have any problem taking horses from captured soldiers, but he did have a problem with his men stealing horses from locals. One of the early members of his band, George Searcy, rustled fifteen horses from the area around Blue Springs, Missouri. When Quantrill discovered his theft, he hanged Searcy from the nearest tree and returned the horses to their owners, some of whom were Union sympathizers.[259]

Quantrill's military etiquette changed when Major General Henry Halleck issued his Order No. 2, on March 13, 1862. The order stated that since Major General Price was issuing commissions to "certain bandits in this State [Missouri], authorizing them to raise 'guerrilla forces,' for the purpose of plunder and marauding, . . ." he should "know that such a course is contrary to the rules of civilized warfare, and that every man who enlists in such an organization forfeits his life and becomes an outlaw." Halleck went on to say that "if captured, [guerrillas will not be] treated as ordinary prisoners of war, but will be [hanged] as robbers and murderers."[260] From that point on, Quantrill decided that if he and his men were going to be treated as "robbers and murderers," they might as well be "robbers and murderers." If one of his men was captured and executed, he went a little further and executed several Union soldiers.

Most historians agree that Quantrill was an able commander. His strategy of dispersing his bushwhackers after every raid was one example of his skill. After each raid, he and his men would hide out, often for weeks, either in the houses of supporters or in the thickets and ravines of western Missouri. John McCorkle, another of Quantrill's guerrillas who later recorded his experiences, described makeshift camps inside caves he and his companions shared far away from civilization when things got hot.[261] Quantrill ensured that his men had the finest horses they could buy, borrow, or steal. Union cavalry soldiers who gave chase, on the other hand, generally rode inferior government-issued nags. Each guerrilla was armed with multiple Colt Navy revolvers, and each honed his skills with target practice until he was a crack shot. While Civil War rifled muskets were generally considered superior for accuracy, they had to be reloaded after each shot; with multiple revolvers, however, Quantrill's men could get off dozens of deadly shots.

Quantrill became a skilled commander, but because he had no prior military experience, he had a steep learning curve that—early on—almost cost him and his men their lives. He learned of Halleck's Order No. 2 shortly after it was issued, and the first individuals his band encountered several days later were a Union sergeant and a toll collector. His men shot both of them in cold blood. That night, Quantrill and his men stopped to have dinner and sleep in the house of David Tate, a Confederate sympathizer. The bushwhackers were so sure that Union soldiers were miles away that Quantrill posted only two guards near the house, who probably fell asleep. Unbeknownst to them, the 2nd Kansas Cavalry was scouring the area trying to track them down. The Union soldiers knew, or at least suspected, that David Tate was a Confederate sympathizer, so Major James Pomeroy was sent with his squadron to arrest Tate for questioning as to the whereabouts of Quantrill and his men. Major Pomeroy had no idea that Quantrill and his men were inside Tate's house, so when he walked up and banged on the door, he received a rude answer when Quantrill, who had been awakened with the commotion outside, fired a shot through the door. Pomeroy immediately ordered his men to start firing on the house. But when he heard women and children screaming, he ordered his men to stop and allowed the family to leave. Quantrill was in a bind. The house was surrounded, the federal soldiers were pouring lead into the house, and, although the log walls absorbed most of the shots, there was no easy way out. Then Major Pomeroy again ordered his men to stop firing, and yelled at Quantrill to surrender or he would set the house on fire and roast the bushwhackers alive. His men set the house ablaze.

Quantrill coolly told his men they were in a tight spot, but that was their best chance for survival was to follow him. So they dashed out the door, firing as they went, and escaped into the woods. Pomeroy's men were so intent on watching the building burn, they were not prepared for the dash out of the house and only fired off a few shots, killing one bushwhacker. Not long after, Quantrill and his men were again surprised by Union troops. They escaped again, but after the second close call, Quantrill made sure that whenever his men were staying together, they posted enough sentries at strategic entry points so they would not be caught off guard again.

In July 1862, Union Major James Gower learned that Quantrill and his bushwhackers were in the area, and decided that he was going to be the hero who captured the guerrilla band. One of his officers, Captain Martin Kehoe, picked up Quantrill's trail, but this time, the guerrilla leader had ample warning and set up an ambush for the federal cavalry. The bushwhackers got off the first shots, killing several of Kehoe's men. Kehoe pulled his men back to regroup. Quantrill probably thought Kehoe and his men were retreating, so he pushed the attack. What Quantrill did not know, however, was that Kehoe had sent word to Gower, who was bringing up a much larger contingent. Kehoe's and Gower's combined forces attacked and caught Quantrill and his men in a trap. Quantrill divided his forces into small squadrons, and miraculously, they escaped. He learned another important lesson in guerrilla warfare—avoid engaging in pitched battles at all costs.[262]

Quantrill and his men were organized and fully functioning as guerrillas when the Confederate Congress passed the Partisan Ranger Act in April 1862, which gave them pay, supplies, and ammunition and allowed Quantrill to call himself "Captain." They continued to operate somewhat independently, but when called upon, they were expected to join up with the regular Confederate Army. Such was the case in the summer of 1862, when the Confederates tried to gain a foothold in Missouri; Quantrill and his men joined in the effort, but when the regular army pulled out in the fall, Quantrill and his guerrillas remained in the area.

When the Confederate Army pulled out of western Missouri, Quantrill and his bushwhackers returned to their guerrilla tactics. His fame spread, and new recruits eagerly joined. Two of the new recruits were John McCorkle and his brother Jabez. Years later, John McCorkle recorded his experiences with Quantrill.[263] Just after midnight, on September 7, 1862, Quantrill and 140 of his men rode into Olathe, Kansas, yelling and firing their guns. They weren't expecting opposition, but they found 125 Union militiamen standing in a line of defense. The bushwhackers ordered their surrender, and all but one complied; he and about a dozen or so civilians were gunned down. In addition to the killings, the guerrillas robbed the locals of all their horses, money, and jewelry. They forced the men to strip down to their underwear and took their clothing.[264]

A little over a month later, on October 17–18, Quantrill and his men hit a community in Kansas again. This time Shawneetown (present-day Shawnee), not far from Kansas City, was the target. As they were riding into town, they encountered a Union Army wagon train loaded with supplies, protected by an infantry escort. Everyone was asleep. When the bushwhackers came swooping in, the soldiers were caught by complete surprise and fifteen were killed. Quantrill and his men continued into town, robbed the citizens of their valuables, killed a number of civilians, and took several hostages, but unlike the previous raids, they then burned nearly the entire town to the ground.

Later in the fall and winter of 1862, as Quantrill's fame was escalating with Confederate supporters, and as his infamy was growing among Unionists, he decided that he deserved a higher level of recognition from the Confederate government. He left his bushwhackers behind in Arkansas and traveled to Richmond, Virginia, where he met with James Sedden, the Confederate Secretary of War. John Newman Edwards, one of Quantrill's earliest and most sympathetic biographers, learned about the meeting from Senator Louis T. Wigfall of Texas, who was present. Quantrill requested a commission as a Confederate colonel, under the Partisan Ranger Act. This commission would legally sanction his leadership of the guerrilla band, with the full backing of the Confederate Government. Sedden refused to give Quantrill his commission, no doubt based on what he had heard of Quantrill's increasing brutality. Quantrill returned to his men, but reported that he did, indeed, receive a commission as colonel. Not wise to the truth, his men from that point on called their leader "Colonel Quantrill." Younger later learned that Quantrill did not receive his commission, and reported as much in his autobiography.[265]

While Quantrill was away, some of his bushwhackers lay low, others followed his lieutenants on raids of their own, and still others joined up with Confederate commands in Arkansas. When he returned in January as "Colonel" Quantrill, he started to pick up where he left off. His band was also picking up new recruits, either as individual members, or as smaller guerrilla forces who chose to join Quantrill, such as Bill Anderson and his band of bushwhackers, who joined in early 1863. Anderson was born in Kentucky, and went with his family first to Missouri, then to Kansas, where they took advantage of the land available there. Anderson's parents were southern sympathizers who favored slavery, although they did not own any slaves themselves. Anderson probably orchestrated the disappearance of a wagon train and all of its contents, although he was never charged with the theft.

"Bloody Bill" Anderson Courtesy of the State Historical Society of Missouri.

Bill and his brother formed a small band, along with Arthur Baker, a local judge and Confederate sympathizer, stealing horses from Kansas and transporting them to Missouri. Baker was captured by Jayhawkers and was paroled, at which time he turned on his partners. Baker shot and killed Bill's father in an argument, which so enraged Bill that he his brother and two other associates killed Baker, locking him in his house and setting it on fire.

Anderson moved to Missouri and started gathering his own following of guerrillas. Eventually, when Anderson joined forces with Quantrill, he and his men had no problem killing Union and Confederate civilians. When Quantrill caught wind of the practice, he was so incensed, he threatened to kill "Bloody Bill" (this was quickly becoming his nickname) Anderson if he didn't stop killing Confederate civilians. The two men eventually made an uneasy peace, but they were never entirely comfortable working with each other.[266]

As Quantrill and particularly "Bloody Bill" were becoming more brazen and bloodthirsty in their attacks, the Union Army tried different strategies to deal with the guerrillas. First, Major General Halleck declared guerrillas as outlaws. Next, Halleck targeted the families of guerrillas, knowing—or at least suspecting—that they were aiding the bushwhackers. If women, children, and non-fighting men provided, or if they were suspected of providing, any type of aid to the enemy, they would be considered "belligerents." They could be detained and questioned, and if there was enough suspicion of complicity, Union commanders could incarcerate them, move them from the hostile area, and even burn their houses and farms. On the other hand, if Missourians could prove that they were noncombatants, and were not connected in any way with the guerrillas, they were left alone.

Halleck's order allowed some flexibility for his commanders. Brigadier General Thomas Ewing Jr., who was appointed as commander of Union forces in the border area in the spring of 1863, interpreted Halleck's policy to err on the side of suspecting anyone with any inkling of possible support for the guerrillas to be guilty of spying. Ewing came from a prominent Ohio family. His father, Thomas Ewing Sr., had served in the US Senate and in the cabinets of several presidents. Thomas Jr. attended Brown University and was his father's secretary while he served as the Secretary of the Interior under Zachary Taylor. The family took in William Tecumseh Sherman, who would later become one of the most important Union generals in the Civil War, as a foster child after Sherman's father died, leaving his mother with eleven children and no money. Sherman and Thomas Ewing Jr. were close in age and were raised together. Then Sherman married Thomas's sister and became his brother-in-law. Thomas Jr. moved to Leavenworth, Kansas, during the territorial period, practiced law, and aspired to be one of the first US senators from Kansas. He was unsuccessful in that effort, but he was appointed as the first chief justice of the Kansas Supreme Court. He resigned his post in 1862 and was appointed as colonel of the

11th Kansas Infantry. Although he had no prior military experience, he proved an able commander, and after leading his regiment in several successful battles, he was promoted to brigadier general in charge of the border area.

Ewing's order to arrest noncombatants was drastic. There was no question that Quantrill and his gang and other bushwhackers were supported by many. Cole Younger and John McCorkle in their later memoirs wrote of the many houses in which they were fed and offered beds. On one occasion, McCorkle wrote that they were sitting down to a meal at one house, but when the scouts reported that the Union cavalry was in the vicinity, they left dinner sitting on the table and moved on to another house, where their new hosts fed them instead.

The Union Army started carrying out Ewing's order in the spring of 1863. Soldiers arrested women and even teenage girls suspected of aiding the bushwhackers. Some were caught red-handed with caches of ammunition and powder in their houses. Others, who had large quantities of rough butternut-colored material, were considered guilty of making the distinctive blouses worn by nearly all guerrillas. If someone was transporting large quantities of food, the assumption was that the supplies were intended for guerrillas. Still others were jailed because they had a great deal of cash in their possession. Many were considered guilty simply because they knew or were related to the bushwhackers. Bill Anderson's three sisters, who were all teenagers—the youngest, Jenny, was only thirteen—were among those detained. Cole Younger's cousins, who also were the sisters of Riley Crawford, one of the youngest members of Quantrill's band, were held. John McCorkle's sister, Charity Kerr, and his widowed sister-in-law, Nannie McCorkle, were captured as well. Nannie was the widow of John's brother, Jabez, who died when he accidentally dropped his rifle and the discharge killed him. John McCorkle reported that his sister and sister-in-law were arrested while hauling food from Kansas City.

The arrested women were put in makeshift jails in Kansas City, Missouri, without any legal protections, and most were held until they could be transported to St. Louis. Some were quickly released if they could prove their innocence. One of the buildings in which they were housed was a three-story structure—commonly referred to as the Thomas Building—on Grand Street. The building was owned by the noted artist George Caleb Bingham, who had added the third story for his studio, which was unoccupied at the time. The women were held on the second floor. The first floor housed a Jewish grocery establishment and the soldiers who guarded the women.

The soldiers removed some of the support beams on the first floor to provide more space to maneuver. From the time the building was used as a makeshift jail, there were reports that the building was unsafe. Cracks appeared in the walls, and plaster was crumbling, leaving white dust almost everywhere. Fearing that the structural integrity was severely compromised, the soldiers and the proprietor who ran the grocery business moved out of the building. They later reported that they informed Ewing and others that the building was unsafe and that the women should have been moved.

On August 13, 1863, catastrophe struck. At about dinner time, the entire building collapsed, taking the adjoining building down with it; or maybe the adjoining building collapsed first, taking the Thomas building with it. No one knew for sure. Soldiers and bystanders rushed to the scene and started removing beams and rubble, pulling survivors from the wreckage as quickly as they could. Four women were killed instantly, including Josephine, the fifteen-year-old sister of Bill Anderson, and Charity Kerr, John McCorkle's sister. Jenny Anderson, Bill's youngest sister, was severely injured with two broken legs, cuts and bruises, and a damaged back, and was crippled for the remainder of her life. Jenny had been chained to a bed for unruly behavior, and there was no chance to protect herself. In all, seventeen women and girls, one boy, and one soldier were victims of the disaster. Nannie McCorkle, John's sister-in-law, managed to leap from the building when it collapsed. She survived.

Even to this day, no one can say for sure why the building collapsed, but recriminations and accusations began immediately. To the guerrillas and rebel sympathizers, the military had purpose-fully damaged the building, claiming that Ewing had ordered the removal of the support beams, hoping that the building would col-lapse. Probably the removal of structural members was a contrib-uting factor. Others claimed to have observed hogs rooting around the foundation, which further undercut the structure. Some noted that a sudden gust of wind caused the already unstable structure to tumble. Another likely factor was that the third story added for Bingham's studio was structurally unsound.

On August 14, one day after the building's collapse, Ewing sent a proposal to his superior, Major General Scofield, which was one of the most ill-advised missives in the Civil War. He recommended posting Field Order No. 10, which formalized his earlier directive for his soldiers to arrest suspected supporters of guerrillas. Officers were authorized to arrest and send to the local provost-marshal anyone who aided or encouraged the guerrillas. In particular, "the wives and children of known guerrillas, and also women, who are the heads of families and are willfully engaged in aiding guerrillas, will be notified by such officers to remove out of this district and out of the State of Missouri forthwith." They would be allowed to take household goods and livestock, and if they did not comply will-ingly, they would be escorted "to Kansas City for shipment south." Scofield approved the order, and it was posted on August 18.

To Quantrill and his bushwhackers, the collapse of the building and Field Order No. 10 were the final straw. John McCorkle would later simply say: "we could stand no more." For one thing, many of their loved ones were killed or maimed, but for another, women were the victims, and to this Victorian society, and even to the most violent guerrillas, women were still held in chivalric high esteem. They should never have been placed in a situation in which they could be injured or killed. In their earlier raids, there was only one report of a woman being injured, and that was claimed as an acci-dent.[267] There was no doubt in their minds that Ewing had orches-trated the collapse of the building, and if that were not enough, now he was escalating the effort to arrest their loved ones and send them out of the state.

The disaster on August 13 certainly was a catalyst for Quantrill's Raid on Lawrence, but he had been planning the raid for some time. Fletcher Taylor, one of Quantrill's lieutenants, spent a week in Lawrence, disguised as a cattle trader, doing a reconnaissance of the town several days before the Thomas Building disaster. He returned to Quantrill's camp and reported that Lawrence was poorly garrisoned, and that the troops stationed there were in a camp some distance from town. Plus, Taylor noted that the streets were wide and easy to ride through. Taylor made his report to Quantrill, Bill Anderson, and other guerrillas—over three hundred in all. Cole Younger later reported that after they heard the report, Quantrill said: "you have heard the report. It is a long march." Quantrill continued, pointing to the potential hazards, particularly if they encountered soldiers. He concluded by asking his men: "What shall it be? Speak out Anderson!"

Anderson answered, "Lawrence or hell," and did so, according to Younger, with fire "flashing in his eyes as he recalled the recent wreck from which his sisters had been taken in Kansas City." Anderson added that he had but "one proviso, that we kill every male thing." Up to this point, when Anderson and his men were involved in any attacks, they generally were ruthless, killing more victims than most. But after his sisters were killed and maimed in the building collapse, everyone agreed that he came completely unhinged, and from that point until the end of his short life months later, killing others was no longer a means to an end, but a means in and of itself. Some of his companions reported that he would literally foam at the mouth when he anticipated a killing spree.

After Anderson made his reply, Quantrill went around the room and asked his lieutenants to vote on the proposal to attack Lawrence. After he had queried everyone, he asked if all had voted; no one spoke, so Quantrill said, "Lawrence it is; saddle up."[268] During the vote tally, everyone agreed on Lawrence as the target, and that killing as many men as possible was the goal. Younger's brother-in-law, John Jarrett, added that it would be great if they could burn everything to ground as well. Cole Younger and John McCorkle were in agreement that if the venture accomplished nothing else, killing Jim Lane would make everything worthwhile.

On the evening of August 20, 1863, many of the citizens of Lawrence came to the Eldridge House hotel to listen to a Mr. Winchell discuss the potential for the Union Pacific Eastern Division railroad coming to their town. H. E. Lowman, editor and proprietor of the *Lawrence State Journal*, reported the meeting several months later. He wrote that the meeting ran until about 10:30 p.m. He and his colleagues stayed after the meeting and talked until about midnight. "When we reached the street and were bending our steps homeward," he reported, "a most strange and inexpressible sense of impending danger came over us. . . . When we reached home we found it impossible to shake off the singular impression that some unseen catastrophe was at hand." He continued, "Quantrell [*sic*] had decided to destroy Lawrence. . . . That was well authenticated. . . . There was evidence enough . . . that he would be most likely to strike when the people were the least watchful and the most certain of their safety. . . . When the first gun was fired and the first unearthly chorus of yells startled the air at the opening of the terrible slaughter which will make the 21st of August, 1863, forever memorable in the annals of Kansas, we were aroused and knew without a moment's hesitation what the tumult meant."[269]

14 Lawrence or Hell

QUANTRILL AND HIS BUSHWHACKERS MOVED very quickly from plan to action. John McCorkle reported 150 guerrillas in the raiding party; Cole Younger counted 310, which was probably closer to the actual number. The logistics of traveling through Kansas with so many men, and without a major confrontation with Union troops, was a major feat. As Quantrill prepared for the attack, he sent a contingent of fifteen men south as a diversion, hoping to draw attention away from the main objective.

As Quantrill guerrillas started heading west, fifty additional guerrillas, who heard the news of Quantrill's mission, joined the party. The expanded group bumped into Confederate Colonel John Holt, who was leading one hundred recruits to join the Confederate Army further south. Holt thought it would be good for his recruits to have a baptism of fire, and joined Quantrill. That brought the number of soldiers and bushwhackers to somewhere between 400 and 450.

Quantrill chose to travel overland, away from any normally traveled routes. They left on the evening of August 20 and screened their movements with outriders. A Union scout saw and reported the guerrillas to his commander, Captain J. A. Pike, at about 7:00 in the evening. Pike reported the sighting to other border commanders, but he made no effort to attack Quantrill, nor did he warn any of the Union outposts or towns further west.

Quantrill and his men continued on their journey through the dark. They passed through several tiny communities, and in one—Gardner—they encountered Union soldiers who asked their business. They reported that they were a Union cavalry unit, headed to Lawrence to have their horses shod. According to Albert Castel, whose account of Quantrill and his guerrillas is highly regarded by historians, the bushwhackers were able to fool the Union soldiers because they wore blue uniforms on this and other raids.[270] According to most reports, the night was pitch-dark. To make sure they were headed in the right direction, each time they encountered someone, they forced the hapless individual to guide them, and in most cases, when that person's services were no longer needed, the raiders shot him. One of their guides was a young boy, whom Quantrill released when he had guided them part of the way.[271]

At about 5:00 on the morning of August 21, Quantrill and his men reached Lawrence. About two miles out of town, they came to the farm of the Reverend S. S. Snyder, the minister of the United Brethren Church in Lawrence. He was an early riser and was milking his cow. Two of the bushwhackers rode into his yard and killed him. Rev. Cordley speculated that Rev. Snyder was singled out because he had volunteered to serve as a lieutenant of colored troops. Rev. Snyder was the first casualty. Riding about a mile further, the guerrillas met Hoffman Collamore, the sixteen-year-old son of the mayor. Young Collamore was out riding, carrying a shotgun to go hunting. He did not think anything of the men, since many were wearing blue, but when they started shooting at him, he took off on his horse and nearly escaped, but he and his horse were hit. He had the sense to lie still as if he were dead, and the guerrillas left him alone. He was lucky and recovered.

Another individual with luck on his side was Joseph Savage, one of the earliest settlers in Lawrence, who arrived with the second Emigrant Aid Company party in 1854. Savage's eyesight was failing him, and part of his morning ritual was to wash his eyes. He heard horses outside, but with his poor eyesight, he thought they were Union troops. Two of Quantrill's men knocked on his door, but he was not ready to receive anyone quite yet, and when he finally opened the door, the bushwhackers were leaving his yard.[272] The next group of people Quantrill's men encountered was not as fortunate.

From the scouting report of Fletcher Taylor, Quantrill knew that the garrison of Union soldiers was stationed just outside of the main part of town. This camp was the first target. Many of the soldiers there during Taylor's visit were transferred elsewhere, replaced by new recruits. Among them were African American men preparing to join one of the black regiments. Since it was dawn, the sentries had left their posts. So without any warning, and since nearly all the soldiers were sound asleep, the attack was a complete surprise. When the bushwhackers rushed the camp, the soldiers had no chance to find or load their weapons. Seventeen were killed, and the rest scattered. After giving chase for a short distance, the guerrillas turned their attention to the town.[273]

Their first stop was the Eldridge Hotel, the most prominent building in town, built on the site of the Free State Hotel that had been destroyed by Border Ruffians several years earlier. A curious thing happened when Quantrill and his men rode up to the hotel. Captain A. R. Banks, provost marshal for Kansas, waved a white flag from a window, surrendering the hotel. He then came down to meet with Quantrill and asked for permission to escort the guests from the hotel to safety. Quantrill agreed, and the guests were escorted to the nearby City (some referred to it as the Whitney House) Hotel, where they were promised safety if they stayed there. Quantrill, as Charley Hart, was a guest in the hotel when he lived in Lawrence. He felt he had been treated well and promised the owner that if he, his guests, and the Eldridge guests stayed put, they would be safe. He placed the City Hotel off limits, ordering his men not to touch the hotel or anyone inside. The fate of the Eldridge Hotel was different. Quantrill allowed his men to ransack the hotel, carrying away everything of value. Quantrill then ordered his men to put the Eldridge Hotel to the torch.[274]

Quantrill's brief humanitarian gesture was indeed brief. Their first target was US Senator James Lane. They knew he was in town, and when the shooting started, Lane surmised that he would likely be their first target. So, still dressed in his nightshirt, he ran to a nearby cornfield; he kept going until he felt he was safe. Rev. Cordley later reported the conversation between Mrs. Lane and Quantrill when the guerrillas came to her door. Quantrill knocked and said he "wanted to see the general." She told them "he was not in." They broke up his furniture, smashed the piano, and then set the house on fire. When he left, Quantrill tipped his hat to Mrs. Lane, and "wished her to give his compliments to General Lane and tell him he would have been very glad to meet him." Mrs. Lane assured him that "Mr. Lane would be no less glad to meet him under different circumstances, but it was not convenient that morning."[275]

The bushwhackers found out that "Doc" Jennison was not in town, but ex-Governor Charles Robinson was, so his house was another target. Robinson was planning to leave in his carriage, and he was getting his team and wagon ready in his large stone barn when the attack started. He believed he would have his best chance for survival if he remained in the barn, and although the raiders rode by several times, they stayed away.

The bushwhackers had learned that stone and brick buildings—like Robinson's barn—could be fortresses, and they avoided them. They also stayed away from ravines and wooded areas, fearing that they might be ambushed from these hiding places. Many who made it to these havens were, for the most part, safe, but everything and everyone else were fair game. Many soldiers, some of whom were home on furlough, and a large percentage of African Americans escaped as well. They knew that they likely were prime targets. Several elderly handicapped African American men were not able to escape, including one ninety-year-old preacher who was known around town as "Old Uncle Frank," who had escaped from slavery on a plantation in Virginia. He thought he had found a haven in Lawrence, but he was gunned down by Quantrill's men. Old Uncle

Frank was like the vast majority of victims, peaceful residents who had no reason to believe they would be targeted.

Later, townsfolk who survived the carnage reported that after the bushwhackers burned the Eldridge Hotel and visited Senator Lane's house, they divided into groups of six or eight. Each carried two to eight revolvers in his belt—some armed also with carbines—as they went about their butchery. Several of Quantrill's men were stationed on Mount Oread to watch for any oncoming rescuers. Quantrill made it clear that women or girls were not to be harmed, but men or boys big enough to hold a gun were targets. While women were safe, nothing was to stop the raiders from killing husbands in the clutches of their wives. There were reports of guerrillas literally pulling women's arms away to get a killing shot at their husbands. One woman reported that her neck was grazed by the bullet—shot at nearly point-blank range—that killed her husband. Many of the victims were shot multiple times to make sure they were dead, and in places where there were piles of corpses, the marauders rode by and unloaded their revolvers into the pile just to make sure their dirty deeds were done.

Some of the killings were particularly gruesome. Murdering men in front of their wives and children was disgraceful. There were several instances where husbands were killed, then thrown into their houses, which were then set on fire while their wives and families watched. Two teenagers, James Perine and James Eldridge, worked as clerks in the Country Store and lived upstairs. When the bushwhackers came into the store, they ordered the two boys to open the safe. They said they did not have the key, so the raiders said if they went and got the key and opened the safe, they would be spared. They got the key, opened the safe, and for their efforts both were shot and killed on the spot. Another gentleman, a Mr. Burt, was standing in front of his house, and a guerrilla asked him for his money. He complied, and as the culprit took his wallet with one hand, he shot Mr. Burt with the other. Another (or maybe the same ruffian) asked a Mr. Murphy for a glass of water. As Mr.

Murphy handed him the glass, the bushwhacker shot him with his free hand.

One incident, however, transcended all others for its barbarity. D. W. Porter owned a small gun shop on Massachusetts Street. His store, in a small wooden building, was very close to the action, and he and a friend decided their best chance was to remain in the store. They were not disturbed for quite some time, but as the day and the raid wore on, many of the guerrillas had found ample supplies of liquor and were getting quite drunk. In this inebriated state, several came in to Mr. Porter's store and shot him and his colleague, but did not kill them. Then they set the store on fire, bound the two men, and threw them into the inferno while they were still alive. The two men begged for mercy, but the thugs left them in the blaze until they were dead.

Rev. Cordley had just returned from Kansas City, where he had traded pulpits with his friend, the Reverend Louis Bodwell. He later said he was happy to be home because he felt safe, whereas in Kansas City, he was fearful for his safety since it was close to the guerrillas' haunts. He woke up early on the morning of the twenty-first and was delighted because the day looked lovely. He heard a commotion a mile or so away but did not think much about it. But then, off in the distance "there came in sight the head of a column of horse-men, rushing forward at a furious speed, the reins over the horses' necks, and the men sitting freely in their saddles with revolvers in hand, and firing continuously. . . . They passed about three hundred yards from my door in plain sight and wheeled to the left just in front of my house. They rode five or six abreast, and were splendid horsemen. They were desperate-looking men . . . belted about with revolvers, some carrying as many as six. Most of them also carried carbines." As the bushwhackers came closer, Rev. Cordley, his wife, and Rev. Bodwell left and walked to the Kansas River, where they hid out in the brush. They were safe, but their house was burned to the ground. They were fortunate that they did not draw the atten-tion of the Quantrill's men because Rev. Cordley later discovered that Quantrill had singled him out for execution since he was a minister and supported escaped slaves.[276]

There were some miraculous escapes. One young African American man, as soon as he heard the shooting, started running, and he did not stop until he reached the Wakarusa River, some four miles distant. He climbed a tree, thinking that would be the safest place to hide. Sometime later, though, he noticed that when the raiders had left Lawrence, they were coming right to his hiding spot. He somehow managed to stay hidden as Quantrill and his men rode directly under the tree. Troy Strode, an African American blacksmith, had a patch of tomatoes in his front yard. He grabbed his money and hid in his garden of tomatoes. His shop was burned, but he was safe. A Union officer escaped from the recruit camp by running away, with the bushwhackers in hot pursuit. He ran into the home of a black family, found a woman's dress, threw it on, along with a nearby sunbonnet, and sauntered out the back door. The guerrillas did not think to ask the "woman" where the soldier was. Mr. Winchell, the representative from the railroad who had addressed the people of Lawrence the night before, ran into the home of Dr. Charles Reynolds, the former rector of the Episcopal Church, who was away as a chaplain in the army. Mrs. Reynolds helped Winchell shave off his beard; then, she and a friend dressed him in women's clothing and put him in a chair wrapped in blankets with cups and medicine bottles all around. When the raiders finally came calling she asked the men to please not bother poor "Aunt Betsie"—actually Mr. Winchell—who was very ill. They left them alone.

The most remarkable escape was that of the Reverend H. D. Fisher, the minister of the Methodist church, who had been chaplain of a Kansas regiment serving in Missouri. With the bushwhackers' special hatred for ministers, and particularly for any who were also chaplains, Rev. Fisher was a prime target. As soon as he heard the commotion and knew what was happening, the reverend started to leave, but he quickly realized that his best chance of survival was to remain in his house. He had an unfinished cellar, so he hid there.

The guerrillas came and demanded to see Rev. Fisher. The raiders came in, started looking all around the house, and then decided he was in the cellar. Mrs. Fisher said they were welcome to look there if they wanted, and even offered them a lantern. Rev. Fisher had crawled up into an unfinished area and they did not see him, but they were still convinced he was somewhere in the house, which they set on fire, hoping to smoke him out. Mrs. Fisher tried to save what she could from the house, while at the same time putting out the flames everywhere they were lit, but ultimately, she was not able to control the fire. So she concentrated her fire-fighting efforts on the area where her husband was hiding. Eventually, she realized she was losing ground, and she told her husband to come out. He crawled through a small window, and as soon as he was out, Mrs. Fisher wrapped him in a rug and piled furniture she had rescued on top of him. Although Quantrill's men were watching the house while it burned, somehow Mrs. Fisher hid her husband until the house was reduced to ashes.

Mary Savage also helped her husband escape, but just before they fled, she witnessed a member of her church gunned down in the street. "We had not gone more than a mile when we saw one of our neighbors and a member of the same church running from his house and two of the bushwhackers after him," she wrote. "They were just taking aim at him as we drove up. Joseph [her husband] comprehended the whole thing in a moment and jump[ed] from the buggy [and] was over the fence and into the cornfield in a second, while I sat almost stupefied with horror at the scene before me. They shot Mr. Langly [their neighbor] three times and I can never efface from my memory the look and cry of anguish that he gave as he fell, the blood running in streams from his wounds."[277]

Many more women were not able to save their spouses. Sarah Fitch summoned the strength to write about the raid weeks later, and she probably captured the despair of many. "That demon [one of Quantrill's men]," she wrote, "who was there swearing—shouting, screaming in our dear little parlor, with his revolver cocked in one hand, the matches lighted to fire our home in the other—I felt there was no mercy there . . . for all passed much more quickly than I can write it, that my heart almost stopped its beating—and in utter despair, I almost doubted if there was a God who loved us." The raider shot her husband in cold blood, then burned her house to the ground.

Fifty years following the raid, Jetta Dix was finally able to tell her story. Her husband, Ralph, operated a blacksmith and carriage shop in downtown Lawrence. She made extra money running a boarding house on the third floor of their house. Jetta, like many others, did not know what to make of the early morning commotion, but when Thomas Pardee, an African American man who worked for Ralph, rushed into their house and told the family to hide, she looked out the window and realized that the danger was real. She hid her three-year-old son and her eighteen-month-old twin daughters in a coal shed, under the care of the family's African American maid. She pleaded with her husband to hide as well. But Ralph was so sure that the men of Lawrence would rally and get the guns from the arsenal—which was about a block from their house—that he refused to seek a hiding place. Jetta saw her brother-in-law, Frank Dix, shot, and she ran to try to help him. As she was holding Frank, a guerrilla shot him again—the bullet grazing her face. Her husband, and other men who had ventured outside their houses, were immediately captured by Quantrill's men. They were promised protection if they would turn over their money and valuables. Jetta started running to her husband and the other men; she stumbled over a rock pile, and at that moment a thug shot the prisoners, including her husband. "I stood, completely dazed and rigid as I saw men falling to the right and left," she later reported. "I could not get to my husband at once, as the guerrillas were coming in every direction, riding through the ally, right over the dead bodies, between the buildings and the street."[278]

Mayor George W. Collamore seemed to have escaped the carnage. When the bullets started flying, he was certain he would be a target, so he and a friend climbed down into the well behind his house. The guerrillas could not find him, but they burned his house to the ground. As the house was burning, Mrs. Collamore called to her husband, who responded. But later, after the bushwhackers had left town, she went back and this time there was no response. The mayor's friend, Captain J. G. Lowe, climbed into the well, but after a few minutes, he did not respond either. When yet another went into the well, he found that all three men were dead. Captain Lowe slipped and fell, but Mayor Collamore and his friend, Pat Keefe, likely suffocated. The well was close to the house, and the house fire sucked the oxygen from the well, killing both men.[279]

Quantrill and his men were in Lawrence for about four hours, from roughly 5:00 a.m. to 9:00 a.m. They left nearly as abruptly as they came—once their lookouts were sure the dust clouds coming from the East meant that soldiers were on their way to the rescue. Nearly all the men assembled and headed out of town, quickly and orderly. At least one straggler, Larkin Skaggs, a former "hard shell" and fallen Baptist minister, wanted to get in one last lick. He was very drunk and headed to the City Hotel, where he wanted to get even with a young woman from whom he had taken a ring earlier, which Quantrill forced him to return. Quantrill apparently had a romantic relationship with the woman when he was living in Lawrence as Charley Hart, and, as the story went, he had given her the ring. Skaggs rode up to the hotel, killed the proprietor, Nathan Stone, and wounded two others. Then he realized that he had been left behind and hurried to catch up. John Speer, the young son of the newspaper editor, picked up a dropped gun, aimed, and hit Skaggs, knocking him from his horse. The townspeople immediately pounced on Skaggs and made sure he was dead. The raid was over.[280]

John McCorkle and Cole Younger described the raid, but both descriptions were brief. McCorkle wrote that most of those killed were Jayhawkers, but "in the raid, a few innocent men may have been killed but this was not intentional." Younger devoted a little

Quantrill's Raid on Lawrence, Kansas, *Harper's Weekly* (September 5, 1863).
Library of Congress.

more attention to the massacre, but picked his words carefully. He
reported that "Bloody Bill" Anderson claimed to have killed fourteen, which no one disputed. He said only one woman, an African
American woman, was killed, but by accident. He then went on
to describe how he personally saved the lives of many potential
victims. He claimed that because he was such a kind, gentle, and
heroic person in Lawrence, the beneficiaries of his "kindness" later
vouched for and helped him receive a reprieve from prison after
the bank robbery in Northfield, Minnesota, years later. Younger
wrote that his brother-in-law, John Jarrett, had his horse shot out
from under him. Younger rescued him, but Jarrett had to leave
behind his saddle and a saddlebag, carrying $8,000, "for the ben-
efit of widows and orphans of Missouri."[281] That last statement,
no doubt, was intended to gild the Robin Hood image. When
the bushwhackers returned to Missouri, they split their spoils
among themselves, and not with—as far as we know—widows and
orphans.

As soon as it was clear that the raid was over, Rev. Cordley and others hurried to the scene of the bloodbath, to see if there was anything they could do. "The first man I met," reported Rev. Cordley, "was John Speer, editor of the *Lawrence Republican*. He was covered with ashes and soot as if he had been through the fire. He grasped my hand eagerly, and said, 'I want you to help find my boy. They have killed one, and the other I cannot find. He slept in the printing-office, and I expect he was burned with the building.' So we went where he said the bed stood, and raked about among the embers in the cellar with poles, but could find no signs of his boy, and no signs of him were ever found."

After tending to as many survivors as possible, Rev. Cordley and his wife found Rev. Bodwell; they were greatly relieved that he had survived. They then went to the site of the Cordley's house. "All that remained was a bed of embers and ashes," he wrote. "Not a book or sermon, not a letter or paper, not a relic of childhood or memento of [any] friend was saved. As we stood silently looking at the desolate scene, Mrs. Cordley quietly wept. Bodwell turned to her and said in his gentlest tones: 'Don't cry, Mary. You have got all you asked for. We are all here.' No more tears were shed for the ruined house. So many all about us were carrying heavier sorrows. . . . [We were] thankful at our own escape."[282]

Following the raid, all who were able gathered around Senator Lane, who had emerged from his hiding place, and thirty-five men started in pursuit of Quantrill and his gang. The guerrillas were not hard to follow. They torched every house they encountered, with the smoke marking their trail. Lane and his men gave chase, but all they could do was nip at Quantrill's heels. They spotted the bushwhackers, but with the small party it would have been suicide to attack. Lane sent messages back to Lawrence for every able-bodied man to join them. He then led his men along the left flank of the guerrillas, in hopes of enough men joining him along with the cavalry for an attack. Indeed, the cavalry was coming to the rescue. Quantrill's lookouts were right about the dust clouds they saw when they called off the raid and started their retreat.

Major P. B. Plumb led some 250 men in pursuit, and when he spotted smoke south and east of Lawrence, he rightly assumed that Quantrill and his men were in retreat. Major Plumb knew that Quantrill's ultimate goal was to reach Missouri, so he headed directly south in an attempt to cut the guerrillas off. Not far from the community of Prairie City, Major Plumb's and Senator Lane's forces met, and Lane informed Plumb that his men had spotted Quantrill's men on the other side of a cornfield. His men were preparing to attack the rear of the guerrillas. Lane requested that Plumb should circle around and meet the bushwhackers as they came out of the field. Then Lane directed Lieutenant Rankin to lead his men on the charge. The problem was that the Lawrence men, in their haste, had mounted whatever was available, so when Lieutenant Rankin started the charge with his beautiful, high-spirited steed, the rest of the men, riding farm horses, mules, donkeys, ponies, and just about everything else, were not able to keep up, so he called off the charge. Two of Major Plumb's companies continued, and although they were not quick enough to meet the guerrillas when they emerged from the corn patch, they gave chase. Plumb's and Lane's men reached where the raiders had briefly stopped; they saw piles of plunder—calico cloth, saddles, trinkets, and other items—left behind. Quantrill avoided the potential encounter and continued on.

Plumb's and Lane's men began to gain on the guerrillas, and Quantrill skirted a cornfield near the house of a man by the name of Josiah Fletcher. Lieutenant Rankin knew the area and informed Major Plumb that they could take another route—a shortcut—that would place them in front of Quantrill. Sure enough, when they emerged from the cornfield, the bushwhackers were right in front of them. But to attack, the Union soldiers first needed to take apart a rail fence. They dismounted to dismantle the fence, and at that moment, a small contingent of bushwhackers charged, and the dismounted soldiers were disoriented just long enough that Quantrill and his main body escaped. For the remainder of the day, the cavalry tried to gain the advantage, but Quantrill's rear guard kept them at bay. By nightfall, the pursuit was pretty much over. Quantrill and his men stopped to rest for an hour or so and to feed their horses. John McCorkle said that none of the men had closed their eyes for two days and two nights, and that it was impossible to stay awake. After the brief rest, the guerrillas continued and did not stop until they reached their old hiding places on the Grand River in Cass County, Missouri, by daybreak.[283]

When Lane and his posse returned to Lawrence after their futile effort to overtake the guerrillas, they and the rest of the town's survivors faced the grim task of burying the dead and rebuilding the town. No one was ever able to determine an exact number of the fatalities. The official number was 183 dead, but a more accurate number was probably closer to 200, or maybe even higher.[284] There were dead bodies everywhere, in some places in heaps. Near the livery stable, seventeen bodies were in a pile. In another location were five bodies in addition to charred remains where bodies were left to burn in the buildings. In some cases, it was days before anyone could even enter some of the still-smoldering buildings. One immediate problem was what to do with the corpses. Many of the town's carpenters were victims, and those who survived had lost their tools in the raid. Several stacks of lumber remained, however, and there were plenty of charred nails from the burned buildings, so the men did the best they could to assemble makeshift coffins. But some bodies were so badly disfigured that the townspeople dug a common grave containing fifty-three unidentified victims. After a week, most of the bodies were buried.[285]

Dealing with the loss of so many lives was beyond description. The near-total destruction of the town was catastrophic as well. Seventy-five buildings—nearly the entire business district—were destroyed. One building was left standing, but the two young men who worked there were dead on the floor. Over one hundred houses were completely destroyed; others were partially burned. Even the houses that were rescued from total destruction were ransacked of all of their contents. Most Lawrence residents had only the clothes they were wearing and nothing else. The guerrillas took all of the women's jewelry they could carry, and one raider even had the audacity to steal the bracelet that had belonged to a small child who had died. When Amelia Read, the child's mother, protested, the scoundrel replied that "I guess she won't need it anymore." Many residents had so little left, their earthly possessions could be carried in wheelbarrows. In addition to the loss of clothing, valuables, and furniture, food was either destroyed or taken. When the townsfolk took an inventory of food, they found only two sacks of flour in the entire town.

Of the citizens whose houses had survived, nearly all opened their dwellings to the homeless. Almost immediately, farmers from the surrounding area and the residents of Leavenworth, Topeka, Wyandotte, and elsewhere started bringing food, clothing, and other essentials to the stricken populace. Residents from St. Louis quickly raised and donated $10,000 for interest-free loans for rebuilding the town, and when the loans were repaid, they refused to accept the principal, part of which went toward building the new state university. If anyone in town had two articles of clothing—such as a man who had two coats—he gave one away. The devastation was horrendous, but the outpouring of generosity was remarkable.

Two days after the raid, East Coast newspapers carried the grim story. The *Boston Sunday Herald's* headlines read: "Horrible Atrocities." The paper went on to say that the Quantrill "affair [was] the most fiendish of the war! Parents [were] shot down with their children clinging about them." *Harper's Weekly,* one of the most widely read magazines of the period, featured an image of the burned-out remains of Lawrence and wrote that "no other such instance of wanton brutality has occurred during the American war." Other news outlets carried similar stories.[286] It's not clear exactly when Amos Lawrence heard the news of the raid, but shortly thereafter, he again dug into his pocket and sent $5,000 to the town to aid the widows and orphans. As with the money donated from St. Louis, Lawrence's generous gift became part of the seed money to establish the University of Kansas in Lawrence.

The generosity shared with Lawrence from around the country could not heal the permanent wounds suffered by the eighty-five women who were instantly widows, nor their 250 children who were left fatherless. An estimated one-third of the population left town, never to return. Most of the eighty-five widows, however, stayed on, determined to help rebuild the town. Some remarried, others did not, and many who remained eked out livings by renting out space in boarding houses, taking in laundry, or other jobs. With the perseverance of these women and the steadfastness of the residents who stayed, the town of Lawrence was rebuilt, and although the scars remained, the new town was bigger and better than before. Rev. Cordley later said that "the sentiment for rebuilding was universal. Everybody said: 'We must put Lawrence right back better than she was.'"[287]

15 O God, the Heathen Are Come into Thine Inheritance

ON AUGUST 30, 1863, NINE days after the massacre, Rev. Cordley later recalled: "so we laid our dead away, and turned our attention to the living." Since it was Sunday, the survivors spontaneously gathered in the Plymouth Congregational Church for a memorial service. "Most of [the women] had only the clothes they had escaped with on the morning of the raid. The men were in their working clothes." Rev. Cordley continued: "Rev. Grosvenor C. Morse, of Emporia . . . assisted in the service. . . . Neither of us felt that we could say anything, or that anything ought to be said. We had a brief devotional service, and dismissed the congregation, and they went away in silence. Of the service itself, I remember little beyond its profound solemnity." He did recall the scripture Rev. Morse selected—Psalm 79—and how appropriate it was for the service: "O God, the heathen are come into thine inheritance. The dead bodies of thy servants have they given to be meat unto the fowls of the heaven, the flesh of thy saints unto the beasts of the earth." In his brief devotional, Rev. Cordley offered: "My friends, Lawrence may seem dead, but she will rise again in a more glorious resurrection. Our ranks have been thinned by death, but let us 'close-up' and hold the ground. . . . The conflict may not be ended, but the victory must be ours. We may perish but the principles for which we contend will live."[288]

Revs. Cordley and Morse offered comfort to the grieving residents of Lawrence, but everyone knew Quantrill and his men were still out there somewhere, and it took little to set off panic. Rev. Cordley wrote that "a farmer two or three miles below the town had been burning some straw." Someone spotted the smoke, he "mounted his horse and galloped into town, screaming at the top of his voice: 'they are coming again, they are coming again; run for your lives. . . .' The report spread like wild-fire, and in a few minutes, men, women, and children were wildly running down the different streets towards the river, uttering the most piercing screams as they ran."[289] Nothing came of this alarm or others, and shortly after the raid, two companies of Union soldiers were permanently stationed in Lawrence for the duration of the war. They built fortifications, armed with artillery pieces, and had a commanding view of a wide area, so they could easily see any invasion from any direction. Men who earlier had remained on the sidelines joined the Kansas volunteers, including Rev. Cordley, who became "a member of the rifle company. . . . We had armed ourselves with repeating rifles."[290]

With the presence of the military, the fear of another attack was never far away until the war was over. But the impetus to rebuild the town was stronger than fear, and Rev. Cordley recalled that the restoration "of Lawrence became a sort of religious obligation." The townspeople agreed that "Lawrence must be rebuilt at all hazzards [sic], and rebuilt at once, . . . and in an incredibly short time it began to take form." The grocery business of Ridenour & Baker was completely destroyed. Mr. Ridenour's house and its contents were gone as well. Further, his partner, Mr. Baker, not only lost everything but was so severely injured in the raid, he nearly lost his life. But even as their place of business was still smoldering, workers began clearing away the debris, quickly started building a new store, and brought in groceries for sale. Before long, they were back in business in a bigger and better facility.

The Simpson brothers, who owned one of the town's banks, survived the attack, but their bank building was destroyed. Miraculously, the bank's vault and its contents remained intact. They hired workers to build a temporary wooden structure around the vault, and opened for business. Then—and this became the norm—they hired builders to build a sound foundation and erected a solid brick bank building around the temporary frame structure. Mr. W. E. Sutliff, who had lived in Lawrence for six years, had built up one of the largest clothing stores in town. Like many others, he lost his stock and his building. He immediately decided to build a bigger store, with more and higher-quality of clothing, and before long he was back in business.

Mr. B. W. Woodward, a druggist, also lost his building and goods. He had been contemplating moving his business to a larger and more centrally located site even before the raid. He moved to a better location, built a larger drug store, and offered a larger variety of medicines. Mr. J. G. Sands, an early resident of Lawrence, ran a harness business in a wooden building, which was destroyed along with the contents. Like many others, he started rebuilding imme-diately with a brick and stone edifice. He restocked even before the building was finished and posted one of the cleverest, and in many ways defiant, advertisements, which read: "ESTABLISHED IN 1855; STOOD THE DROUGHT IN 1860; TOTALLY DESTROYED IN 1863; DEFIES ALL COMPETITION IN 1864."[291]

One of the most important businesses up and running again was the *Lawrence State Journal* newspaper office. The *Journal* appeared again on October 1, 1863, with the headline: "To Our Patrons. This is a juvenile Kansas State Journal. Next week we promise it shall look better." Mr. H. E. Lowman, the editor, reported that the offices were in a cellar. He asked for the good people of Kansas to subscribe for $2 a year, and asked any who had subscriptions that had not expired before the raid to notify him so their newspapers would continue. Lowman also sounded the optimism for a bigger and better town. "Lawrence," he wrote, "expands into brick and mortar walls. We [the newspaper, will] develop into power presses and printing material."[292]

In the November 12, 1863 edition of the *State Journal*, the editor reported that a new steam-powered press had arrived from

Chicago, and that he hoped he could start publishing a daily news-paper when the press was in operation. In the same edition, the paper reported that a telegraph line was connected to his office for instant national news. In the news department, the paper reported that the long-awaited bridge across the Kansas River—which was under construction and damaged in the raid—was nearly complete. Further, the railroad, which would revolutionize transportation for Lawrence, was still scheduled for completion by January 1864. A week later, in the November 19 edition of the *Journal*, the editor noted that he toured the town and reported that 137 buildings were either under construction, rebuilt, or completed after the raid. Some were small, temporary structures, mostly for the laborers and mechanics who were helping to rebuild the town. Yet many were underway, built with stone and brick, "that would be an ornament to any city."[293]

Even John Speer, who lost two sons in the raid, put a positive spin on Lawrence's future when his newspaper, the *Kansas Daily Tribune*, started up again in December 1863. "Hurrah for Lawrence," Speers wrote. He continued: "Talking about a Phoenix arising from its ashes . . . Lawrence has done it. . . . One hundred and forty new houses already gone up, and business flourishing like a green bay tree. Bridges, railroads, and other little matters attended to, and now a daily paper, The *Tribune*, in full blast."[294]

There was a great deal of optimism for the town and its future. But the human condition is such that it was impossible for every-one to simply ignore what had happened and move on. The nearly one-third of the population who left after the massacre clearly were not looking toward the bright future in Lawrence. For the families of the two hundred victims—the ones who remained in town—life was going to be difficult for some time. Then there were some who simply could not cope with what had happened. Kansas historian Katie Armitage described one such Lawrence resident in a recent article in *Kansas History*. Fred Read lost his store and everything in it, valued at $10,000. His wife, Amelia, was the woman from whom one of Quantrill's men took a bracelet that had belonged to their deceased infant daughter. Read and his wife survived, and she saved their house although the guerrillas had tried to burn it to the ground. So, while the Reads' financial losses were devastating, they had their home and they had each other. But not long after Quantrill and his men left town, Fred Read crawled into a liquor bottle and did not crawl out again for several weeks. His wife was so concerned about his health that she had him locked up in the city jail to dry him out. The story did, however, have a happy ending. Read was released from jail, quickly recovered from his inebriated state, rebuilt his business—it was far more successful than before the raid—served on the city council, and became a leading force and was successful in obtaining relief funds from the state for Lawrence residents impacted by Quantrill's Raid.[295]

Quantrill doubtless was on the minds of many Lawrence residents as they rebuilt their town. He most definitely was in the constant thoughts of Brigadier General Ewing. After the raid, the general remained in command in the border region. August 1863 had been a horrendous month for him. His plan to arrest and imprison women who supported the guerrillas was a disaster. Quantrill had pulled together one of the largest bands of guerrillas to nearly obliterate Lawrence. His trusted aide, Major Plumb, failed to capture Quantrill and his men. On August 25, Ewing issued his General Order No. 11 in the hopes of—once and for all—ending the guerrillas' reign of terror on the Missouri-Kansas border.

His order stated that "all persons living in Jackson, Cass, and Bates counties, Missouri, and in that part of Vernon included in this district, [with some exceptions] are hereby ordered to remove from their present places of residence within fifteen days from the date hereof." Inhabitants who could "establish their loyalty to the satisfaction of the commanding officer of the military station near their present place of residence will receive from him a certificate stating the fact of their loyalty, and the names of the witnesses by whom it can be shown." These individuals or families were required to move "to any military station in this district, or to any part of the State of Kansas, except the counties of the eastern border of the State. All others shall remove out of the district." In other words, all residents in the area identified in the order, whether loyal to the Union or not, were required to move.[296]

Ewing hoped to achieve several objectives with his order. First, he wanted to preempt Jim Lane, who was threatening to raise a huge army to obliterate everything and nearly everyone with any connection to the Confederacy in the border areas of Missouri. Second, he thought that by removing everyone—loyal and disloyal citizens—from the border area, all support for the guerrillas would vanish. Third, he believed that by placing the army in charge of carrying out this order, he could keep the Kansas Jayhawkers, and the more radical and brutal faction—the Red Legs—away from wreaking vengeance on Missourians.

His first goal was successful. Lane raised an army of about one thousand Kansans who were heading toward the border, but Ewing sent his troops to meet them at the border, and Lane backed off. His second objective was partially successful, but mostly not. As loyal and disloyal residents were forced to leave their homes and farms, they left behind hay, grain, farm animals, and smokehouses full of meat. The intent was for the army to either gather or destroy everything, but the soldiers were so busy moving people, they did not have time to take care of anything else. So, in the short term, the guerrillas helped themselves to the abundance of food, forage, and animals. Finally, although Ewing's intention was to move residents, he wanted the houses and outbuildings to remain intact so that when hostilities ended, the Missourians could return to their homes with everything pretty much intact. This backfired almost completely, for most of his soldiers were Kansans who were so incensed with the Lawrence Massacre, they destroyed and burned many houses, barns, and other outbuildings.

Caleb Bingham, who despised Ewing even before the collapse of his building with the makeshift jail for female "belligerents," grew

even more vocal in his hatred after the general issued General Order
No. 11. He wrote a letter to Ewing, saying that if he went ahead
with his order he would make the general "infamous with pen and
brush." Bingham did just that, and in 1868, he painted his famous
General Order No. 11, showing the harsh treatment Missourians suffered under the order. He also used his pen, and several years later,
he wrote a letter to the editor of the *St. Louis Republican* describing the exodus of Missourians. "Dense columns of smoke arising in
every direction marked the conflagrations of dwellings," he wrote,
"many of the evidences of which are yet to be seen in the remains
of seared and blackened chimneys, standing as melancholy monu-
ments of a ruthless military despotism which spared neither age, sex,
character, nor condition."[297]

Finally, Ewing's Order No. 11 did nothing to lead to the capture of Quantrill and his men. They managed to reach Missouri
following the raid, losing only a handful of their compatriots. As
had become their practice, when they reached Missouri, the men
scattered. With Union patrols moving residents from their homes

George Caleb Bingham, *Order No. 11.* Cincinnati Art Museum.

and looking for the bushwhackers, Quantrill and his men were constantly on the move. They hid during the day and helped themselves to the food and forage left behind by the exiles at night. By the end of September 1863, after a couple of close calls with federal soldiers, Quantrill and most of his men decided to head south for the winter. Some stayed behind in Missouri, but about four hundred guerrillas—including new recruits—followed Quantrill. On their way to Indian Territory (present-day Oklahoma), the lead party of bushwhackers, under the command of one of Quantrill's lieutenants, Dave Poole, came across a recently constructed Union fort at Baxter Springs. Many of the white and African American federal troops were outside the fort eating their lunch, and Poole and his men decided to attack. Poole sent word back to Quantrill that his men had initiated the attack, and as the main party of guerrillas was heading toward Baxter Springs, they encountered a large wagon train of Union soldiers. The wagons, as it turned out, were escorting Union Major General James G. Blunt, who was on his way from Fort Scott to Fort Smith in Arkansas. Blunt later reported that since Quantrill and his men "were dressed in blue uniform[s] and carried our [the Union] flag, they were at first supposed to be federal troops, but a doubt arising as to whether they were friends or enemies, I approached their line, alone, to ascertain their true character, and when within three hundred yards of them, they opened a fire on me." Blunt then ordered his escort and accompanying troops "to return the fire and charge their [the guerrilla] line, [but] I discovered that the entire escort (who were new recruits) had broken at the first fire of the enemy, and were flying in disorder over the prairie." What Blunt did not report was that he was barely able to escape on his magnificent horse, but was forced to leave behind his belongings, including his sword and general's commission. Blunt did, however, report that "in this affair eighty-seven men, including escort, clerks, teamsters, servants, and musicians were killed. All who fell wounded or were taken prisoners were inhumanely murdered."[298] Quantrill lost only two men.

The guerrillas made their way to Texas, where they set up their winter camp. When Quantrill and his men arrived in Texas, many of the animosities that had been brewing between the bushwhackers rose to the surface. Some felt guilty for their participation in the Lawrence Massacre. They had no problem killing Union soldiers, especially Jayhawkers and Red Legs, but the wanton massacre of innocent civilians was too much. Others were upset with how Quantrill was managing his followers. They had understood that the plunder from Lawrence and other raids would be distributed among the dispossessed and destitute families who had suffered during the war, only to find that Quantrill allowed and even encouraged the spoils to be distributed among the bushwhackers, with the lion's share going to some of his lieutenants. And still others were just plain tired of living the transient life of guerrillas. They seldom slept in the same place for more than a night or so, and they generally had made their beds in their remote hideouts. Plus, they missed their families and homes.

About forty members of the band left. Some, such as Bill Gregg, left to join up with the regular Confederate Army. Cole Younger accepted an appointment to go into New Mexico Territory on a mission to recruit new Confederate soldiers, which was a complete failure. He continued on his journey to California, ending up in San Francisco, where he spent the remainder of the war living with his uncle.

In addition to the unease among bushwhackers, many Confederate commanders were uncomfortable in the presence of Quantrill and his men in or near their encampments. Major General Sterling Price liked Quantrill and approved of his exploits, but other Confederate leaders thought the bushwhackers were no better than common criminals and wanted nothing to do with them. To control the guerrillas, Price listened to his lieutenants and ordered Quantrill to re-form his men under a more orderly command, reducing the number of guerrillas to eighty-four, with Quantrill at the head with three lieutenants under him.

But the discipline this structure implied quickly dissolved. Since their earliest encounters and partnership, Quantrill and "Bloody Bill" Anderson had maintained an uneasy peace. It did not take long for their partnership to evaporate. Quantrill had one of Anderson's men killed for thievery, which so incensed Anderson that he took his followers and left. The breakup was so complete, Quantrill's and Anderson's men even engaged in several skirmishes while in Texas. Things went from bad to worse for Quantrill. In a heated argument with George Todd—who had been one of his lieutenants from the earliest days—Quantrill was humiliated and surrendered his command to Todd. Quantrill left Texas with a small contingent of his followers and went into hiding in Missouri.[299]

In the spring of 1864, the bushwhackers, now under the separate commands of Anderson and Todd, headed back to Missouri. A new recruit joined Anderson's band—Frank James's sixteen-year-old kid brother, Jesse. The teenager had been itching to join the guerrillas for some time and was finally allowed to do so. Jesse James quickly

Jesse James (age seventeen) as member of Quantrill/Anderson Guerrillas. AF Eisenbahn Archive, Alamy Stock Photo.

learned the ways of the guerrillas and took full part in the attacks, which were more frequent and bloody than in the past.

Late in the summer of 1864, the bushwhackers joined forces with Major General Price, who led a small army into Missouri, attempting to reestablish a Confederate presence in the state. Price's first target was St. Louis, where he planned to capture the large Union arsenal there. The city and garrison were too heavily armed, so he moved on to his next objective, Jefferson City, the state capital, which was also well defended. Price skirted these two cities and started heading west. Brigadier General Thomas Ewing Jr. followed Price, and on the morning of September 27, Price turned and attacked the federals, driving them into the defenses at Fort Davidson, near Pilot Knob. Technically Price won this battle because after repeated assaults, the Union soldiers pulled out of Fort Davidson that night, blowing up the fort's powder magazine. But the victory was costly for Price; he lost many more men than his Union counterparts, gaining virtually nothing of military value.

The same day Price was attacking Fort Davidson, "Bloody Bill" Anderson orchestrated a massacre that added to his reputation for brutality. Anderson and his men were in Centralia, Missouri, dressed in blue Union uniforms as was their custom. While there, a passenger train pulled in to the station with 125 passengers—civilians and soldiers—on board. Anderson called for an officer to step off the train. Sergeant Thomas Goodman bravely obeyed, thinking that he would be shot, but he hoped that the remaining soldiers would be spared. Instead, Anderson ignored Goodman, and he and his eighty guerrillas killed the remaining twenty-two soldiers who were heading home on leave after the Battle of Atlanta. Each was shot multiple times, mutilated, scalped, then thrown back on the train, which was set on fire and sent on down the tracks. Goodman was held as a prisoner for ten days, but managed to escape.

The telegraph operator in Centralia sent a message reporting the attack, and later that afternoon, Union Major A. V. E. Johnston, with 155 men of the newly formed 39th Missouri Infantry

Regiment (Mounted), rode into Centralia. These soldiers were raw recruits with little or no battle experience. John McCorkle, reported that George Todd, Quantrill's successor, did not participate in the Centralia Massacre and that he reprimanded Anderson for his brutality, but when word came that Johnston was heading toward Centralia, Todd and his men joined forces with Anderson for the ensuing battle. They set a trap for the federals, and Johnston rode right into it. The major saw the bushwhackers dismounting, and thinking they were planning for a battle on foot, he ordered his men to also dismount, directing some to take the horses to the rear. Then he formed his men into a line of battle. As it turned out, the guerrillas were simply tightening the girths on their saddles for the ensuing battle. They remounted and charged the soldiers, who were on foot, with their revolvers blazing. The federals were armed with single shot Enfield rifles; some were able to get off one shot; then, with the bushwhackers bearing down on them, they panicked and ran. Of the 155 Federals, 123 were killed, including Major Johnston, whom, as Frank James later reported, was killed by his brother, Jesse.

After the massacre and battle at Centralia, the bushwhackers, as was their common practice, scattered throughout the countryside. After several days, Todd's men regrouped and joined up with Price's army, which had been moving west toward Kansas City. On October 21, Todd was scouting ahead for Price near Independence, and on top of a hill, he was mortally wounded by a sharpshooter. He died a short time later. During their time together, the guerrillas had grown very close as comrades, and the death of George Todd was particularly devastating. On many occasions, he led a charge, and had seemed to have a charmed life because up until this fatal shot he had not been hit or even grazed from enemy fire. His death was terribly hard for John McCorkle. Todd had asked for McCorkle to hurry to his bedside; McCorkle was not able to reach him in time, and later in his memoirs, he wrote simply: "I loved Todd more than a brother."[300]

Bill Anderson did not join up with Price and continued bush-whacking in western Missouri. On October 26, 1864, Union Lieutenant Colonel Samuel P. Cox and his 350 militiamen, who had been tracking Anderson, finally caught up with the guerrillas in the small hamlet of Albany, Missouri. Unlike Major Johnston, who led new recruits against the bushwhackers, Cox was leading a force of veterans, and he was a skilled commander. Anderson, who was leading about eighty men, appears to have looked upon the situation as another Centralia: he formed his men and charged. Like the federals at Centralia, many of Cox's men were dismounted, but instead of panicking and running, they held their ground in fixed positions and kept up a constant and disciplined fire. Recognizing that their situation was not like Centralia, most of the guerrillas instinctively fell back to reorganize. Anderson and one compatriot, however, continued riding ahead in the charge. Anderson was shot from his horse and probably was dead before he hit the ground. His men tried in vain to reclaim his body, but were unsuccessful.

"Bloody Bill" Anderson shortly after he was killed. Wikimedia Commons. Public domain.

The Union soldiers had a trophy, and they carted Anderson's body to the nearby town of Richmond. They checked his belongings to make sure they had indeed killed "Bloody Bill"—false rumors had been circulating for weeks that he had been killed—and when they were sure, they placed him on display and photographed his corpse. Finally, they buried "Bloody Bill" in an unmarked grave in the local cemetery. "Bloody Bill" Anderson was only twenty-four or twenty-five when he was killed.[301]

The losses of Todd and Anderson within a week of each other were devastating to the Confederate guerrillas and a cause for jubilation on the Union side. To make matters even worse for the Confederates, on October 23, right between these two deaths, Price was dealt a stunning defeat at Westport, Missouri, that nearly annihilated his army. Faced by federals, led by Major General Samuel R. Curtis in his front, and dogged from behind with the Union cavalry led by Major General Alfred Pleasanton, Price was in a fix. He could have attempted a retreat to the south, but he instead decided to attempt to attack one enemy force at a time. He attacked Curtis's Army of the Border first, throwing attack after attack at his position. Curtis's men held firm. Understanding that he quickly would be caught in a vise—as Pleasanton came up toward his rear—he retreated south. For all intents and purposes, his campaign was over, thus ending any Confederate threat to Missouri. There was one more battle, the Battle of Mine Creek in Kansas on October 25, which had the distinction of being one of the largest cavalry battles in the war. For James Montgomery, the Battle of Mine Creek brought the border conflict to a fitting conclusion. He had earlier resigned his commission due to poor health, but when he found that Price was headed in his direction, he rejoined. The Battle of Mine Creek, in which Montgomery and his son participated, was fought, as he later wrote, "in sight of my place," near Mound City. Price's army was nearly destroyed, and with the defeat, the Confederate menace in Missouri and Kansas was over.

As Price's army moved west, the people of Lawrence again were fearful that they were the target. But with troops permanently stationed there for protection, and with the Confederates on the run, they finally felt secure. They and most Kansas residents still very much supported the war effort, but as 1864 progressed, many other northerners were growing tired of the war that seemed to have no end. When the offensives in the East and the South seemed to be going nowhere, the frustration with the war effort increased. The Army of the Potomac, now under the command of Lieutenant General Ulysses S. Grant, was unable to defeat Confederate General Robert E. Lee in the Overland Campaign in Virginia. Major General William T. Sherman, leading the Union's Military Division of the Mississippi, was making progress through Georgia, but like Grant, his army was not able to score a knockout blow to the Confederates. By late summer, it was becoming clear to President Lincoln that there was a strong, almost inevitable probability that he would not be reelected in November.

Circumstances changed dramatically when Sherman captured the major Confederate railroad hub city of Atlanta on September 2, 1864. Public opinion in the North started to swing back in favor of Lincoln, and victory now seemed to be within reach. Further, to boost the chances for reelection, many Union soldiers were furloughed and allowed to return to their homes, with the not-too-subtle purpose of allowing them to vote in the upcoming election. They had fought to secure a clear victory, and they did not want their efforts wasted. In fact, the twenty-two soldiers killed by "Bloody Bill" Anderson in Centralia were heading home ostensibly to vote in the November election.

Kansas probably would have voted to reelect Lincoln no matter what. But with the local Union forces finally running the Confederates out of the area, with the death of "Bloody Bill" Anderson, with Quantrill out of the picture, and with the news that Sherman had taken Atlanta, there was no question who Kansans would vote for the first time they could vote in a Presidential election.

Not surprisingly, President Lincoln won by seventeen thousand to four thousand votes. Republicans also overwhelmingly won the state legislature, electing eighty-five of the one hundred seats. This was also good news for James Lane. At the time, the state legislature elected US senators, and the new legislature convened on January 10, 1865. Three days later it elected Lane to a second term as a US senator from Kansas by an overwhelming margin.[302]

For all intents and purposes, the war ended for Kansans when Price's Confederate Army was driven from the border area. But the war continued in the South and the East. President Abraham Lincoln was inaugurated for his second term on March 4, 1865. Less than a month later, on April 2, the Union Army broke through the Confederate lines near Petersburg, Virginia, which spelled the beginning of the end for the Confederacy. Two days later, President Lincoln and his young son Tad toured the smoldering ruins of Richmond, Virginia, just vacated by the Confederate government. Then on April 9, General Lee surrendered to Lieutenant General Grant at Appomattox Courthouse, ending the war. The people of Lawrence rejoiced when news arrived that the Civil War was over. Their joy quickly changed to sadness when just days later they learned that President Lincoln had been assassinated.

The war ended, but the pride of soldiers' service from Lawrence and the rest of Kansas continued. Many Kansas veterans joined the Grand Army of the Republic (GAR), a social, economic, and political advocacy group established shortly after the war ended. At its peak in 1890, the GAR counted nearly five hundred thousand members nationwide. Kansas had more than eighteen thousand members in 478 posts, which was larger, per capita, than in any state in the Union.

Most local GAR posts built their own halls, which often functioned as local community centers. Members also pooled their resources—in many cases matched with federal funds—to provide homes and funds for the widows and orphans of Civil War soldiers, as well as to care for disabled or elderly veterans, and bury and mark the graves of their members. They also leveraged federal Civil War claim funds and raised additional money to build the Memorial Building in Topeka, completed in 1911. The building housed the GAR's state headquarters as well as the Kansas State Historical Society.

As a national organization, the GAR welcomed African American veterans. By 1894, a total of 167 Kansas black members joined GAR posts in Atchison, Fort Scott, Kansas City, Lawrence, Leavenworth, and Topeka. The Lawrence branch was named the Samuel Walker Post in honor of the man who fought in battles during "Bleeding Kansas," the Civil War, and who for a number of years was the Douglas County Sheriff and the City Marshal of Lawrence.[303]

The year the GAR Memorial Building was completed in 1911 was significant for another reason: the grande dame of Kansas, Sara Robinson, died at age eighty-four. After the war, she recorded her recollections of Quantrill's Raid and the Civil War in Kansas. She had outlived most of her contemporary free-state pioneers. She observed firsthand the trials, tribulations, and triumphs in Lawrence. She was jubilant when Kansas became a free state, electing her husband as its first governor. Looking back, she rejoiced that her home and her nation had "a peace that would be lasting, that would come when it should be heralded; . . . that the whole nation was free—slavery being abolished."[304]

Epilogue: From Ashes to Immortality

LOOKING BACK ON THE EARLY years of Lawrence, Rev. Cordley recalled that in the spring of 1865, with the Confederate Army's surrender, "after ten years of disturbance in one form or another, we were to enjoy what Governor Geary was fond of calling, 'the benign influences of peace.'" He continued, writing that "it was so comfortable to feel that we could retire at night without fear of alarm, and work by day without fear of attack. We need no longer start at every unusual sound, nor scan with care every unusual sight. This was a luxury we had not enjoyed since the beginning of the settlement ten years before. One hardly needs to say that we enjoyed it as few people enjoy peace and quiet."[305]

Peace also brought prosperity. On the heels of Quantrill's Raid, three transportation improvements dramatically changed Lawrence's economic trajectory. Since its founding, the Kansas River never was a reliable transportation route. Plans were in the works for years to build a bridge, and during the Civil War, investors—including Josiah Miller, the former editor of one of Lawrence's first newspapers—pulled together the necessary funds to begin construction. The project was nearing completion when Quantrill and his men came to town. Seven workers and a subcontractor were killed in the massacre, and the principal investors lost almost everything, but they quickly regrouped, resumed construction, finished, and opened the bridge for business in December 1863.

Lawrence Bridge 1863. Public domain.

The bridge was a major improvement, but the real prize—or actually real prizes—came when the Kansas Pacific Railroad made Lawrence a major stop in 1864,[306] and the Leavenworth, Lawrence, and Galveston Railroad included Lawrence on its route in 1867. The railroads provided more reliable and efficient transportation; they also provided jobs. The official census for Lawrence in 1860 counted 1,645 inhabitants. By 1870, the population had exploded to 8,320. A large majority of the new residents arrived in the second half of the decade, changing the community's demographic and geographical makeup. New England residents, who dominated the population earlier, were now only a little more than 20 percent of the total population. Residents from the Upper Midwest and the Upper South made up about 30 percent each, and about 20 percent came from Europe. German immigrants made up the majority of the latter group, establishing an enclave of residences and businesses in East Lawrence. African Americans still composed a sizable part of the population.[307]

New houses and new business buildings sprang up all over town, mostly replacing those lost in the raid. With the new bridge, the area north of the Kansas River started growing as well. One of the few buildings to survive was one of the oldest and most prominent buildings in town—the Plymouth Congregational Church. It was a symbol of the old, established New England abolitionists who had first settled Lawrence. The church continued to grow during the war, so that by 1864, the congregation started exploring the possibility of constructing a new edifice on a location closer to the center of town. Momentum and enthusiasm for a new house of worship grew, and shortly after the war, the church board directed the newly established Society of the Plymouth Congregational Church to find a building site, hire an architect, and raise $15,000 for the new building.

The Society hired John G. Haskell as its architect. Haskell was the perfect choice. He was quickly developing the reputation as the finest, most creative architect in the state—he was hired to design the new state capitol building in Topeka. His father, Franklin Haskell, was a charter member of the church. And, with the design commissions he had accepted to this point in his career, this was his first church.

Many church members were more interested in cost and function rather than in style, but Haskell responded with what would become his motto, that "beauty costs no more than ugliness." He created an edifice with "angles, projections, and towers," incorporating elements of the Gothic and Renaissance Revival styles in his exterior treatment. The front featured four brick-engaged columns, with spires extending about ten feet above the façade, stained glass windows, and an elaborate pipe organ. The church was dedicated in May 1870, and the other churches in town dismissed

Plymouth Congregational Church, Lawrence, Kansas. Photo by Bhall87, placed in public domain in Wikimedia Commons.

their congregations to allow their parishioners to attend the event. Haskell's church still stands, and over the years, ancillary structures have been added to meet the needs of the growing congregation.[308]

As Plymouth Church was under construction, one of the town's newest congregations, made up of many of the town's newest residents, decided to build a new church as well. The English Lutheran Church—whose members, ironically, were mostly Swedish and German—wanted to integrate into the community and learn to speak English as quickly as possible. Organized in 1867, the congregation was small and not well-off financially, but it wanted Haskell to design the new building. Haskell agreed and graciously donated plans for a simple, but elegant, Gothic Revival structure. The exterior was built with rough-cut stone; lancet windows and a larger lancet entrance were the primary Gothic Revival features. The entrance at the

Old English Lutheran Church, Lawrence, Kansas. Photograph by CP&Associates, Architects and Planners.

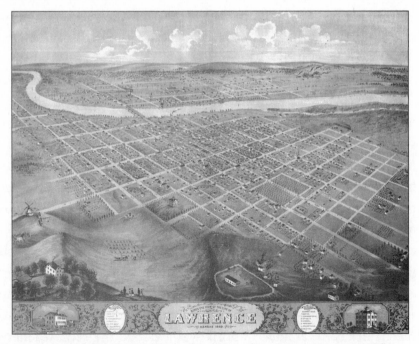

Panorama titled "Bird's Eye View of the City of Lawrence, Kansas 1869." Library of Congress.

right side of the church was topped by a simple steeple with lancet windows that mimicked the main windows. The church was quietly dedicated on December 18, 1870, and became a symbol of the new Lawrence.[309]

Once Kansas became a state, the establishment of institutions of higher education became a top priority. Lawrence placed itself in a position as the potential home of one of these colleges. Almost simultaneous with the first shovels turning over the soil in Lawrence, the people planned to eventually build a college on Mount Oread in the center of town.

In 1863, as the legislature was poised to select a site for the state university, Lawrence positioned itself as one of three possible locations, in competition with Manhattan and Emporia. At the outset, Manhattan seemed the most desirable location. The town's leaders offered Bluemont Central College, with its stone building, a one-thousand-volume library, science facilities and equipment, along with its 120 surrounding acres, to the state as its contribution. Lawrence offered $15,000 in cash for the new university. Emporia offered forty acres but no cash. Manhattan appeared to be in the driver's seat.[310]

Just before the state legislature was poised to vote on the location of the university, the Lawrence supporters mounted a huge lobbying effort, and on February 20, 1863, Governor Carney signed the law giving the university to Lawrence. Later, William Miller reported that his brother, Josiah—the same Josiah who helped build the bridge and edit one the town's first newspapers—who at the time also was Lawrence's postmaster, engineered the "vote getting" effort, bribing the legislators with $5 each. Just before the vote, Josiah noticed that he had missed two prospective members, and he slipped them $4 apiece to ensure a favorable vote. While Manhattan and Emporia lost out on the state university, Manhattan received the state agricultural and mechanics college, and Emporia was awarded the state teacher's college.[311]

So the people of Lawrence bribed the state legislature, promising $15,000 in cash—which it did not have—to locate the state university in their town. Now they had to deliver. The legislation required the city to come up with the full amount by November 1, 1863.[312]

Of course, no one counted on the horrific catastrophe of Quantrill's massacre in August, which made the prospect of raising the necessary funds by the deadline seem impossible. But not long after the raid, Charles Robinson contacted Amos Lawrence and asked if he would give the city the full $15,000 in cash to meet the deadline. Lawrence agreed to give $10,000, and Kansas Governor Thomas Carney agreed to loan the remainder from his personal account, paving the way for the University of Kansas to open on September 12, 1866.[313]

For its first couple of years, the university struggled. There were plenty of students, but nearly all were in the preparatory program and were not ready for college. Money was tight, and to make matters worse, the legislature cut its funding. In 1868, just when the

John Fraser, Chancellor, University of Kansas, 1867–1874. Kenneth Spencer Research Library, University of Kansas.

situation seemed bleakest, the board of regents hired John Fraser as its new chancellor. Chancellor Fraser and the regents convinced the City of Lawrence to float bonds for $100,000 for new buildings. Lawrence was well on its way toward recovery from Quantrill's Raid, and the town's leaders quickly grasped that in addition to railroads and industries, keeping up with the expansion of its university was a wise investment.

Fraser brought in new faculty and exerted his considerable energy to build the University of Kansas into a real university, moving away from being a preparatory school. On June 11, 1873, the university held its first commencement in the newly completed University Building—which was designed by John Haskell—graduating four students. With its emphasis on admitting women as well as men, Flora Ellen Richardson was a member of the first graduating class, as well as the class valedictorian.[314]

Just as the university and the town of Lawrence were truly beginning to prosper, the nationwide Panic of 1873 dealt the town and the college a severe blow. Lawrence was down, but it was not out.

University Hall (later Fraser Hall) 1882, Kenneth Spencer Research Library, University of Kansas.

With the two railroads and the means to ship and receive goods, the fledgling manufacturing sector grew. It received a big boost when several entrepreneurs raised the capital to build a dam on the Kansas River to provide power. Floods, ice, and bankruptcy delayed the project, but in 1879 the dam was completed, providing power to several factories. Using a cable transfer system that produced 1,500 horsepower with the capability to power multiple factories five miles away, Lawrence became a manufacturing center.[315]

Lumber-, paper-, and gristmills dominated the manufacturing industry, but with the new power source, Lawrence quickly became one of the major manufacturing centers for barbed wire. The Consolidated Barb Wire Company—which combined three factories into one—produced most of the barbed wire for Kansas and was a major supplier for the western United States. Another industry that thrived with the building of the dam was the Wilder Brothers Shirt Factory.[316]

While industry in Lawrence was on the upswing, farmers in the surrounding area had dealt with the ups and downs of growing crops since they had first settled the area. But the economic and environmental crises in 1873 were particularly devastating. As if these factors were not enough, the railroads that were so important for shipping agricultural products gouged farmers with shipping costs. To face these multiple issues, farmers banded together to collectively improve their situation. Twenty-eight farmers near the small community of Vinland, about a dozen miles south of Lawrence, organized a chapter of the Patrons of Husbandry (commonly referred as the Grange) in 1873. Collectively, they purchased feed, seed, and machinery at wholesale prices for their members. Their Grange Hall, built in 1883 and still standing, provided a center for social activities on the second floor and a store for farm supplies on the first.[317] The national Grange organization provided financial aid to farmers in times of hardship, and in time, it negotiated more favorable freight costs on railroads. In many ways, the Grange harkened back to the free-state movement from years earlier. The antislavery residents joined forces to protect their homes and businesses and to ensure that the state they were creating was free. In much the same way, Grangers joined together for their common economic and social interests.

Agriculture and industry in Lawrence and the surrounding area provided opportunities for a new educational institution, which opened in 1884. The local US congressman, Dudley Haskell, brother of architect John Haskell, was instrumental in locating the United States Indian Industrial Training School in his hometown. Haskell Institute—the name was later changed to honor the congressman, who died before the school opened—was created in an era in which white American liberalism and guilt led to the belief that the survival of American Indians could only happen if the children were placed in government-run Indian schools. The purpose was to separate children from their Indian culture and make them into "white, Christian" American farmers, domestic workers, or

Amos Adams Lawrence, Harvard University Portrait Collection, gift of Friends of Amos Lawrence to Harvard University, H190.

laborers. The people of Lawrence embraced the new school, believing that they were doing their part to save America's indigenous people from extinction.[318]

After the turmoil of "Bleeding Kansas" and the Civil War, and as Lawrence was developing into a modern community, Rev. Dr. Cordley (the University of Kansas awarded him with an honorary doctor of divinity degree in 1874) sat down to write the history of his adopted town. As the coda, he wrote that "the people of Lawrence were not lovers of strife. Her people were lovers of order and peace. . . . Now peace had come after all these years of strife. And it was peace that would stay."[319]

In the spring of 1884, Amos Lawrence decided to finally accept the invitation that had been on the table for thirty years—to visit the town in Kansas that bore his name.[320] He had been ill off and on during the past winter, and he hoped the trip would improve his health. Since he would turn seventy in a couple of weeks, he knew that time was running out for a visit, so Lawrence, his wife, his daughter, and Dr. Samuel A. Green, the former mayor of Boston, boarded a train and headed west. When they arrived in Lawrence on May 27, 1884, Lawrence and his party were escorted to Dr. Charles Robinson's house, which was their headquarters during their visit.

Amos Lawrence's visit was a momentous occasion for the town. Many knew that without his generosity thirty years earlier, the town might well have never been built. Plus, his huge monetary gift, some twenty years earlier, was a critical piece in the establishment of the University of Kansas in Lawrence. So the organizers rolled out the red carpet, planning a week of events to honor their guest and to show off their community. On the first day, the group toured the town and ended up at the University of Kansas, where the faculty presented Lawrence with a resolution that recognized his "generosity which laid the corner-stone of the system of higher education in this commonwealth." They also invited him to participate in commencement exercises, scheduled toward the end of his visit.

His schedule for the remainder of the visit included participating as a special guest for Decoration (Memorial) Day, visiting in Topeka, and attending a huge picnic as the guest of honor. Charles Branscomb, the man whom Lawrence and the board of the Emigrant Aid Company sent to scout for a location for the first settlement, planned a special dinner as well. At the conclusion of the festivities in Lawrence, Amos Lawrence and his party were scheduled to continue on their journey to Colorado.

The schedule was so ambitious it would have exhausted a younger man. Lawrence was not young and was still recovering from his winter ailments. After a couple of days, he cut short his trip and returned to Boston. In his diary he wrote that "the reception was so generous and overwhelming that it was too much." Later, Lawrence intimated to his son that because he was a very private man who shunned public attention, being placed in the limelight made him very uncomfortable.[321]

Even though Amos Lawrence cut short his visit, the time he spent at the University of Kansas was important to him. Higher education was something he vigorously supported throughout his life. From the time he graduated from Harvard, he supported his alma mater with his energy and his money. In 1847, he donated $10,000, matched by the Methodist Church, to establish Lawrence University in Appleton, Wisconsin, which became the second coeducational college in the country. When he helped to create Lawrence, Kansas, he never wavered in his goal to help create a college there. During his visit to the University of Kansas, his hosts noted that a portion of his financial donation to help found the university was used to ensure that the children who survived Quantrill's Raid, as well as children of Kansas soldiers killed in the Civil War, would be exempt from paying any tuition or fees.[322] Lawrence continued his practice of generously giving his time and money to those in need until his death in 1886.

The "stark mad abolitionists" who came to Lawrence in the 1850s probably would be pleased to see that the town they created remains a liberal island in the current sea of Kansas conservatism. In the 2016 presidential election, Donald Trump defeated Hillary Clinton in Kansas 57 percent to 36 percent. In Douglas County (where Lawrence is located), however, Clinton defeated Trump 63 percent to 29 percent. The abolitionists who founded Lawrence were the radicals of their day, on the far left side of the antislavery movement. In many ways, they were out of step with other antislavery advocates. But they successfully made Kansas a free state and played a significant role in bringing the nation into the recognition of the evils of the institution of slavery.

The pioneers would also be pleased to know of their continuing legacy. When fourth graders study Kansas history, their teachers take to them to the significant sites in Lawrence that are important to the early history. And each year, on the Saturday closest to the anniversary of Quantrill's Raid (August 21), the Douglas County Historical Society, the Watkins Museum, Freedom's Frontier, Lawrence Parks and Recreation, and other organizations sponsor tours, lectures,

Monument to Quantrill victims in Lawrence, Kansas. Kansas State Historical Society.

musical programs, and a wide variety of special events. Included are tours of the historic Oak Hill Cemetery located on land set aside by the citizens of Lawrence to honor the victims of Quantrill's Raid. Volunteers read the names of all of victims of the raid. Tour participants see the graves of the many early Lawrence residents—James Lane, the Haskell brothers, John Speer, Charles and Sara Robinson, and many others. They also are directed to the monument erected in 1895 to the victims of Quantrill's Massacre. While there, the tour guides remind the group of sacrifices early Lawrence residents suffered in its important role in the struggle to rid the nation of slavery.

Appendix: What Happened to the Players in This Story?

WHEN WE LAST ENCOUNTERED **ANTHONY Burns**, he was led to a ship in Boston Harbor, in chains, awaiting his return to slavery. In the first four months of his return to captivity, things went from bad to worse for Burns. His owner, Charles F. Suttle, sent him to a Richmond slave jail where he was held in chains, which left him permanently crippled and in ill health for the remainder of his short life. Immediately after his capture, the abolitionist community of Boston tried to purchase his freedom, offering as much as $1,200. Suttle instead sold him to David McDaniel, a slave trader, from Rocky Mount, North Carolina, for $910.

In the spring of 1855, a group of African Americans in Boston bought his freedom for $1,300. Burns returned to Boston and eventually studied theology at Oberlin College and Fairmont Theological Seminary in Cincinnati. In 1858, he went to Maine, where he prepared a traveling exhibit called "The Grand Moving Mirror," portraying the "degradation and horror of American slavery." Burns planned to travel with the exhibition through New England, but his ill health thwarted his plans. In 1860, he became the minister at a Baptist church in Indianapolis. He then moved to the Zion Baptist Church in Saint Catherines, Upper Canada (present-day Ontario). Burns died in Canada at age twenty-eight in July 1862 from consumption (tuberculosis), never having regained his health.

Not long after his visit to Kansas, **Amos Adams Lawrence** again joined forces with Eli Thayer to establish the "Utah Emigrant Aid Company," modeled on the Kansas group, with the purpose of encouraging non-polygamous non-Mormons to migrate to Utah. The effort flopped, mostly because Utah Mormons recognized that their only path to statehood required the abolition of polygamy. Lawrence continued his lifelong practice of generously giving his time and money to Harvard and temperance programs, and by helping individuals in need, whether they were people who had worked for him, schoolmates or friends who had fallen on hard times, or even people he did not know. His family continued to be the most important part of his life, and remained his greatest source of strength and joy right up until his death in 1886.

Eli Thayer was elected as a Republican to Congress, where he served from 1857 to 1861, his second term as chairman of the Committee on Public Lands. He never lost his itch to start up new communities. He tried to duplicate his effort in Kansas by organizing the town of Credo in Virginia (later part of West Virginia) as well as his partnership with Lawrence to flood Utah with non-Mormons. Both endeavors were unsuccessful. Later in life, he engaged in railroad and other business pursuits, and he unsuccessfully ran for Congress again in 1872. His legacy, however, was always tied to the Emigrant Aid Company. Amos Lawrence later said that "he [Thayer] never faltered in his faith, and he inspired confidence everywhere." Eli Thayer lived in Worcester until his death in 1899.

The **Reverend Thomas Wentworth Higginson** volunteered for, and quickly rose to the rank of captain in, the 51st Massachusetts Infantry in the Civil War. He was wounded in action in August 1862. When he recovered, he was appointed colonel of the 1st South Carolina Volunteers—made up almost entirely of former slaves. The 1st South Carolina later became the 33rd US Colored Troops (USCT). The USCT along with the 54th Massachusetts black infantry regiment participated in the assault on Fort Wagner, as depicted in the film *Glory.* Higginson recorded his experience in

Army Life in a Black Regiment (1870), in which he described his experiences commanding his regiment, and for posterity he wrote down the Negro spirituals his men sang around the campfire in their own dialect. "Until the blacks were armed," he wrote, "there was no guaranty of their freedom. It was their demeanor under arms that shamed the nation into recognizing them as men."

Following the war, Higginson "discovered" Emily Dickinson. As a regular contributor to the *Atlantic Monthly*, in one of his articles he encouraged young, aspiring writers to publish their works. Thirty-one-year-old Emily Dickinson responded, sending along four poems. Following the first encounter, the two corresponded frequently, and after Dickinson died in 1886, Higginson edited and published Dickinson's poems. After a long and very fruitful life, Higginson died in 1911 at the age of eighty-seven.

The **Reverend Henry Ward Beecher** continued as minister at Plymouth Congregational Church in Brooklyn for the remainder of his life. He was at odds with American theologians in that he embraced Darwin's theory of evolution as compatible with the Bible. During the early 1870s, however, his personal life and reputation took a severe beating. Elizabeth Tilton, a member of his congregation, confessed to her husband, Theodore, that she had had an affair with Beecher. Through much of his entire ministry, there were innuendoes that Beecher's wandering eyes had led to affairs with female congregants. But this affair took on a life of its own. The media picked up the story, which provided some of the juiciest headlines of the time. Eventually, Theodore Tilton sued Beecher for adultery in 1875. Beecher was exonerated with a hung jury, and his church exonerated him as well, but the episode nearly broke him financially. He continued as a popular lecturer and eventually recouped his finances. He died, solvent again, in 1887.

Senator James H. Lane was a staunch supporter of Lincoln for reelection. He also ran for reelection to the US Senate and won. As a senator, Lane had supported most of the administration's policies and was firmly in the camp of the Radical Republicans concerning issues relating to African Americans. He often went well beyond the administration, supporting increased rights for blacks—especially former slaves. But after President Lincoln's assassination, when Andrew Johnson became president, Lane did a complete about-face, supporting Johnson's reconstruction policies, including the president's veto of the Civil Rights Bill. In addition, there were revelations of questionable financial dealings concerning government contracts. He lost the support of his constituents almost overnight. Tragically, Lane shot himself on July 1, 1866, while visiting his brother-in-law in Leavenworth. He died ten days later.

Lane was one of the most colorful, interesting, and enigmatic politicians in Kansas history. His suicide at age fifty-two not only ended his life but in many ways ended a major part of the early history of Kansas. Few were as fascinating or as controversial, loved or hated with as much passion as James Henry Lane.

Charles and Sara Robinson remained in Lawrence for the remainder of their lives. Charles was instrumental in the establishment of the University of Kansas in Lawrence and served on the board during much of its early years. He helped found the Kansas Historical Society and served as its president. He also was president of Haskell Indian School. Charles died in 1894, but Sara lived almost another twenty years. According to her biographer, she "used her pen to fight those she saw as trying to rewrite Kansas history," especially those who attempted "to denigrate her husband's legacy in order to promote the memory of James Lane." [323] The Robinsons left no heirs, so when Sara died, she left much of their considerable estate to the University of Kansas. Much of the present campus is built on land they donated.

Dr. John Doy left Lawrence to promote his book *The Narrative of John Doy, of Lawrence, Kansas: An Unvarnished Tale in the East* and to drum up support for Abraham Lincoln's election in 1860. In 1861, his son Charles was killed in an ambush in Moneka, in south-central Kansas. In 1862, John moved his family to Battle Creek, Michigan. In 1869, he was convicted of procuring an abortion for a young woman, and committed suicide with an overdose of morphine while awaiting sentencing, claiming he would never go to jail again.

In 2005, an archeological team from Washburn University found what was likely the site of John Doy's house. The team excavated the foundation and found a rich collection of artifacts from the 1850s time frame. The students knew absolutely nothing about John Doy before they started the project, and they were intrigued with his story, which supplemented the archeological discoveries. [324]

When **William Clarke Quantrill's** guerrilla band split into the factions led by "Bloody Bill" Anderson and George Todd in 1864, Quantrill lay low in Missouri, but following the deaths of Anderson and Todd in October, he again resumed leadership of a much smaller band and led his guerrillas into western Kentucky.[325] Quantrill and his men wore Union uniforms and claimed to be part of the 4th Missouri Cavalry, and as its leader, he used the pseudonym of Captain Clarke. He and his men had some success in Kentucky, and found Confederate sympathizers who provided shelter and food, but eventually, the Union forces recognized who he was and started pursuing him in earnest. Major General John M. Palmer, the commanding officer in Kentucky, assigned Edwin Terrell the exclusive charge to pursue Quantrill, with orders to bring him back dead or alive. Terrell caught up with Quantrill on May 10, 1865, several weeks after nearly all Confederate forces had surrendered. Quantrill was shot in the spine, paralyzed, and transported to a prison hospital in Louisville, where he died on June 6.

While Quantrill was lingering between life and death, he became a devout Roman Catholic and was given last rites. He was buried in an unmarked grave in a local cemetery. The disposition of his remains became a truly bizarre story. One of Quantrill's boyhood friends, William W. Scott, claimed to have brought Quantrill's remains back to Dover at the request of Quantrill's mother. Scott also tried to sell some of Quantrill's bones to collectors. Then, in the early 1990s, the Missouri division of the Sons of Confederate Veterans arranged for some of Quantrill's remains to be taken from Ohio and reburied in a Confederate cemetery in Higginsville, Missouri.

The story of Quantrill and his guerrillas did not end with his death. Several members of his band embarked on lives of crime after the war. Many of Quantrill's men stayed in touch with one another and started holding reunions, which continued until nearly all members were dead. Today, the William Clarke Quantrill Society continues to perpetuate his legacy.[326] Numerous films and books, in both fiction and fact, continue the story of William Clarke Quantrill and his guerrillas.

For some of Quantrill's and "Bloody Bill" Anderson's gangs, their Civil War adventures were but a beginning. **Cole Younger** and **Frank** and **Jesse James** achieved more fame or notoriety—depending on

Cole Younger advertisement for lecture of his life story at Steger Opera House, Bonham, Texas in 1913. Fannin County (Texas) Historical Commission.

one's point of view—after the Civil War. In one of the most famous crimes in American history, Cole Younger, his brothers Jim and Bob Younger, Frank and Jesse James, and several others attempted to rob the First National Bank of Northfield on September 7, 1876. Cole later wrote that they targeted this bank because they understood it was owned by two former Union generals, Benjamin Butler and Adelbert Ames. Whatever the reason, the attempted robbery was a complete disaster for the Younger-James Gang. Not intimidated by the outlaws, the townspeople grabbed their guns and started firing at the robbers from nearly everywhere. Two townspeople and two outlaws were killed, and a posse trapped and caught the three Younger brothers not far from the scene of the crime. All three pled guilty to avoid the noose. Cole survived his brothers, was released from prison in 1901, and made a nice living on the lecture circuit telling his life story until he died in 1916 at the age of seventy-two.

The James brothers managed to escape and made their way to Nashville, Tennessee. When the James brothers arrived in Nashville, they assumed new names and lived peaceful lives for the next three years. **Jesse** grew restless, though. He moved back to Missouri and organized a new gang and started robbing banks again. Two of his gang members were Bob and Charley Ford. Unbeknownst to Jesse, Bob Ford had a secret arrangement with the governor of Missouri, Thomas T. Crittenden—that he would bring in Jesse James for a reward. On April 3, 1882, while Jesse James was standing on a chair in his living room to clean a dirty picture hanging on the wall, Bob Ford shot him in the back. Jesse was thirty-four when he was killed. **Frank** decided he did not want to meet the same end as his younger brother, and five months after Jesse was killed, he surrendered to Governor Crittenden. He was tried and acquitted of several of his crimes. Frank James did a number of odd jobs for the remainder of his life, but he eventually returned to his family farm and charged twenty-five cents for tours of the famous outlaws' home. He died there in 1915 at age seventy-two.

Frank James at age fifty-five, 1897. Library of Congress.

When **John Geary** left Kansas, he went first to Washington, DC, where he did his best to bring the nation's attention to the perils in Kansas. He returned to his farm in Pennsylvania, remarried (his first wife died before he went to Kansas), and intended to lead a quiet life as a farmer. All of that changed with the outbreak of the Civil War. Geary raised the 147th and 28th Pennsylvania Infantry regiments and became colonel of the latter. He was soon promoted to the rank of brigadier general and led his troops against Thomas J. "Stonewall" Jackson in the Shenandoah Valley Campaign in the Battle of Chancellorsville, in May 1863, and in the Battle of Gettysburg, defending the far right flank of the Union Army on Culp's Hill. Later in 1863, his division was transferred to Chattanooga. In the Battle of Wauhatchie, Geary's son, Edward, was wounded in the battle and died in his father's arms. He distinguished himself in the Battle of Lookout Mountain, the entire Atlanta Campaign, Sherman's March to the Sea, and the Carolinas

Campaign. In his military service in the Mexican War and the Civil War, Geary was wounded ten times.

After the war, Geary returned to Pennsylvania as a war hero. He served two terms as the Republican governor of Pennsylvania from 1867 to 1873, and had a solid reputation for attacking the political influence of the railroads and vetoing many special-interest bills. On February 8, 1873, less than three weeks after leaving the governor's post, Geary died from a heart attack while preparing breakfast for his infant son. He was fifty-three years old.

Late in the Civil War, **Dr. Charles Jennison** commanded a Kansas militia brigade in the action against Sterling Price in the battles of the Little Blue, Independence, Westport, Marais des Cygnes, Mine Creek, and Newtonia. After Price was pushed out of Missouri, however, Jennison returned to his old "Jayhawking" ways. He was court-martialed, found guilty, and cashiered out of the militia on June 23, 1865. He and his men were charged with burning the homes of defenseless women and children and hanging three men who claimed to be Union supporters. Following the war, Jennison settled in Leavenworth, Kansas. During his guerrilla days, he developed a keen eye for superior horseflesh. He bought a ranch and raised what were considered some of the finest race and trotter horses in the state. He also entered the political arena. He was elected to the city council, served for a time as the ex-officio mayor, then ran and won a seat in the Kansas House of Representatives in 1865, in which he served two terms. In 1871, he was elected and served one term in the Kansas Senate. He remained in Leavenworth, where he died in 1884.[327]

James Montgomery resigned from his Union commission, but agreed to again serve to drive out Sterling Price's Missouri Expedition in October 1864. Montgomery took command of the 6th Kansas Militia Regiment and saw action at the Battles of Big Blue, Westport, Mine Creek, and Marais des Cygnes. After the war, Montgomery returned to his farm in Linn County and also returned to his earlier profession as a preacher. He led the First Day Adventist church congregation in Linn County until his death in December 1871.

George Washington Brown was one of the most influential persons in Lawrence during the territorial period. His *Herald of Freedom* newspaper was the town's principal news source in the 1850s. After the *Lawrence Republican* drove his paper out of business in 1859, he moved to and helped found the city of Emporia. In 1860, after Brown learned of George Bissell's and Edwin L. Drake's success in drilling for oil on Oil Creek near Titusville, Pennsylvania, he decided to try his hand at drilling for oil. He dug three moderately successful oil wells in Miami County, Kansas. In 1865, he left for the more lucrative oil fields of Pennsylvania, but did not stay long. After several months, he settled in Rockford, Illinois, where he lived for the remainder of his life. His principal activity was writing a biography of John Brown and about territorial Kansas. The remainder of his life turned out to be quite long—he died in February 1915 at the age of ninety-four.

John Speer felt the full brunt and pain of Quantrill's Raid of 1863. His eldest son John was killed, and his son Robert was presumed burned in the *Lawrence Republican* office. As did many of his contemporaries, Speer dabbled in politics. He was a delegate to the 1864 national Republican convention, and voted to renominate Lincoln for President. Speer also served in both the Kansas Senate and House of Representatives, and he was appointed as the Kansas State Printer and a United States revenue collector. He further was instrumental in the establishment of the University of Kansas and Baker University. His first love, though, was managing newspapers and writing, which consumed most of the remainder of his life. One of his greatest passions was venerating his dear friend, James Lane. Speer wanted to do all he could to ensure that future Kansans would hold Lane in as high esteem as did he. So in 1897, he wrote and published the *Life of Gen. James H. Lane, The Liberator of Kansas.* Late in life, Speer moved to Denver to live with his daughter. There must have been something about newspaper work in Kansas, because, as with George Brown, Speer lived to the ripe old age of eighty-eight.

The other member of the early Lawrence newspaper triumvirate, **Josiah Miller,** left the newspaper business after the Border Ruffians destroyed his printing office and press. His paper had struggled anyway, so there was little incentive to get back into the business. Miller campaigned for John C. Frémont for president in 1856, then returned to Lawrence, where he became the probate judge for Douglas County. Miller was elected to the first Kansas State legislature, but resigned when he was appointed as the first Lawrence postmaster, which was a financially lucrative position. He was selected to the three-member committee to select the site for the University of Kansas. In 1863, Miller was appointed as paymaster for the army, with the rank of major. After the Civil War, Miller was a principal mover and shaker to rebuild Lawrence after the raid. He invested in and promoted the Leavenworth, Lawrence, and Galveston Railroad, and was a partner in the Lawrence Bridge Company as well as the Lawrence Dam Water Power and Manufacturing Company.

One of Josiah Miller's most valuable contributions was the collection of letters he left behind: to his parents in South Carolina during his early time in Lawrence, and to his brother and others later. He was articulate and inclusive, and often he did not hold back on his passions, capturing the events of the times. Unlike the other early editors, Miller died at the relatively young age of forty-two in 1870, following surgery in St. Louis to amputate his leg.[328]

Samuel Walker, one of the ablest free-state military leaders, carried his military prowess into the Civil War. He rose up through the officer ranks, receiving a brevet (temporary) promotion to brigadier general. Mid-1865, Walker led the 16th Regiment Kansas Volunteer Cavalry on the ill-fated (for the whites, successful for the Indians) Powder River Expedition. The venture, under the overall command of Major General Grenville Dodge, was intended as a punitive attack on the Sioux, Cheyenne, and Arapaho Indians. When the expedition ended, Walker led his troops back to Fort Laramie, where he and his soldiers mustered out of service.[329]

Following his Civil War service, Walker remained with the Kansas militia and rose to the rank of major general. He was elected sheriff of Douglas County, Lawrence City Marshal, and as a Republican to the Kansas State Senate. He remained in Lawrence for the remainder of his life and died in 1893.

John G. Haskell continued designing buildings in Kansas as the state architect and in his private practice. The National Register of Historic Places lists twelve structures designed by Haskell in its inventory for Kansas—everything from modest schoolhouses to the state capitol.[330] He continued working up until his death in 1907 at age seventy-five. One building Haskell designed toward the end of his career that brought great satisfaction was the Douglas County (Kansas) Courthouse. The county never had its own county building until Haskell was selected as the architect and designed a building, which was completed in 1904.

The **Reverend Dr. Richard Cordley** left Lawrence in 1875 to pastor a Congregational church in Flint, Michigan. He remained in Flint for three years. He then returned to Kansas as the minister of the Congregational Church in Emporia, where he remained until 1884. Rev. Cordley returned to Plymouth Congregational Church in 1884, where he remained until his death in 1904. From contemporary accounts, at the end of his life he was afflicted with what he called "a creeping paralysis," likely something such as Parkinson's disease. To deliver his last sermon, shortly before he died, he had to be assisted to the pulpit.

Several years after his death, Rev. Cordley's congregation published a collection of his sermons. From this sample, Rev. Cordley's sermons were theologically sound, not long, and each offered practical advice to his parishioners. His style was to feed his congregation from the scripture, not to condemn them, and from the friendly way in which he spoke to his audience, it was clear that his church members loved him. But his influence went well beyond his congregation. At his memorial service, the Reverend Samuel A. Riggs, a fellow Congregational minister, offered the eulogy, saying that "of the men, young, vigorous, and strong, who came then [in the 1850s] no one has made a deeper and more enduring impression upon Lawrence and the State than Richard Cordley."[331]

Notes

1   The basic framework established with the Northwest Ordinance has been the basis for admitting new states since 1787. Alaska and Hawaii, the two most recently admitted states, met milestones similar to those established by this ordinance.

2   William Parker Cutler and Julia Perkins Cutler, *The Life, Journals and Correspondence of Rev. Manasseh Cutler, LLD* (Cincinnati: Robert Clark and Company, 1888), 203–334. Rev. Cutler recorded his trip and his experiences in his journal. His grandchildren published his papers in 1888, and it is now available online at: https://books.google.com/books/about/Life_Journals_and_Correspondence_of_Rev.html?id=HRAXAAAAYAAJ.

3   Letter in its entirety can be found at: https://www.loc.gov/exhibits/jefferson/159.html.

4   Quoted in: http://edsitement.neh.gov/lesson-plan/kansas-nebraska-act-1854-popular-sovereignty-and-political-polarization-over-slavery.

5   Quoted in: https://www.nps.gov/liho/learn/historyculture/peoriaspeech.htm.

6   George Hilliard to Francis Lieber, June 1, 1854, cited in: James M. McPherson, *Battle Cry of Freedom: The Civil War Era* (New York: Oxford University Press, 1988), 120.

7   Article IV, Section 2, paragraph 2 read: "No Person held to Service or Labor in one State, under the Laws thereof, escaping into another, shall, in Consequence of any Law or Regulation therein, be discharged from such Service or Labor, but shall be delivered up on Claim of the Party to whom such Service or Labor may be due." The text of the Fugitive Slave Act of 1850 can be found at: avalon.law.yale.edu/19th_century/fugitive.asp.

8   Some estimates were as high as $100,000.

9   In this oft quoted letter, Lawrence goes on to say that he hopes the people of Massachusetts will "stand by the laws until they are repealed," but

he also noted that "Massachusetts never can be made hunting ground for masters to pursue their runaways." Amos Adams Lawrence to Giles Richards, 1 June 1854, Amos Adams Lawrence Papers, Massachusetts Historical Society, Boston (Hereafter cited as Lawrence MSS); also quoted in Jane H. and William H. Pease, *The Fugitive Slave Law and Anthony Burns: A Problem in Law and Enforcement* (Philadelphia: J. B. Lippincott Company, 1975), 53.

10　Taken from the Biographical Sketch for the Lawrence MSS.

11　Ibid., Diary entry 7 January 1854. One of his charities was to pay for relocating former slaves to Liberia, Africa. On January 27, 1854, he noted in his diary that he gave $2,400 to Mr. and Mrs. Appleton to send eighty former slaves to Liberia.

12　Statutes at Large, 33rd Congress, 1st Session, Chapter 59, 277ff. The Kansas-Nebraska Act can be found at: http://www.ourdocuments.gov /doc.php?flash=true&doc=28.

13　Franklin Pierce was the nephew of Lawrence's stepmother, Lawrence MSS, Diary, 13 April 1854.

14　Lawrence MSS, Diary, 30 May, 3 June 1854.

15　Ibid., 18, 25 June 1854.

16　William Lawrence, *Life of Amos A. Lawrence: with Extracts from his Diary and Correspondence* (Boston: Houghton, Mifflin and Company, 1888), 78.

17　Eli Thayer, *A History of the Kansas Crusade: Its Friends and Its Foes* (New York: Harper and Brothers, 1889), 24.

18　Lawrence, *Life of Amos A. Lawrence*, 80-81.

19　Lawrence MSS, Diary, 19 August, 3 September 1854.

20　In 2003, Brown University President Ruth J. Simmons appointed a Steering Committee on Slavery and Justice to investigate and issue a public report on the University's historical relationship to slavery and the transatlantic slave trade. The committee produced *Slavery and Justice report of the Brown University Steering Committee on Slavery and Justice*, detailing the role of the Brown family in the slave trade, and the university's role over time in confronting historical injustice and slavery's legacy. The report can be found at: brown.edu/Research/Slavery_Justice /documents/SlaveryAndJustice.pdf.

21　Webb's letter is included in www.territorialkansasonline.org/~imlskto/ cgi-bin/index.php?SCREEN=show_transcript&document_id= 100368SCREEN=search&submit=search&search=Thomas%20H.%20 (Hopkins),%201801–1866%20Webb&startsearchat=0&searchfor =authors&printerfriendly=&county_id=&topic_id=&document_ id=100368&selected_keyword=

22　www.territorialkansasonline.org/~imlskto/cgi-bin/index .php?SCREEN=show_document&document_id=101815&SCREEN

_FROM=search&submit=search&search=Thomas%20H.%20
(Hopkins),%201801–1866%20Webb&startsearchat=0&searchfor=authors

23 Quoted in Samuel A. Johnson, *The Battle Cry of Freedom: New England Emigrant Aid Company in the Kansas Crusade*, (Lawrence: University of Kansas Press, 1950),14.

24 Hale's book and its influence are described by Cora Dolbee in her 1933 article in the *Kansas Historical Review*. Cora Dolbee, "The First Book on Kansas: The Story of Edward Everett Hale's 'Kanzas and Nebraska,'" *Kansas Historical Review* 2 (May 1933), 139–181. An electronic version can be found at: www.kancoll.org/khq/1933/33_2_dolbee.htm.

25 Lawrence MSS, Diary, 28 October 1855; www.territorialkansasonline .org/~imlskto/cgi-bin/index.php?SCREEN=view_image&file _name=h000436&document_id=100126&FROM_PAGE=; and http://www.territorialkansasonline.org/~imlskto/cgi-bin/index.php? SCREEN=show_document&document_id=100125&SCREEN _FROM=search&submit=search&search=Lyman%20,%20 1775–1863%20Beecher&startsearchat=0&searchfor=authors

26 www.plymouthchurch.org/our_history.php

27 Sam Houston's Speech Opposing the Kansas-Nebraska Act (February 15, 1854), quoted in: www.tsl.state.tx.us/exhibits/civilwar/documents/before/sam-houston- feb15–1854–1.html. President John F. Kennedy featured Sam Houston's speech as a chapter in his *Profiles in Courage*. (New York: Harper Brothers, 1956), 93–109. As the only southern Senator to oppose the Kansas-Nebraska Act, his action temporarily derailed his political career in Texas.

28 The 1854 treaty with the Delaware Indians can be found at: digital. library.okstate.edu/kappler/Vol2/treaties/del0614.htm; the 1829 treaty can be found at: digital.library.okstate.edu/kappler/Vol2/treaties /del0304.htm.

29 The entire "Plan of Operation" can be found at: www.territorialkansasonline .org/~imlskto/cgi-bin/index.php?SCREEN=show_document&- document_id=101532&SCREEN_FROM=keyword&selected _keyword=Massachusetts%20Emigrant%20Aid%20 Company&startsearchat=5

30 Quoted in Don W. Wilson, *Governor Charles Robinson of Kansas* (Lawrence: University of Kansas Press, 1975), 5.

31 Nicole Etcheson, "Labouring for the Freedom of This Territory: Free-State Kansas Women in the 1850s," *Kansas History: A Journal of the Plains* 21 (Summer 1998), 77.

32 Biographical information from Ibid., 1–11.

33 Charles Robinson, *The Kansas Conflict* (New York: Harpers and Brothers, 1892),69; cited from http://books.google.com/books?id=AvZ5AAAAMAAJ &pg=PA1&source=gbs_toc_r&cad=4#v=onepage&q&f=false

34 The Pre-emption Law of 1841 was widely used for the settlement of Kansas. It provided that a squatter (head of household, who could be a married man, a single man, or a widow, all over twenty-one) could claim 160 acres of government land, on which he/she squatted, for no less than $1.25 an acre, as long as he/she was an American citizen, or intended to become a citizen, and had squatted on the land for at least fourteen months.

35 Ibid., 69–73.

36 Colonel James Blood described the selection of what became Lawrence in an article appearing in the Lawrence *Journal* (January 12, 1891). He wrote that Branscomb wanted the settlement to be on the Wyandot Reservation, but that he (Blood) had pointed out the complications in settling on Indian land, and instead recommended the site on the Kansas River, since it was south and west of the Delaware Reservation, and thus not encumbered and could be settled and claimed under the Preemption Law of 1841.

37 John Doy published his biography privately in 1860, titled *The Narrative of John Doy of Lawrence, Kansas* (1860), 5, which is available at: http://quod. lib.umich.edu/g/genpub/ABJ5091.0001.001?rgn=main;view=fulltext . Just so that readers would not think he embellished any part of the story, the subtitle read: "A Plain, Unvarnished Tale."

38 Ibid., 6.

39 Ibid., 7

40 B. R. Knapp, article published in the Boston *News* (August 9, 1854). Article was reproduced in A. T. Andreas, *History of the State of Kansas* (Chicago: Andreas's Western Historical Publishing Company, 1883), 312.

41 Doy, *Narrative of John Doy*, 8.

42 Andreas, *History of Kansas*, 313.

43 Lawrence MSS, Diary, 27 August, 3, 24 September 1854.

44 Andreas, *History of Kansas*, 313.

45 Lawrence MSS, Diary, 9, 29 October 1854.

46 http://www.territorialkansasonline.org/~imlskto/cgi-bin/index .php?SCREEN=show_transcript&document_id=102336SCREEN =immigration&submit=&search=&startsearchat=&searchfor=&printer friendly=&county_id=&topic_id=129&document_id=102336& selected_keyword=

47 Manhattan native Kevin G. W. Olson has written a delightful and comprehensive history of Manhattan, Kansas, describing the early settlement, the establishment of Kansas State University, and everything else in the town's early history. The dust jacket says that Olson has gone from growing up in the "Little Apple" (Manhattan, Kansas) to working in the "Big Apple" (New York). Kevin G. W. Olson, *Frontier Manhattan: Yankee*

Settlement to Kansas Town, 1854–1894 (Lawrence: University of Kansas Press, 2012).

48 Samuel Johnson discusses many of these organizations in his *Battle Cry of Freedom*, 65–71; Russell Hickman, "The Vegetarian and Octagon Settlement Companies," *Kansas Historical Quarterly* 2 (November 1933), 377–85; "Vegetarians for Kansas," *Herald of Freedom*, April 28, 1855

49 www.territorialkansasonline.org/~imlskto/cgi-bin/index.php?SCREEN =show_document&SCREEN_FROM=immigration&document _id=102650&FROM_PAGE=&topic_id=135

50 The entire census is reproduced at: search.ku.edu/search?q=1855%2Bcen-sus&btnG=Search&site=TKO&sort=date%3AD%3AL%3Ad1&out-put=xml_no_dtd&ie=UTF-8&oe=UTF-8&filter=0&client=default_ frontend&proxystylesheet=TKO. For some districts, the individual census sheets are different than the totals at the end. For example, when counting the number of enslaved people in District 16, the total is thir-ty-eight, but the summary at the end lists thirty-three. For the totals here, I used the numbers on the sheet (i.e., thirty-eight for District 16).

51 The 1855 Kansas Territorial census also is available on the Kansas Genealogy website at: skyways.lib.ks.us/genweb/archives/troubles.html.

52 Andreas, in his *History of Kansas*, wrote that Knapp sent his report to the Boston *News* on this date in August. The Boston *News* might have existed in 1854, but I could not find a reference to this source. Andreas's histories are generally very reliable, so the reference is almost certainly correct. Andreas, *History of Kansas*, 313.

53 Ibid.

54 Doy, *Narrative of John Doy*, 10.

55 Joseph Savage, "Recollections of 1854," *Western Home Journal* 4 (14 July1870). These recollections are available online at: www.territori-alkansasonline.org/~imlskto/cgi-bin/index.php?SCREEN=transcripts /savage_joseph

56 Andreas, *History of Kansas*, 314.

57 The "new" Plymouth Church will be discussed in greater detail later in this volume in Chapter 17.

58 "A Valuable Letter," *Herald of Freedom*, October 21, 1854. The complete run of the *Herald of Freedom* is available online at: http://chroniclinga-merica.loc.gov/lccn/sn82006863/1855–01–06/ed-1/seq-2/

59 *Herald of Freedom*, January 13, 1855.

60 Charles Robinson to Amos Adams Lawrence, December 18, 1854. Typescript of the letter can be found at: www.territorialkansasonline .org/~imlskto/cgi-bin/index.php?SCREEN=view_image&file _name=k302423&document_id=102491&FROM_PAGE=

61 Richard Cordley, *History of Lawrence: From the First Settlement to the Close of the Rebellion* (Lawrence, Kansas: E. F. Caldwell, 1895), 24–26.

62 Reports of the number of emigrants in the third group vary from 160 to 200. Reports of the number that returned to the East vary as well, from one-third to two-thirds. Louise Barry, "The Emigrant Aid Company Parties of 1854," *Kansas Historical Quarterly* 12 (May 1943): 146–150.

63 Ibid., 115–155.

64 Lawrence, *Life of Amos Lawrence*, 85.

65 The letters above and the diary entry are included in Lawrence, *Life of Amos A. Lawrence*, 85–86.

66 Found at: www.territorialkansasonline.org/~imlskto/cgi-bin/index.php? SCREEN=show_transcript&document_id=100408SCREEN=key-word&submit=&search=&startsearchat=15&searchfor=&printer-friendly=&county_id=&topic_id=&document_id=100408&selected _keyword=Lawrence,%20Amos%20Adams,%201814–1886.

67 Amos A. Lawrence to Charles H. Branscomb, September 26, 1855. Found at: www.territorialkansasonline.org/~imlskto/cgi-bin/index.php ?SCREEN=show_document&document_id=100416&SCREEN_ FROM=keyword&selected_keyword=Lawrence,%20Amos%20 Adams,%201814–1886&startsearchat=15.

68 Lawrence's public persona was that of an antislavery advocate, not a "stark mad abolitionist," as he wrote his uncle in a private correspond-ence. His protestations aside, most Emigrant Aid Company settlers in Kansas probably fell within the abolitionist camp. They advocated an immediate end to slavery, and they believed the best means to accomplish that goal was to not allow slavery to gain a foothold in Kansas. Cited in Lawrence, *Life of Amos A. Lawrence*, 86–88.

69 Louise Barry, "The New England Emigrant Aid Company Parties of 1855," *Kansas Historical Quarterly* 12 (August 1943): 227–68.

70 *Herald of Freedom*, March 10, 24, and April 28,1855; O. S. Fowler, *A Home for All, or Gravel Wall and Octagon Made of Building New, Cheap, Convenient, Superior, and Adapted to Rich and Poor* (New York: Fowler and Wells: 1854).

71 Cordley, *History of Lawrence*, 30–32.

72 Nichole Etcheson, *Bleeding Kansas: Contested Liberty in the Civil War Era* (Lawrence: University Press of Kansas, 2004), 56–59. In 1856, Congress investigated the elections in Kansas as well as the Wakarusa War (which will be discussed later in this study in Chapter 5), and other events in Kansas Territory (1855–1856). The investigation and subsequent report was called the Howard Report. It can be found at: quod.lib.umich. edu/m/moa/AFK4445.0001.001/290?rgn=full+text;view=image. The

section dealing with the 1855 Territorial Election in Lawrence can be found on pages 148–151.

73 A copy of Robinson's letter can be found at: www.territorialkansasonline .org/~imlskto/cgi-bin/index.php?SCREEN=show_transcript&document_id=102359SCREEN=keyword&submit=&search=&startsearchat=10&searchfor=&printerfriendly=&county_id=&topic_id=&document_id=102359&selected_keyword=Robinson,%20Charles,%20 1818–1894.

74 Etcheson, *Bleeding Kansas*, 60–61.

75 Sara T. L. Robinson, *Kansas, Its Interior and Exterior Life: Including a Full View of its Settlement, Political History, Social Life, Climate, Soil, Productions, Scenery, etc.* (Boston: Crosby, Nichols, and Company, 1856), 65. This book can be found at: books.google.com/books?id =CHgFAAAAQAAJ&printsec=frontcover&source=gbs_ge_summary_r&cad=0#v=onepage&q&f=false.

76 Johnson, *Battle Cry of Freedom*, 103.

77 Cited in Robinson, *Kansas, Its Interior and Exterior Life*, 80–83.

78 Cordley, *History of Lawrence*, 38–39.

79 Robinson, *Kansas, Its Interior and Exterior Life*, 70.

80 Lawrence MSS, Diary, 10 July 1855.

81 Lawrence confirmed the donation in his diary (Ibid, 23 July 1855)

82 Abbott's entire reminiscence can be found at: www.territorialkansasonline.org/~imlskto/cgi-bin/index.php?SCREEN=show_document&document_id=102421&SCREEN_FROM=keyword&selected_keyword=Abbott,%20James%20Burnett&startsearchat=40. The *Herald of Freedom* announced that the shipment of five boxes, marked "books," arrived safely on the *Emma Harmon* steamboat. To the surprise and pleasure of everyone, they discovered that the parts for one hundred Sharps rifles were in the boxes. *Herald of Freedom*, July 21, 1855.

83 *New York Times*, February 8, 1856.

84 Wilson, *Charles Robinson*, 27.

85 Quoted in Ibid, 28.

86 The term "Garrisonian" referred to the followers of William Lloyd Garrison, publisher of the *Liberator* newspaper, and a radical abolitionist, who condemned the government for not ending slavery, and the United States Constitution for protecting slavery. Ibid., 28–30; Robinson, *Kansas Conflict*, 171–72.

87 Ibid., 173–74.

88 Wilson, *Charles Robinson*, 31–33.

89 Josiah Miller, editor of the Lawrence *Free State* newspaper, to his parents, October 15, 1855. A copy can be found at: www.territorialkansasonline.org /~imlskto/cgi-bin/index.php?SCREEN=show_document&document

_id=101642&SCREEN_FROM=keyword&selected_keyword
=Shannon,%20Wilson,%201802–1877&startsearchat=0.

90   Dale E. Watts, "How Bloody was Bleeding Kansas? Political Killings in
     Kansas Territory, 1854–1861," *Kansas History: A Journal of the Central
     Plains* 18 (Summer 1995): 116.

91   Most American history textbooks still use the Hoagland Commission
     data of two hundred as the number of deaths from "Bleeding Kansas."
     The Hoagland Claims Commission was appointed by Congress in 1859.
     It met in Kansas, and its duty was to determine if any Kansas residents
     were entitled to compensation as a result of the events in "Bleeding
     Kansas." It is not entirely clear how the commission arrived at the num-
     ber of two hundred killed during the territorial period in Kansas.

92   Cited in Watts, "How Bloody was Bleeding Kansas," 117.

93   Ibid., 116–29.

94   Isaac Goodnow, "Narrative, the Murder of Charles Dow," Isaac
     Goodnow Collection, Kansas State Historical Society, 1856.

95   Robinson, *Kansas Conflict*, 184–86.

96   Ibid., 187

97   Etcheson, *Bleeding Kansas*, pp. 81–83.

98   Robinson, *Kansas Conflict*, pp. 188–94.

99   Kristen Tegtmeier Oertel, *Bleeding Borders: Race, Gender, and Violence in Pre-
     Civil War Kansas* (Baton Rouge: Louisiana State University Press, 2009), 77.

100 Ibid, pp. 199–203; Etcheson, *Bleeding Kansas*, pp. 84–87.

101 Ibid, pp. 87–88.

102 Robinson, *Kansas, Its Interior and Exterior Life*, pp. 164–65.

103 Robinson, *Kansas Conflict*, p. 212.

104 Robinson, *Kansas, Its Interior and Exterior Life*, pp. 164–65.

105 Robinson, *Kansas Conflict*, 219–20.

106 "Lawrence A Year Ago," *Herald of Freedom*, July 28, 1855. Articles
     about new businesses, churches, schools, and the athenaeum appeared
     in the Herald as they were established during 1855.

107 *Herald of Freedom*, January 12, 1856.

108 For those who are not familiar with what an athenaeum is, it was a term
     for libraries or literary societies, or both, commonly used in the early
     1800s. *Herald of Freedom*, July 28, 1855.

109 Robinson, *Kansas, Its Interior and Exterior Life*, 66.

110 Ibid., pp. 177–79, 191–94.

111 Joseph Savage, "Recollections of 1854," 22.

112 James C. Malin, "Housing Experiments in the Lawrence Community,
     1855," *Kansas Historical Quarterly* 21 (Summer 1954): 95–121.

113 In a balloon-framed structure, vertical lumber would run the length of
     the structure from the foundation to the roof rafters, with each floor
     attached to the framing lumber.

114   Ibid; Johnson, *Battle Cry of Freedom*, pp. 169–70.

115   Text of the Kansas-Nebraska Act can be found at: memory.loc.gov /cgi-bin/ampage?collId=llsl&fileName=010/llsl010.db&recNum=300.

116   Johnson, *Battle Cry of Freedom*, pp. 115–16.

117   The expression "Fabian policy" was common at that time. It referred to the Roman Consul and general, Fabius Maximus (third century BC), whose nickname was the "delayer," because in the Second Punic Wars, he hit at the enemy's supply lines and vulnerable points rather than attempting a full-scale attack, and thus saved his army to fight another day. Amos Lawrence to Charles Robinson, January 31, 1856, found at: www.territorialkansa-sonline.org/~imlskto/cgi-bin/index.php?SCREEN=show_transcript&-document_id=101083SCREEN=keyword&submit=&search=&start-searchat=20&searchfor=&printerfriendly=&county_id=&topic_id=&-document_id=101083&selected_keyword=Lawrence,%20Amos%20 Adams,%201814–1886.

118   Johnson, *Battle Cry of Freedom*, pp. 124–25 and 163–66.

119   Ibid., p. 163.

120   M. W. Delahay to Genl. C. Robinson, Col. J. H. Lane & others, February 16, 1856. Found at: www.territorialkansasonline.org/~imlskto/cgi-bin /index.php?SCREEN=show_document&document_id=100646&SCREEN _FROM=keyword&selected_keyword=Pierce,%20Franklin,%20 1804–1869&startsearchat=5.

121   Quoted in Robinson, *Kansas Conflict*, pp. 225–26.

122   Howard Committee Report, p. 67, 109.

123   Samuel Johnson noted that the assailant wasn't known for twenty-five years after the attack. He quoted from Leveret W. Spring in his *Kansas: Prelude to the Civil War* (1907) that the culprit was J. F. Filer. Johnson, *Battle Cry of Freedom*, p. 156n.

124   Ibid., pp. 157–58.

125   Cordley, *History of Lawrence*, iii, 42.

126   The US Constitution defines treason in Article III, Section 3: "Treason against the United States, shall consist only in levying war against them, or in adhering to their enemies, giving them aid and comfort." The author of the indictment was careful to precisely define treason on constitutional grounds.

127   The indictment and report or arrests are found at: http://www.kansas memory.org/item/228352/text.

128   Etcheson, "Laboring for the Freedom of This Territory," 82–83.

129   Oertel, *Bleeding Borders*, 132; Sarah Robinson, *Kansas: Its Interior and Exterior Life*, 8.

130   Oertel, *Bleeding Borders*, 61, 64. Kristen Tegtmeier Oertel provides detailed information about women in Kansas in her book. Nicole

Etcheson also does a wonderful job with the same subject in her article "Laboring for the Freedom of This Territory."

131 Robinson, *Kansas Crusade*, pp. 261–62.

132 The text of the indictment can be found at: www.kansasmemory.org/item/228352/text, and Johnson, *Battle Cry of Freedom*, p. 158.

133 Transcript of Learnard's letter is found at: www.territorialkansasonline.org/~imlskto/cgi-bin/index.php?SCREEN=show_document&SCREEN_FROM=border&document_id=100232&FROM_PAGE=&topic_id=69.

134 Full speech, along with interruptions for hoots, yells, waving hats, etc., and Atchison's profanity is found at: www.territorialkansasonline.org/~imlskto/cgi-bin/index.php?SCREEN=show_document&SCREEN_FROM=border&document_id=103035&FROM_PAGE=&topic_id=69. There is some dispute as to whether Atchison actually made this speech or another one at the same time as to how women should be treated. The version quoted here is from Joseph Pomeroy Root, subsequently elected the state's first lieutenant governor, who was a prisoner at the time, who heard and claimed that what he reported was very close to what Atchison said.

135 The full text of Sumner's speech can be found at: eweb.furman.edu/~benson/docs/sumnerksh2.htm.

136 Lawrence, *Life of Amos Lawrence*, p. 122.

137 Shortly after the Wakarusa War, Brown wrote to his wife, describing the "war," its aftermath, and conditions in Kansas at the time. The letter can be found at: www1.assumption.edu/ahc/kansas/JohnBrownWakarusa.html.

138 Exodus 21:24, Leviticus 24:20, and Matthew 5:38–48.

139 Few Americans have had more biographies written about them than John Brown. They have tended to fall into two interpretations. Some have viewed Brown as a crusader, willing to give his life for the noble cause of ending slavery. Many recent biographies fall into this category. In this interpretation, Brown was a major catalyst for bringing on the Civil War and thus ending the institution of slavery. Others see Brown more as a madman, crazed with his passion to end slavery, who probably did more to damage the antislavery cause than help it. Of the recent biographers, David S. Reynolds' *John Brown, Abolitionist: The Man Who Killed Slavery, Sparked the Civil War, and Seeded Civil Rights* (New York: Vintage 2006) is one of the more comprehensive biographies on Brown. His interpretation tends more toward Brown as a crusading idealist, in the vein of earlier writers like W. E. B. Du Bois. I borrowed from his description of the killings along Pottawatomie Creek in pp. 138–78

140 Etcheson, *Bleeding Kansas*, 114–118.

141 Cordley, *History of Lawrence*, 108–09.

142 John Doy, *Narrative of John Doy*, 13–16.

143 Ibid., 17; Thomas Bickerton testified as part of the Journal of Investigations in Kansas on December 5, 1856, describing his life's story up to that point and his involvement in the Border Wars. His entire testimony can be found at: www.territorialkansasonline.org/~imlskto/cgi-bin/index.php ?SCREEN=show_document&document_id=101584&SCREEN_ FROM=keyword&selected_keyword=Abbott%20howitzer& startsearchat=0.

144 Cordley, *History of Lawrence*, 115–18.

145 Doy, *Narrative of John Doy*, 17. A description of the battle of Fort Titus was reported in the *New York Times*, August 17, 1856. This article and a further description of the battle can be found at: www.lecompton-kansas.com/page/the-battle-of-fort-titus. A number of artifacts from the battle are on exhibit at the Territorial Capitol/Lane Museum in Lecompton, at the Kansas Museum of History in Topeka, and Watkins Community Museum in Lawrence.

146 Cordley, *History of Lawrence*, 123.

147 Frank W. Blackmar, *Kansas: A Cyclopedia of State History*, 1 (Chicago: Standard Publishing, 1912), 270.

148 Robinson's letter (August 16, 1856) is at: www.territorialkansasonline. org/~imlskto/cgi-bin/index.php?SCREEN=show_transcript&doc-ument_id=100176SCREEN=keyword&submit=&search=&start-searchat=0&searchfor=&printerfriendly=&county_id=&topic_id=&-document_id=100176&selected_keyword=Treason.

149 Lawrence, *Amos Lawrence*, p. 111.

150 Cordley, *History of Lawrence*, 126–37.

151 Letter from Charles Robinson to Sara Robinson (September 20, 1856) is found at: www.territorialkansasonline.org/~imlskto/cgi-bin/index.php? SCREEN=show_transcript&document_id=101131SCREEN=keyword &submit=&search=&startsearchat=75&searchfor=&printerfriendly =&county_id=&topic_id=&document_id=101131&selected _keyword=Robinson,%20Charles,%201818–1894.

152 Wilson, *Charles Robinson*, 48

153 *Herald of Freedom*, November 1, 1856.

154 Quoted in Howard N. Meyer, *The Magnificent Activist: The Writings of Thomas Wentworth Higginson* (1823–1911) (New York: Da Capo Press, 2000), 79.

155 Ibid., 82.

156 Ibid., 88.

157 Ibid., 98–100.

158 The definitive work on the Whig Party is Michael F. Holt, *The Rise and Fall of the American Whig Party: Jacksonian Politics and the Onset of the Civil War* (New York: Oxford University Press, 1999).

159 "Presidential Result," *Herald of Freedom*, November 15, 1856.

160 Until the ratification of the Twentieth Amendment to the Constitution, the presidential inauguration took place on March 4.

161 Etcheson, *Bleeding Kansas*, 137.

162 Robinson, *Kansas Conflict*, 339–40.

163 The full text of Buchanan's Inaugural Address can be found at: www .bartleby.com/124/pres30.html.

164 Cordley, *History of Lawrence*, 141–42; in the April 18, 1857 edition of the *Herald of Freedom*, George Brown ran several stories about the appointment of Walker as governor, his biography, and a note that he hoped Walker would not give in to pressure from the pro-slavery faction, but would be balanced in his administration.

165 "Filling Up," Ibid.; the Reverend Ephraim Nute, the Unitarian minister in Lawrence, reported similar numbers of daily arrivals, with estimates as high as three thousand per day, cited in Johnson, *Battle Cry of Freedom*, 241.

166 Quoted in Ibid., 251.

167 The text of Lawrence's letter can be found at: www.territorialkansason line.org/~imlskto/cgi-bin/index.php?SCREEN=show_document&-document_id=101698&SCREEN_FROM=keyword&selected_keyword=Lawrence,%20Amos%20Adams,%201814–1886 &startsearchat=30.

168 "Introductory," *Lawrence Republican*, May 28, 1857; "Has the *Herald of Freedom* at All Times Sustained the Position and Policy of the Free State Party in Kansas?" *Lawrence Republican*, June 25, 1857; "A Partisan Press for Partisan Purposes Are Laboring to Crush It," *Herald of Freedom*, June 27, 1857.

169 We will visit the Eldridge Hotel again a little later in this volume during the Quantrill Raid in 1863. In modern Lawrence, another Eldridge Hotel stands on the same spot as the Free State Hotel, and several websites claim it is haunted, one going so far as to call it a "hotel with a boo!"

170 "No Vote," *Herald of Freedom*, May 2, 1857.

171 Etcheson, *Bleeding Kansas*, 145–49.

172 The text of the Dred Scott decision can be found at: https://www.loc. gov/rr/program/bib/ourdocs/DredScott.html

173 "The Grasshopper Falls Convention," *Herald of Freedom*, September 5, 1857.

174 Cordley, *History of Lawrence*, 148–51; "Fraudulent Returns," *Herald of Freedom*, October 17, 1857.

175 "The Time for Legislation," Ibid.

176 The text of the Lecompton Constitution can be found at: http://www .kansasmemory.org/item/90818.

177 T. Dwight Thatcher, who was a delegate to the Leavenworth Constitutional Convention (it meets later), recalled the process of creating the Kansas Constitution in his address as he was leaving his position as president of the Kansas State Historical Society in 1883. His speech is included in Cutler, *History of the State of Kansas*, Territorial History, Part 54, the "Story Retold," found at: http://www.kancoll.org/books/ cutler/terrhist/terrhist-p54.html#THE_STORY_RETOLD

178 Quoted in www.territorialkansasonline.org/~imlskto/pdf/tko_lesson_ pop_sov.pdf.

179 Cordley, *History of Lawrence*, 159–60.

180 Charles Robinson, *The Kansas Conflict*, 378–80.

181 Diane Miller, "To Make Men Free: The Underground Railroad in Bleeding Kansas" (May 2008), found at: www.nps.gov/subjects/ugrr /discover_history/upload/UGRR-in-Kansas.pdf, 10–13.

182 Charles Robinson, *The Kansas Crusade*, 380.

183 Ibid, 277–80; Miller, "To Make Men Free," 13.

184 Lawrence, *Life of Amos A. Lawrence*, 122–30.

185 Ibid, 135–38.

186 Dr. Doy's description is in his *Narrative of John Doy*, 25–115. There is a well-done documentary of his adventure available on YouTube at: www .youtube.com/watch?v=1–4T2xh61s0.

187 There were discrepancies in the story. Doy had Fisher's barbershop in Lawrence; Nute in Leavenworth. Doy had his pursuers shooting at him; Nute did not.

188 Etcheson, *Bleeding Kansas*, 204; James B. Abbott, "The Rescue of Dr. John W. Doy," in Sheridan, *Freedom's Crucible*, 22.

189 Ibid., 25.

190 Cordley, *History of Lawrence*, 163.

191 Richard Cordley, *Pioneer Days in Kansas* (Boston: Pilgrim Press, 1903), 122–36.

192 Dennis M. Dailey, "Josiah Miller, an Antislavery Southerner: Letters to Father and Mother," *Kansas History: A Journal of the Central Plains* 36 (Summer 2013): 71.

193 Richard B. Sheridan has put together a wonderful book on the Underground Railroad in Lawrence and Douglas County, Kansas. He compiled all of the documents he could find, and in the ending commentary, he answers as many questions as he can about the railroad. Richard B. Sheridan, Editor and Compiler, *Freedom's Crucible:*

The Underground Railroad in Lawrence and Douglas County, Kansas, 1854–1865 (Lawrence: University of Kansas, Division of Continuing Education, 1998).

194 Ibid., 67–74.

195 Ephraim Nute to Unknown Recipient (February 24, 1859). Full text of the letter can be found at: http://www.territorialkansasonline.org/~imlskto /cgi-bin/index.php?SCREEN=show_document&document_id=102721 &SCREEN_FROM=keyword&selected_keyword=Fisher,%20 Charley&startsearchat=0.

196 Robinson, *Kansas Conflict*, 383

197 The full text of the Leavenworth Constitution can be found at: www. territorialkansasonline.org/~imlskto/cgi-bin/index.php?SCREEN =show_document&document_id=102076&SCREEN _FROM=keyword&selected_keyword=Leavenworth%20Constitution &startsearchat=0.

198 William E. Connelly, *A Standard History of Kansas and Kansans* (Chicago and New York: Lewis Publishing Company, 1918), transcribed by Carolyn Ward, for the Internet version, at: skyways.lib.ks.us/genweb /archives/1918ks/v2/945.html.

199 Data here comes from: www.kshs.org/kansapedia/wyandotte -constitutiona-convention/17884.

200 Ibid, 19–20: also, an article in the Kansas State Historical Society describes Lincoln's visit in more detail: www.kshs.org/kansapedia/ abraham-lincoln-in-kansas/12132; Another more detailed book on Lincoln's visit and his connection with Kansas is Carol Dark Ayres, *Lincoln and Kansas: Partnership for Freedom* (Manhattan, KS: Sunflower University Press, 2001).

201 "The Herald of Freedom," *Lawrence Republican*, December 29, 1859.

202 Kansas State Historical Society, *Wyandotte Constitution,* at: www .kansasmemory.org/item/90272.

203 "Glorious Intelligence! Kansas in the Union!" *Lawrence Republican* (January 31, 1861).

204 Lawrence, *Life of Amos A. Lawrence*, 152–167.

205 Robert E. May, *The Southern Dream of a Caribbean Empire, 1854– 1861* (Gainesville: University Press of Florida, 2002), 216–217, 243.

206 Ibid., 183–206; James McPherson devoted a chapter to the New England Brahmins in his book, *The Mighty Scourge: Perspectives on the Civil War* (New York: Oxford University Press, 2007), 145–154. McPherson was fascinated that of the 578 Harvard graduates, most of whom served in the 2nd Cavalry and the 20th Massachusetts Infantry, and most who likely could have avoided service, ninety, or nearly six- teen percent, were killed in action.

207 Cordley, *History of Lawrence*, 179–80. In the military hierarchy of the Civil War, regiments were the primary units. A full regiment was made up of one thousand men, divided into ten companies of one hundred men each. A colonel generally was the commander of a regiment. Three to five regiments would make up a brigade, generally commanded by a brigadier general. Two to four brigades would make a division; multiple divisions made a corps; and multiple corps made an army.

208 Richard W. Hatcher III and William Garrett Piston, eds., *Kansans at Wilson's Creek: Soldiers Letters from the Campaign for Southwest Missouri*, Volume 3, Studies of the Civil War in the Trans-Mississippi Theater (Springfield, MO: Wilson's Creek National Battlefield Foundation, 1993), 8–9.

209 Ibid. This volume features letters written by Leavenworth-area soldiers and one correspondent to the Leavenworth *Daily Times*, leading up to and including the Battle of Wilson's Creek. Most of the correspondents are identified, but for this particular letter, the writer is identified simply as "M." The editors speculate that "M" likely was Sgt. Mentzer through a process of elimination.

210 "Whipping Volunteers Under Major Sturgis," *Lawrence Republican* (July 15, 1861).

211 "A Soldier Executed," *Lawrence Republican*, from the collection at Wilson's Creek National Battlefield, nd.

212 Statistics can be found at: http://www.kshs.org/p/civil-war-sesquicentennial/16839. By comparison, New York State contributed just over 9 percent of its entire population.

213 Quoted in Richard B. Sheridan, "The Contrabands in Lawrence and Douglas County," in Sheridan, ed., *Freedom's Crucible*, 107.

214 Richard Cordley, "The Contrabands in Lawrence, Kansas," in ibid., 98.

215 Quoted in ibid., 99–101.

216 Ibid., 102–103; Nathan Wilson, "Congregationalist Richard Cordley and the Impact of New England Cultural Imperialism in Kansas, 1857–1904," *Great Plains Quarterly* 24 (Summer 2004): 190–92.

217 These excerpts are from a collection of letters from Lt. Levant L. Jones to his wife, Hattie Jones, in the Missouri State Historical Society. The letters were written between June 8 and August 9, 1861.

218 William Garrett Piston and Richard Hatcher, *Wilson's Creek: The Second Battle of the Civil War and the Men Who Fought It* (Chapel Hill: University of North Carolina Press, 2000), 338–339.

219 Edward R. Nash to Hattie Jones, August 18, 1861, included in the collection of letters from Levant L. Jones to Hattie Jones, Missouri State Historical Society.

220 These statistics are taken from the 1st Kansas Volunteer Infantry Regiment, regimental history, which can be found at: http://www.kansasguardmuseum.org/dispunit.php?id=3. The National Park Service states that the 1st Kansas Infantry Regiment is seventh on the list of Northern units suffering the largest number of killed, wounded, or mortally wounded in any one engagement during the Civil War. But it has a different number of casualties with 106. National Park Service, "Facts About the Battle of Wilson's Creek, August 10, 1861."

221 Hatchet and Piston, *Kansans at Wilson's Creek*, 78fn.

222 "The Martyrs of Freedom," *Lawrence Republican*, August 29, 1861.

223 In 1944, Kirke Mechem had fun, noting that "several weeks ago that noble myth, the Kansas Jayhawk, was attacked on the grounds that it is attempting to become a real bird. A group of educators had discovered that one of their own textbooks not only tells little children that it is real but that it is a native of this locality. Faced with this dilemma, the school men naturally appointed a committee. As a result, an open season was declared on the Jayhawk and for a time there was a good deal of excited shooting, principally in the newspapers. When the smoke cleared away it was hard to tell from appearances whether the educators were the hunters or the hunted. Although they claimed they saw feathers fly the only trophy they brought back was the statement out of the textbook, which they announced they would stuff and mount above the committee-room door. But even this turned out to be not completely dead, and from last reports the Jayhawk will still perch in the text, metamorphosed, however, once more into a myth." Kirke Mechem, "The Mythical Jayhawk," *Kansas Historical Quarterly* 13 (February 1944): 1; Another, more recent piece on the Jayhawk was written by Frank Baron. Baron argues that August Bondi, the Jewish radical abolitionist, was the first person to describe the term Jayhawk, and he further claimed that Lane was the first one to use the term. Frank Baron, "James H. Lane and the Origins of the Kansas Jayhawk," *Kansas History: A Journal of the Central Plains* 34 (Summer 2011): 114–27.

224 "The Kansas War, the Disturbances in Southern Kansas—Brown and Montgomery." *New York Times* (January 28, 1859); "Origin of the Word Jayhawking," in "Application to the People of Kansas. Incidents in the Early History of the Territory," *The Allen County Courant* (Iola, Kansas) (May 23, 1868).

225 www.ku.edu/about/traditions/jayhawk/

226 Quoted in William Connelly, *Quantrill and the Border Wars* (Cedar Rapids, IA: The Torch Press. 1910), 412.

227 Stephen Z. Starr, *Jennison's Jayhawkers: A Civil War Cavalry Regiment and Its Commander* (Baton Rouge: Louisiana State University Press, 1973). 27–29.

228 James Montgomery was featured in the film *Glory* (1989) as a racist, revenge-seeking commander of African American troops in South Carolina, who was nearly as unbalanced as John Brown. thttp://www.imdb.com/title/tt0097441/.

229 Quoted in http://www.kshs.org/kansapedia/cool-things-proslavery-leader-s-desk/10309.

230 Starr, *Jennison's Jayhawkers*, 30.

231 Ibid., 31.

232 John Speer, *The Life of Gen James H. Lane: The Liberator of Kansas, with Corroborative Incident of Pioneer History* (Garden City, KS: John Speer, Printer, 1897), 227.

233 Bryce D. Benedict, *Jayhawkers: The Civil War Brigade of James Henry Lane* (Norman: University of Oklahoma Press, 2009), 34–35; Lane's leadership of the "Frontier Guard" is described in Erich Langsdorf, "Jim Lane and the Frontier Guard," *Kansas Historical Quarterly* 9 (February 1940), 13–25.

234 Quoted in Ibid., 37.

235 The American Battlefield Protection Program (under the National Park Service) description of the Battle of Dry Wood Creek, September 2, 1861, found at: http://www.nps.gov/abpp/battles/mo005.htm.

236 *Life of Gen. James H. Lane*, 252.

237 Robinson, *Kansas Conflict*, 434–35.

238 Beccy Tanner, "150 Years Later, Quantrill's Raid on Lawrence Still Stirs Deep Emotions—On Both Sides," *Wichita Eagle* (July 21, 2014).

239 Nicole Etcheson, "Jennison's Jayhawkers," *New York Times* (Opinionator) (December 28, 2011), found at: http://opinionator.blogs.nytimes.com/2011/12/28/jennisons-jayhawkers/?_r=0.; "Seventh Regiment Kansas Volunteer Cavalry (regimental history)," excerpts from Cutler's *History of the State of Kansas* 1883, transcribed by Kathleen Roper, and found at: http://www4.pair.com/justfolk/RegHst1htm.

240 Ibid.

241 Quoted in Etcheson, "Jennison's Jayhawkers."

242 Benedict, *Jayhawkers*, 192–202.

243 Speer, *Life of Gen. James H. Lane*, 253.

244 Ibid., 261–62.

245 Chris Tabor, "Skirmish at Island Mound," posted at: islandmound.tripod.com/casualties.htm.

246 http://www.civilwaronthewesternborder.org/content/1st-kansas-colored-volunteers-later-79th-us-colored-infantry. Today, the Battle

of Island Mound is commemorated in a Missouri State Historic Site: https://mostateparks.com/park/battle-island-mound-state-historic-site

247 Hunter, soon after he arrived in Georgia, issued an order freeing all slaves in the vicinity. That order was quickly rescinded by President Lincoln, as was his second order to recruit former slaves to fight for the Union cause. Eventually, Congress and the president did allow him to start recruiting former slaves into the Union army.

248 Lu Ann Jones and Robert K. Sutton, *The Life and Legacy of Robert Smalls of South Carolina's Sea Islands* (Fort Washington, PA: Eastern National, 2012), 24–25.

249 "The Guerrilla Under Quantrel [*sic*] Have Taken and Plundered Olathe," *Lawrence Journal* (September 11, 1862); "Quantrell [*sic*] There Have Been Fugitive Reports for Weeks," Ibid. (November 6, 1862).

250 Cordley, *History of Lawrence*, 190.

251 "The Boldest Raid Yet!," *Lawrence Journal* (May 14, 1863).

252 Among his soldiers, one who gained fame—or, better stated, infamy— later on was Cole Younger, who along with his brothers and the James brothers were outlaws after the war. Younger related the story of his adventures with Quantrill in his autobiography later in life: from the Amazon.com Kindle edition, Cole Younger, *The Story of Cole Younger, By Himself* (1903). For this book, and for later references to Younger's autobiography, I use the Amazon.com Kindle edition, at: www.amazon.com/Story-Cole-Younger-Himself-ebook/dp/B004TPC6Y0/ref=s-r_1_1?s=books&ie=UTF8&qid=1425493959&sr=1–1&keywords=-cole+younger+autobiography. John McCorkle was another guerrilla who recorded his experiences later. He told this story as fact in his reminiscences, John McCorkle, and O. S. Barton, *Three Years with Quantrill, A True Story*, from the Amazon Kindle edition: www.amazon.com/Three-Years-Quantrill-Western-Frontier/dp/0806130563/ref=sr_1_1?s=books&ie=UTF8&qid=1425597665&sr=1- 1&keywords=john+mccorkle%2Bquantrill. Edward Leslie tells the story, in his biography, but points out that the story is incorrect. Edward E. Leslie, *The Devil Knows How to Ride: The True Story of William Clarke Quantrill and His Confederate Raiders* (New York: Random House, 1996), 35–36.

253 McCorkle, *Three Years with Quantrill*: his story is true and well-documented, and can be found at numerous sources, including, Ibid. 64–81; and www.lawrence.com/news/2006/aug/14/morgan_walker_raid/.

254 Cited in Albert Castel, *William Clarke Quantrill: His Life and Times*, new edition (Norman: University of Oklahoma Press, 1999), 23; Castel goes on to say that William E. Connelly, in his *Quantrill and the Border Wars* (Cedar Rapids, Iowa, 1910), wrote one of the early biographies of Quantrill, which was heavily biased against the bushwhacker.

Connelly included any story, such as Quantrill's sadism as a child, that put Quantrill in a negative light. On the other hand, John Newman Edwards, in his *Noted Guerrillas, or The Warfare on the Border* (St. Louis: Bryan, Brand and company, 1877), put Quantrill in a completely different light. Edwards perpetuated the myth that the guerrillas were Robin Hood–like characters.

255 Henry Younger was murdered in July 1862, and the speculation was that he was attacked by Captain Walley and his soldiers, although no charges were ever brought against him. Younger, *Cole Younger.*

256 Ibid. The study of the average wealth of guerrillas comes from James McPherson, *Battle Cry of Freedom: The Civil War Era* (New York: Oxford University Press, 1988), 785. McPherson credits his information to Don Bowen, "Guerrilla Warfare in Western Missouri, 1861–65: Historical Extensions of the Relative Deprivation Hypothesis," in *Comparative Studies in Society and History* (Cambridge University Press) 49, Jan. 2007 edition (January 1, 1977), 30–51.

257 Younger, *Cole Younger;* and Leslie, *The Devil Knows How to Ride*, 105–106.

258 Castel, *William Clarke Quantrill*, 70–71.

259 McCorkle, *Three Years with Quantrill.*

260 *The War of the Rebellion: A Compilation of the Official Records of the Union and Confederate Armies*, Series I, Volume 8, page 612.

261 McCorkle, *Three Years with Quantrill.*

262 Albert Castel postulated that Quantrill learned from his mistakes during these three incidents, so he really deserves the credit here. I took his analysis a little further, but he set the stage. Castel, *William Clarke Quantrill*, 73–84; John McCorkle reported these incidents in the first person in his reminiscences, which was interesting in that he didn't join Quantrill until August 1862. Clearly, the story was told in the camp, and it seemed to grow, because McCorkle stated that dozens of federals were killed in the battle at the Tate House. McCorkle, *Three Years with Quantrill.*

263 Ibid.

264 One interesting tidbit from this incident was that a local picked up a miniature flag dropped by one of the bushwhackers. The flag is now in the collection of the Kansas Historical Society. http://www.kshs.org/kansapedia/quantrill-s-flag/10154.

265 Edwards, *Noted Guerrillas,*156–58; also quoted in Castel, *William Clarke Quantrill*, 101–03; McCorkle, *Three Years with Quantrill.*

266 Matthew C. Hulbert, "William 'Bloody Bill' Anderson," *Essential Civil War Curriculum* (June 2012), found at: www.essential.civilwar.vt.edu/assets/files/ECWC%20TOPIC%20Anderson%20Bloody%20Bill%20Essay1.pdf.

267Cole Younger did not mention the collapse of the building in his memoirs years later; Darryl Levings, "Mystery Still Surrounds 1863 Jail Collapse, Deaths" *Kansas City Star* (October 3, 2013); Tony O'Brian, "Collapse of the Women's Prison in Kansas City," *Civil War on the Western Border: The Missouri-Kansas Conflict, 1854–1865*, found at: www.civilwaronthewesternborder.org/content/collapse-union -women%E2%80%99s-prison-kansas-city.

268Younger, *Cole Younger.*

269H. E. Lowman wrote this piece and several other features in March 1864. His newspaper office was completely destroyed in the raid, and it took several months for him and his business to get back on its feet. *Lawrence State Journal* (March 24, 1864).

270Castel, *William Clarke Quantrill,* 124–25. When the bushwhackers were in Lawrence, however, Rev. Cordley reported that they were wearing their distinctive butternut blouses. But his account might have been off, in that when they arrived in town, Hoffman Collamore—who appears in a little later in this chapter—said he thought the guerrillas were Union troops because they were wearing blue.

271According to Albert Castel, Quantrill was familiar with the terrain they were crossing, but because the night was so dark, he forced local farmers along the route to guide the guerrillas on their way. Also according to Castel, ten such unlucky souls were forced into service, then were shot when they were no longer needed. Castel, *William Clarke Quantrill,* 125–126.

272Cordley, *History of Lawrence,* 201–02.

273There were varying reports on the number and makeup of the Union recruits. John McCorkle wrote that many of them were "colored." Cole Younger claimed there were two hundred soldiers; others placed the number much lower. McCorkle, *Three Years with Quantrill;* Younger, *Cole Younger.* Rev. Cordley reported that seventeen recruits were killed. Cordley, *History of Lawrence,* 203.

274Ibid., 204–05.

275Ibid., 230; according to Younger, Lane rode off on a fine steed and was chased, but his horse was too fast, and he got away. McCorkle said Lane had three pianos in his house, two that had belonged to people in Jackson County, Missouri—both stories were myths. McCorkle, *Three Years with Quantrill;* Younger, *Cole Younger.*

276Cordley, *Pioneer Days in Kansas,* 179; Wilson, "Congregationalist Richard Cordley," 192.

277A copy of the entire description along with a transcript can be found at: www.civilwaronthewesternborder.org/content/mary-savage-jane-simpson

278 Jan Biles, "Quantrill's Raid: Abomination Against Civilians," *The Topeka Capital-Journal* (June 10, 2015).

279 Much of the description of the raid came from Cordley, *Pioneer Days in Kansas*, 178–89 and Cordley, *History of Lawrence*, 198–232.

280 Castel and Leslie claim that Skaggs had taken a ring from Lydia Stone, the proprietor's daughter. Quantrill had given the girl the ring earlier, and demanded that Skaggs give it back. Rev. Cordley, on the other hand, simply said Skaggs was so drunk he didn't know what he was doing and wanted to kill at least one more to bring his number to thirteen. Castel, Leslie, and others refer to the hotel owned by Stone as the Whitney hotel, where Charley Hart (Quantrill) had stayed. Rev. Cordley referred to it as the City hotel.

281 Younger, *Cole Younger;* McCorkle, *Three Years with Quantrill.*

282 Cordley, *Pioneer Days in Kansas*, 183–85.

283 Cordley, *History of Lawrence*, 233–38; McCorkle, *Three Years with Quantrill;* Castel, *William Clarke Quantrill*, 136–41; Leslie, *The Devil Knows How to Ride*, 245–56.

284 Richard Cordley listed 126 known deaths in his *History of Lawrence* (243–48). A monument erected in Lawrence in 1895 listed 150 deaths. Leslie, in his *The Devil Knows How to Ride* (237), cites the number of 183, printed in the St. Louis *Missouri Democrat*, which was reported by three men from Lawrence who were in charge of the burial party, but they also noted that there were seven additional bodies. Robert Speers's body was never recovered, and not counted, as were a number of others, making the total likely more than 200.

285 Cordley, *History of Lawrence*, 240–42.

286 *Lawrence Journal World* (August 18, 2013).

287 Cordley, *History of Lawrence*, 246–51.

288 Cordley, *Pioneer Days in Kansas*, 220–21: Rev. Cordley's sermon was reported in Plymouth Congregational Church website, at: plymouth-lawrence.com/about-us/history/.

289 Cordley, *History of Lawrence*, 248–49

290 Wilson, "Congregationalist Richard Cordley," 193.

291 Ibid. 249–50.

292 "To Our Patrons . . ." *Lawrence State Journal* (October 1, 1863).

293 "Our Press and Type Have Arrived from Chicago," Ibid. (November 12, 1863); Ibid. (November 19, 1863).

294 Quoted in Katie H. Armitage, "'Out of the Ashes': The Rebuilding of Lawrence and the Quest for Quantrill Raid Claims," *Kansas History: A Journal of the Central Plains*, 37 (Winter 2014–2015): 229.

295 Ibid., 226–41.

296 Albert Castel, "Order No. 11 and the Civil War on the Border," found at: www.civilwarstlouis.com/History2/castelorder11.htm.

297 George Caleb Bingham. "Letter to the Editor," *St. Louis Republican* (February 26, 1877).

298 James G. Blunt, "General Blunt's Account of His Civil War Experiences," *Kansas Historical Quarterly* 1 (May 1932): 248–49. This article is available online at: www.kancoll.org/khq/1932/32_3_blunt.htm.

299 Castel, *William Clarke Quantrill*, 155–72; Younger, *Cole Younger*; McCorkle, *Three Years with Quantrill*.

300 McCorkle, *Three Years with Quantrill*.

301 Castel, *William Clarke Quantrill*, 198–99; not surprisingly, the stories surrounding Anderson's death vary widely. Some have Lt. Col. Cox as a major, leading 150 against 300 guerrillas. Some sources claim that Cox had his men cut off Anderson's head and put it on top of a telegraph pole. The one piece of the story that is clear is that Anderson was dead, confirmed by several photographs of his corpse. A recent account of Anderson's death can be found at: opinionator.blogs.nytimes.com/2014/10/29/killing-bloody-bill/?_r=0

302 Wendell Holmes Stephenson, *Publications of the Kansas State Historical Society Embracing the Political Career of James H. Lane* 3 (Topeka: Kansas State Historical Society, 1930), 147.

303 The GAR dissolved in 1956 when its last member, the last surviving Union Civil War veteran, Albert Woolson, died in Duluth, Minnesota. For more detail about the African American GAR in Kansas, refer to Roger D. Cunningham, *The Black Citizen Soldiers of Kansas, 1864–1901* (Columbus: University of Missouri Press, 2008), 53; Donald R. Shaffer, *After the Glory: The Struggles of Black Civil War Veterans* (University of Kansas Press, 2004), 145.

304 http://www.civilwaronthewesternborder.org/content/robinson-sara; Robinson, Sara T. D. "Personal Recollections of Mrs. Sara T.D. Robinson of the Quantrell Raid of August 21, 1863." Special Collections, University of Missouri-Kansas City.

305 Cordley, *Pioneer Days in Kansas*, 254.

306 The Kansas Pacific Railroad was the same line as the Union Pacific, Eastern Division, mentioned in the earlier chapter—only the name changed.

307 National Register of Historic Places, Thematic Nomination for Lawrence, Kansas (1997), found at: www.lawrenceks.org/assets/pds/planning/documents/lawrencethematicnr.pdf.

308 A detailed history and description of the Plymouth Congregational Church building is in the National Register of Historic Places

Nomination, found at: www.kshs.org/resource/national_register/nomi-nationsNRDB/Douglas_PlymouthCongregationalChurchNR.pdf.

309 A detailed description of the English Lutheran Church can be found in the National Register of Historic Places Nomination, found at: www.kshs.org/resource/national_register/nominationsNRDB/Douglas_EnglishLutheranChurchNR.pdf. In the early 1900s, the congregation outgrew its building and moved to a new church nearby. In the late 1980s, the building was nearly demolished, but a local developer stepped in, and by adaptive re-use converted the church into a suite of professional offices. www.facebook.com/pages/Ashlar-LC-Old-English-Lutheran-Church-Professional-Office-Suites/514738791918570?sk=photos_stream.

310   C. S. Griffin, "The University of Kansas and the Years of Frustration, 1854-64," *Kansas Historical Quarterly* 32, (Spring 1966), 6–16.

311 Ibid., 19–20.

312 In an earlier chapter, we noted that Amos Lawrence offered $11,000 in his Emigrant Aid Company stock to build a college in Lawrence, but before Lawrence could transfer the money, he experienced a temporary financial setback and had to renege on his offer. Frank M. Blackmar, *Higher Education in Kansas*, 27 (Washington, DC: United States Bureau of Education, Circular of Information, in Contributions to Educational History, 1900), 23–24.

313 John H. McCool, "Down, but Not Out," in the University of Kansas history webpage, found at: kuhistory.com/articles/down-but-not-out/.

314 Ms. Richardson lived in Lawrence for the remainder of her life, and her daughter, her granddaughter, her great-grandson, and her great-great grandson all attended and graduated from the University of Kansas. Brian Drake, "Lady First," in the University of Kansas History webpage, found at: kuhistory.com/articles/lady-first/.

315 The cable transfer system is described in www.lowtechmagazine.com/2013/03/the-mechanical-transmission-of-power-3-wire-ropes.html.

316 National Register Thematic Nomination for Lawrence; Cutler's *History of the State of Kansas*.

317 A detailed description of the Vinland Grange Hall, and a history of the Grange chapter in Vinland, the National Register Nomination, can be found at: http://www.kshs.org/resource/national_register/nominationsNRDB/Douglas_VinlandGrangeHallNR.pdf.

318 www.haskell.edu/about/history.php. The school is now called Haskell Indian Nations University, which embraces the rich and diverse native cultures. The current one thousand students, from federally recognized tribes and Alaska Native Organizations throughout the nation, can now

pick from baccalaureate programs in elementary education, American Indian studies, business administration, and environmental science.

319 Cordley, *History of Lawrence*, 269.

320 On August 13, 2013, the *Lawrence Journal-World* newspaper published a delightful article about Amos Adams Lawrence. There was one little problem—the lead read that "while he never visited the city that was named after him . . ." which as you can see above is incorrect. http://www2.ljworld.com/news/2013/aug/18/man-who-gave-lawrence -its-name-amos-lawrence/

321 Lawrence MSS, Diary, June 7, 1884; Lawrence, *Life of Amos A. Lawrence*, 274; "Hon. Amos A. Lawrence," *The Lawrence Gazette* (May 29, 1884); "Hon. Amos A. Lawrence," *The Lawrence Journal* (May 29, 1884); "Hon. Amos A. Lawrence Visit," Ibid. (May 31, 1884).

322 "Information in Regard to the University of Kansas" (Topeka: Kansas Publishing House, 1884).

323 Deborah Keating, "Sara Tappan Doolittle Lawrence," found at: www .civilwaronthewesternborder.org/content/robinson-sara.

324 Steve Fry, "Digging up the Past: Lawrence Site May Yield Home of Abolitionist," (Topeka) *Capital Journal* (June 1, 2005), found at: cjon-line.com/stories/060105/kan_digpast.shtml#.VY2ONflViko.

325 Albert Castell, Quantrill's biographer, noted that several of Quantrill's later guerrillas claimed that their leader's purpose was to head through Kentucky to Washington, DC, for the purpose of assassinating President Lincoln. Other members of his band said that claim was preposterous, and Castel agreed with the latter reports.

326 The society's website can be found at: wcqsociety.com/

327 Starr, *Jennison's Jayhawkers*, 367–82.

328 Miller's letters have been published in: *Dailey*, "Josiah Miller, an Antislavery Southerner: Letters to Father and Mother," 66–89.

329 My great-grandfather Isco Pony Sutton joined Walker on this expedition and mustered out of Company L at Fort Laramie.

330 www.kshs.org/natreg/natreg_listings/search/page:1/arch:Haskell /submit:SEARCH

331 Richard Cordley, D. D., *Sermons [by] Richard Cordley, D. D., For Thirty-Eight Years Pastor of Plymouth Church, Lawrence, Kansas.* (Boston, New York: Pilgrim Press, 1912). Available at: https://archive.org/details/ sermonsbyrichard00cord

Bibliography

Books

Andreas, A. T. *History of the State of Kansas.* Chicago: Andreas's Western Historical, 1883.

Ayres, Carol Dark. *Lincoln and Kansas: Partnership for Freedom.* Manhattan, Kansas: Sunflower University Press, 2001.

Benedict, Bryce D. *Jayhawkers: The Civil War Brigade of James Henry Lane.* Norman: University of Oklahoma Press, 2009.

Blackmar, Frank M. *Higher Education in Kansas.* Volume 27. Washington, DC: United States Bureau of Education, Circular of Information, in Contributions to Educational History, 1900.

_____. *Kansas: A Cyclopedia of State History.* Volume 1. Chicago: Standard Publishing, 1912.

Castel, Albert. *William Clarke Quantrill: His Life and Times,* new edition. Norman: University of Oklahoma Press, 1999.

Connelly, William E. *Quantrill and the Border Wars.* Cedar Rapids, Iowa: The Torch, 1910.

Cordley, Richard. *History of Lawrence: From the First Settlement to the Close of the Rebellion.* Lawrence, Kansas: E. F. Caldwell, 1895.

_____. *Pioneer Days in Kansas.* Boston: Pilgrim Press, 1903.

Cutler, William Parker and Julia Perkins Cutler. *The Life, Journals and Correspondence of Rev. Manasseh Cutler, LLD.* Cincinnati: Robert Clark and Company, 1888.

Cunningham, Roger D. *The Black Citizen Soldiers of Kansas, 1864–1901.* Columbus: University of Missouri Press, 2008.

Edwards, John Newman. *Noted Guerrillas, or The Warfare on the Border.* St. Louis: Bryan, Brand, 1877.

Etcheson, Nichole. *Bleeding Kansas: Contested Liberty in the Civil War Era.* Lawrence: University Press of Kansas, 2004.

Fowler, O. S. *A Home for All, or Gravel Wall and Octagon Made of Building New, Cheap, Convenient, Superior, and Adapted to Rich and Poor.* New York: Fowler and Wells, 1854.

Goodwyn, Lawrence. *The Populist Moment: A Short History of the Agrarian Revolt in America.* New York: Oxford University Press, 1978.

Griffin, Clifford S. *The University of Kansas: A History.* Lawrence: The University Press of Kansas, 1974.

Hatcher, Richard W. III and William Garrett Piston, eds. *Kansans at Wilson's Creek: Soldiers Letters from the Campaign for Southwest Missouri.* Volume 3, Studies of the Civil War in the Trans-Mississippi Theater. Springfield, MO: Wilson's Creek National Battlefield Foundation, 1993.

Holt, Michael F. *The Rise and Fall of the American Whig Party: Jacksonian Politics and the Onset of the Civil War.* New York: Oxford University Press, 1999.

Johnson, Samuel A. *The Battle Cry of Freedom: New England Emigrant Aid Company in the Kansas Crusade.* Lawrence: University of Kansas Press, 1950.

Jones, Lu Ann and Robert K. Sutton. *The Life and Legacy of Robert Smalls of South Carolina's Sea Islands.* Fort Washington, PA: Eastern National, 2012.

Kennedy, John F. *Profiles in Courage.* New York: Harper Brothers, 1956.

Lawrence, William. *Life of Amos A. Lawrence: with Extracts from his Diary and Correspondence.* Boston: Houghton, Mifflin and Company, 1888.

Leslie, Edward E. *The Devil Knows How to Ride: The True Story of William Clarke Quantrill and His Confederate Raiders.* New York: Random House, 1996.

May, Robert E. *The Southern Dream of a Caribbean Empire, 1854–1861.* Gainesville: University Press of Florida, 2002.

McPherson, James M. *Battle Cry of Freedom: The Civil War Era.* New York: Oxford University Press, 1988.

———————. *The Mighty Scourge: Perspectives on the Civil War.* New York: Oxford University Press, 2007.

Meyer, Howard N. *The Magnificent Activist: The Writings of Thomas Wentworth Higginson, 1823–1911.* New York: Da Capo, 2000.

Oertel, Kristen Tegtmeier. *Bleeding Borders: Race, Gender, and Violence in Pre-Civil War Kansas.* Baton Rouge: Louisiana State University Press, 2009.

Olson, Kevin G. W. *Frontier Manhattan: Yankee Settlement to Kansas Town, 1854–1894.* Lawrence: University of Kansas Press, 2012.

Pease, Jane H. and William H. *The Fugitive Slave Law and Anthony Burns: A Problem in Law and Enforcement.* Philadelphia: J. B. Lippincott, 1975.

Peterson, John M. *John G. Haskell: Pioneer Kansas Architect.* Lawrence: Douglas County Historical Society, 1984.

Piston, William Garrett and Richard Hatcher III. *Wilson's Creek: The Second Battle of the Civil War and the Men Who Fought It.* Chapel Hill: University of North Carolina Press, 2000.

Reynolds, David S. *John Brown, Abolitionist: The Man Who Killed Slavery, Sparked the Civil War, and Seeded Civil Rights.* New York: Vintage 2006.

Shafer, Donald R. *After the Glory: The Struggles of Black Civil War Veterans.* Lawrence: University of Kansas Press, 2004.

Sheridan, Richard B, Editor and Compiler. *Freedom's Crucible: The Underground Railroad in Lawrence and Douglas County, Kansas, 1854–1865.* Lawrence: University of Kansas, Division of Continuing Education, 1998.

Speer, John. *The Life of Gen James H. Lane: The Liberator of Kansas, with Corroborative Incident of Pioneer History.* Garden City, KS: John Speer, Printer, 1897.

Starr, Stephen Z. *Jennison's Jayhawkers: A Civil War Cavalry Regiment and Its Commander.* Baton Rouge, Louisiana State University Press, 1993.

Stephenson, Wendell Holmes. *Publications of the Kansas State Historical Society Embracing the Political Career of James H. Lane.* Volume 3. Topeka: Kansas State Historical Society, 1930.

Thayer, Eli. *A History of the Kansas Crusade: Its Friends and Its Foes.* New York: Harper and Brothers, 1889.

Wilson, Don W. *Governor Charles Robinson of Kansas.* Lawrence: University of Kansas Press, 1975.

Books in Electronic Format

Connelly, William E. *A Standard History of Kansas and Kansans.* Chicago and New York: Lewis Publishing Company, 1918. Transcribed by Carolyn Ward, for the Internet version, at: skyways.lib.ks.us/genweb/archives/1918ks/v2/945.html

Cordley, Richard, D. D. *Sermons [by] Richard Cordley, D. D., For Thirty-Eight Years Pastor of Plymouth Church, Lawrence, Kansas.* Boston, New York: Pilgrim Press, 1912. Available at: https://archive.org/details/sermonsbyrichard00cord

Doy, John. *The Narrative of John Doy of Lawrence, Kansas: A Plain, Unvarnished Tale.* Published privately, 1860. http://quod.lib.umich.edu/g/genpub/ABJ5091.0001.001?rgn=main;view=fulltext http://books.google.com/books?id=AvZ5AAAAMAAJ&pg=PA1&source=gbs_toc_r&cad=4#v=onepage&q&f=false

McCorkle, John and O. S. Barton. *Three Years with Quantrill, A True Story.* 1914. Amazon.com Kindle edition: www.amazon.com/Three-Years-Quantrill-Western-Frontier/dp/0806130563/ref=sr_1_1?s=books&ie=UT-F8&qid=1425597665&sr=1- 1&keywords=john+mccorkle%2Bquantrill.

Fowler, O. S. *A Home for All, or Gravel Wall and Octagon Made of Building New, Cheap, Convenient, Superior, and Adapted to Rich and Poor.* New York: Fowler and Wells, 1854.

Goodwyn, Lawrence. *The Populist Moment: A Short History of the Agrarian Revolt in America.* New York: Oxford University Press, 1978.

Griffin, Clifford S. *The University of Kansas: A History.* Lawrence: The University Press of Kansas, 1974.

Hatcher, Richard W. III and William Garrett Piston, eds. *Kansans at Wilson's Creek: Soldiers Letters from the Campaign for Southwest Missouri.* Volume 3, Studies of the Civil War in the Trans-Mississippi Theater. Springfield, MO: Wilson's Creek National Battlefield Foundation, 1993.

Holt, Michael F. *The Rise and Fall of the American Whig Party: Jacksonian Politics and the Onset of the Civil War.* New York: Oxford University Press, 1999.

Johnson, Samuel A. *The Battle Cry of Freedom: New England Emigrant Aid Company in the Kansas Crusade.* Lawrence: University of Kansas Press, 1950.

Jones, Lu Ann and Robert K. Sutton. *The Life and Legacy of Robert Smalls of South Carolina's Sea Islands.* Fort Washington, PA: Eastern National, 2012.

Kennedy, John F. *Profiles in Courage.* New York: Harper Brothers, 1956.

Lawrence, William. *Life of Amos A. Lawrence: with Extracts from his Diary and Correspondence.* Boston: Houghton, Mifflin and Company, 1888.

Leslie, Edward E. *The Devil Knows How to Ride: The True Story of William Clarke Quantrill and His Confederate Raiders.* New York: Random House, 1996.

May, Robert E. *The Southern Dream of a Caribbean Empire, 1854–1861.* Gainesville: University Press of Florida, 2002.

McPherson, James M. *Battle Cry of Freedom: The Civil War Era.* New York: Oxford University Press, 1988.

_____. *The Mighty Scourge: Perspectives on the Civil War.* New York: Oxford University Press, 2007.

Meyer, Howard N. *The Magnificent Activist: The Writings of Thomas Wentworth Higginson, 1823–1911.* New York: Da Capo, 2000.

Oertel, Kristen Tegtmeier. *Bleeding Borders: Race, Gender, and Violence in Pre-Civil War Kansas.* Baton Rouge: Louisiana State University Press, 2009.

Olson, Kevin G. W. *Frontier Manhattan: Yankee Settlement to Kansas Town, 1854–1894.* Lawrence: University of Kansas Press, 2012.

Pease, Jane H. and William H. *The Fugitive Slave Law and Anthony Burns: A Problem in Law and Enforcement.* Philadelphia: J. B. Lippincott, 1975.

Peterson, John M. *John G. Haskell: Pioneer Kansas Architect.* Lawrence: Douglas County Historical Society, 1984.

Piston, William Garrett and Richard Hatcher III. *Wilson's Creek: The Second Battle of the Civil War and the Men Who Fought It.* Chapel Hill: University of North Carolina Press, 2000.

Reynolds, David S. *John Brown, Abolitionist: The Man Who Killed Slavery, Sparked the Civil War, and Seeded Civil Rights.* New York: Vintage 2006.

Shafer, Donald R. *After the Glory: The Struggles of Black Civil War Veterans.* Lawrence: University of Kansas Press, 2004.

Sheridan, Richard B, Editor and Compiler. *Freedom's Crucible: The Underground Railroad in Lawrence and Douglas County, Kansas, 1854–1865.* Lawrence: University of Kansas, Division of Continuing Education, 1998.

Speer, John. *The Life of Gen James H. Lane: The Liberator of Kansas, with Corroborative Incident of Pioneer History.* Garden City, KS: John Speer, Printer, 1897.

Starr, Stephen Z. *Jennison's Jayhawkers: A Civil War Cavalry Regiment and Its Commander.* Baton Rouge, Louisiana State University Press, 1993.

Stephenson, Wendell Holmes. *Publications of the Kansas State Historical Society Embracing the Political Career of James H. Lane.* Volume 3. Topeka: Kansas State Historical Society, 1930.

Thayer, Eli. *A History of the Kansas Crusade: Its Friends and Its Foes.* New York: Harper and Brothers, 1889.

Wilson, Don W. *Governor Charles Robinson of Kansas.* Lawrence: University of Kansas Press, 1975.

Books in Electronic Format

Connelly, William E. *A Standard History of Kansas and Kansans.* Chicago and New York: Lewis Publishing Company, 1918. Transcribed by Carolyn Ward, for the Internet version, at: skyways.lib.ks.us/genweb/ archives/1918ks/v2/945.html

Cordley, Richard, D. D.. [START ITAL]Sermons [by] Richard Cordley, D. D., For Thirty-Eight Years Pastor of Plymouth Church, Lawrence, Kansas[END ITAL]. Boston, New York: Pilgrim Press, 1912. Available at: https://archive.org/details/sermonsbyrichard00cord

Doy, John. *The Narrative of John Doy of Lawrence, Kansas: A Plain, Unvarnished Tale.* Published privately, 1860. http://quod.lib.umich. edu/g/genpub/ABJ5091.0001.001?rgn=main;view=fulltext http:// books.google.com/books?id=AvZ5AAAAMAAJ&pg=PA1&- source=gbs_toc_r&cad=4#v=onepage&q&f=false

McCorkle, John and O. S. Barton. *Three Years with Quantrill, A True Story.* 1914. Amazon.com Kindle edition: www.amazon.com/Three-Years-Quantrill- Western-Frontier/dp/0806130563/ref=sr_1_1?s=books&ie=UTF8&- qid=1425597665&sr=1- 1&keywords=john+mccorkle%2Bquantrill.

Miller, Diane. *To Make Men Free: The Underground Railroad in Bleeding Kansas*. National Park Service, May 2008. www.nps.gov/subjects/ugrr /discover_history/upload/UGRR-in-Kansas.pdf.

Robinson, Charles. *The Kansas Conflict*. New York: Harpers and Brothers, 1892. https://books.google.com/books/about/The_Kansas_Conflict.html?id= AvZ5AAAAMAAJ.

Robinson, Sara T. L. *Kansas, Its Interior and Exterior Life: Including a Full View of its Settlement, Political History, Social Life, Climate, Soil, Productions, Scenery, etc.* Boston: Crosby, Nichols, 1856. books.google .com/books?id=CHgFAAAAQAAJ&printsec=frontcover&source=gbs _ge_summary_r&cad=0#v=onepage&q&f=false.

Younger, Cole. *The Story of Cole Younger, By Himself*. 1903. Amazon.com Kindle edition, at: www.amazon.com/Story-Cole-Younger-Himself -ebook/dp/B004TPC6Y0/ref=sr_1_1?s=books&ie=UTF8&qid= 1425493959&sr=1-1&keywords=cole+younger+autobiography

Articles

Armitage, Katie H. "'Out of the Ashes': The Rebuilding of Lawrence and the Quest for Quantrill Raid Claims." *Kansas History: A Journal of the Central Plains*, 37 (Winter 2014–2015): 226–241.

Baron, Frank, "James H. Lane and the Origins of the Kansas Jayhawk." *Kansas History: A Journal of the Central Plains* 34 (Summer 2011): 114–27.

Barry, Louise. "The Emigrant Aid Company Parties of 1854." *Kansas Historical Quarterly* 12 (May 1943): 115–155.

_____. "The New England Emigrant Aid Company Parties of 1855." *Kansas Historical Quarterly* 12 (August 1943): 227–68.

Dailey, Dennis M. "Josiah Miller, an Antislavery Southerner: Letters to Father and Mother." *Kansas History: A Journal of the Central Plains* 36 (Summer 2013): 66–89.

Dirck, Brian R. "By the Hand of God: James Montgomery and Redemptive Violence." *Kansas History: A Journal of the Central Plains* 27 (Spring-Summer, 2004): 100–116.

Etchison, Nicole. "Labouring for the Freedom of This Territory: Free-State Kansas Women in the 1850s." *Kansas History: A Journal of the Central Plains* 21 (Summer 1998): 68–87.

Griffin, C. S. "The University of Kansas and the Years of Frustration, 1854–64." *Kansas Historical Quarterly* 32, (Spring 1966): 1–32.

Hickman, Russell. "The Vegetarian and Octagon Settlement Companies." *Kansas Historical Quarterly* 2 (November 1933): 377–385.

Hougen, Harvey R. "The Marais des Cygnes Massacre and the Trial and Execution of William Griffith." *Kansas History: A Journal of the Plains* 8 (Summer 1985): 74–94.

Langsdorf, Erich. "Jim Lane and the Frontier Guard." *Kansas Historical Quarterly* 9 (February 1940): 13–25.

Mechem, Kirke. "The Mythical Jayhawk." *Kansas Historical Quarterly* 13 (February 1944): 1–15.

Watts, Dale E. "How Bloody was Bleeding Kansas? Political Killings in Kansas Territory, 1854–1861," *Kansas History: A Journal of the Central Plains* 18 (Summer 1995): 116–129.

Wilson, Nathan. "Congregationalist Richard Cordley and the Impact of New England Cultural Imperialism in Kansas, 1857–1904." *Great Plains Quarterly* 24 (Summer 2004): 184–199

Articles in Electronic Format

Blunt, James G. "General Blunt's Account of His Civil War Experiences." *Kansas Historical Quarterly* 1 (May 1932): 248–49. www.kancoll.org /khq/1932/32_3_blunt.htm

Castel, Albert "Order No. 11 and the Civil War on the Border." www.civil-warstlouis.com/History2/castelorder11.htm

Dolbee, Cora. "The First Book on Kansas: The Story of Edward Everett Hale's "Kanzas and Nebraska" *Kansas Historical Review* 2 (May 1933): 139–181. www.kancoll.org/khq/1933/33_2_dolbee.htm.

Hulbert, Matthew C. "William 'Bloody Bill' Anderson," *Essential Civil War Curriculum* (June 2012). www.essential.civilwar.vt.edu/assets/files/ ECWC%20TOPIC%20Anderson%20Bloody%20Bill%20Essay1.pdf

Savage, Joseph. "Recollections of 1854," *Western Home Journal* 4 (14 July 1870). www.territorialkansasonline.org/~imlskto/cgi-in/index.php?SCREEN =transcripts/savage_joseph.

Manuscript Collections

Amos Adams Lawrence Papers. Massachusetts Historical Society. Boston, Massachusetts.

Issac Goodnow Collection. Kansas State Historical Society. Topeka, Kansas.

Online Manuscript Collections

The texts of American Indian treaties cited in this volume can be found at: digital.library.okstate.edu/kappler/Vol2/treaties/del0614.htm; and digital.library.okstate.edu/kappler/Vol2/treaties/del0304.htm.

Kansas Military History is available at: www.kansasguardmuseum.org.

Important documents, letters, images, and other information encompassing the entire range of Kansas history are available at: www.kansasmemory.org.

[The] "Personal Recollections of Mrs. Sara T. D. Robinson of the Quantrell [sic]Raid of August 21, 1863" can be found in the Special Collections, University of Missouri-Kansas City.

Every conceivable document, letter, image, map, or notable artifact relating to the history of Kansas as a territory is available at: www.territorialkansasonline.org

Online Government Documents

Laws and many documents can be found at the Library of Congress site: memory.loc.gov/ammem/index.html

Laws cited in this volume as well as a wealth of additional government documents can be found at the National Archives site: www.ourdocuments.gov.

Books and government reports are available at: quod.lib.umich.edu/m/moa.

The National Park Service has a wealth of information available on the Underground Railroad at: www.nps.gov/ugrr, and information on soldiers and sailors in the Civil War at: www.nps.gov/civilwar/soldiers-and-sailors-database.htm.

The National Register of Historic Places Nominations for Kansas and other states can be found at: www.nps.gov/nR.

The War of the Rebellion: A Compilation of the Official Records of the Union and Confederate Armies. The full set is available at: ebooks.library.cornell.edu/m/moawar/waro.html.

Newspapers

The Allen County Courant (Iola, Kansas)
Anti-slavery Bugle (New Lisbon, Ohio)
Capital Journal (Topeka, Kansas)
Free State (Lawrence, Kansas)
Herald of Freedom (Lawrence, Kansas)
Kansas City (Missouri) Star
Lawrence (Kansas*) Gazette*
Lawrence (Kansas) *Journal*
Lawrence (Kansas) *Journal World*
Lawrence (Kansas) Republican
Lawrence (Kansas*) State Journal*
(Leavenworth, Kansas*) Daily Times*
The New York Times

Websites

Slavery and Justice Report of the Brown University Steering Committee on Slavery and Justice, detailing the role of the Brown family in the slave trade and the university's role over time in confronting historical injustice and slavery's legacy: brown.edu/Research/Slavery_Justice/documents/SlaveryAndJustice.pdf.

Essays written by notable scholars on Civil War topics related to the Civil War in the West: www.civilwaronthewesternborder.org A variety of stories on Kansas history: www.kshs.org University of Kansas history: www.kuhistory.com *New York Times* article for the sesquicentennial of the Civil War: opinionator.blogs.nytimes.com

Information about the William Clarke Quantrill Society: wcqsociety.com/

Index